"John Lott is the most dogged, intellectually credible, academic defender of the right to keep and bear arms in the United States today. He is also the chief beast in the night to the gun control crowd. His works are must reading for those of us on the front lines in these debates. *The War on Guns* is his best work yet. In it, the reader will find well-documented all the data, statistics, practical, legal, and moral arguments one will ever need to support the natural right to self-defense. The statists will fear this book. Freedom lovers will crave it."

—**HON. ANDREW P. NAPOLITANO**, senior judicial analyst Fox News Channel, and Distinguished Visiting Professor of Law, Brooklyn Law School

"To paraphrase a once-famous commercial slogan, 'When John R. Lott speaks, everyone listens.' Or, at least they should when this leading expert on all matters gun control speaks out so provocatively and persuasively. In his new book, Lott delves into the myriad ways in which anti-gun 'statistics' and 'research' have been used to perpetrate utter falsehoods and misleading propaganda. If there is to be any intelligent, honest, and objective discussion of gun policy in the United States, then *The War on Guns* ought to be required reading."

—**CHARLES J. GOETZ**, Joseph M. Hartfield Professor of Law Emeritus, University of Virginia School of Law

"John R. Lott is a role model for those who do scientific research on important problems. He is objective and logical. He uses the best evidence available—data from natural experiments on the effects of gun regulations—to compare the effects of alternative policies. He fully discloses his analysis, and responds to critics by conducting further research. As a result, his findings have persuaded many people. Lott's scientific approach is the opposite of the advocacy research that fills many academic journals, and which the media delight in reporting. Lott's *The War on Guns* exposes and explains the deceptions used by gun-control advocates. Those who want to live in a safer world will benefit from Lott's findings. Of the many gun regulations to date, there are no scientific comparisons that have found a reduction in crime or death rates."

—**PROFESSOR J. SCOTT ARMSTRONG**, The Wharton School, University of Pennsylvania

"We should all thank and admire John Lott for single-handedly changing the debate on guns from ill-informed rhetoric attacking gun ownership to hard-headed empirical analysis that shows the benefits of allowing law abiding citizens to carry concealed weapons. *The War on Guns* continues this debate by showing that the anti-gun lobby has spent millions of dollars making false and misleading claims about guns. Once again, John Lott provides careful and rigorous empirical analysis that undermines these claims. Kudos to John Lott for having the guts to take on the anti-gun lobby."

—**PROFESSOR WILLIAM M. LANDES**, senior lecturer and Clifton R. Musser Professor Emeritus of Law & Economics, University of Chicago Law School

"John Lott is more responsible than anyone else for arguments that gun ownership in the U.S. increases safety and reduces crime. Arrayed against him are the entire public health establishment and much of the media. In this book, John carefully analyzes many of the arguments made against gun ownership—for example, there are more gun homicides and mass shootings in the U.S. than elsewhere, background checks reduce gun harms, "Stand Your Ground" laws harm African Americans and increase crime—and shows using both statistical and anecdotal evidence that they are incorrect. He also shows that wealthy opponents of gun ownership (such as Michael Bloomberg) finance much fallacious "public health" research on the effects of guns. Anyone interested in the gun debate should read this book, and opponents of gun ownership have an intellectual obligation to confront the arguments."

> —**PROFESSOR PAUL H. RUBIN,** Samuel Candler Dobbs
> Professor of Economics, Emory University

"John Lott's new book, *The War on Guns: Arming Yourself Against Gun Control Lies*, does just that. Lott deals with a wide variety of claims that question the value of firearms for self-defense, providing the analysis and facts the public needs to see through the distortions of gun control advocates. This is a valuable guide to a more balanced understanding of the issue."

> —**PROFESSOR JOYCE LEE MALCOLM**, Patrick Henry Professor of
> Constitutional Law and the Second Amendment, Antonin Scalia Law
> School, George Mason University

"John Lott's new book, *The War on Guns: Arming Yourself Against Gun Control Lies*, is an indispensable source of facts, insights, and cogent argument. Anyone who wants to be informed on the gun control issue has to read this book."

> —**CARLISLE E. MOODY**, Professor of Economics, William and Mary

THE WAR ON GUNS

To Tom: for all
Thanks for all
you do! Thanks also
for being such a
great teacher back
at U Chi H.
Best,

THE WAR ON GUNS

ARMING YOURSELF AGAINST GUN CONTROL LIES

JOHN R. LOTT JR., Ph.D.

REGNERY
PUBLISHING
A Division of Salem Media Group

Regnery® is a registered trademark of Salem Communications Holding Corporation

Cataloging-in-Publication data on file with the Library of Congress
ISBN 978-1-62157-580-1

Published in the United States by
Regnery Publishing
A Division of Salem Media Group
300 New Jersey Ave NW
Washington, DC 20001
www.Regnery.com

Manufactured in the United States of America

10 9 8 7 6 5 4 3 2 1

Books are available in quantity for promotional or premium use. For information on discounts and terms, please visit our website: www.Regnery.com.

Distributed to the trade by
Perseus Distribution
250 West 57th Street
New York, NY 10107

CONTENTS

WHAT IS AT STAKE

The Supreme Court is wrong on the Second Amendment, and I am going to make that case every chance that I get.[1]
—Hillary Clinton to her donors in Greenwich Village, New York City, September 2015.

The Supreme Court has decided on two occasions that the government can't simply ban people from owning guns. The first ruling, *District of Columbia v. Heller,* struck down a handgun ban and gunlock regulations in Washington, D.C. in 2008.[2] Then came *McDonald v. City of Chicago* in 2010, which struck down Chicago's ban and broadened the scope of the previous decision to apply to all of the states.[3] Both of these rulings were made by narrow five to four majorities.

With the passing of Justice Antonin Scalia in February 2016, there are now only four members of the Supreme Court who oppose gun bans. One of these four—Justice Anthony Kennedy—is now over eighty years old.

The liberal members of the Supreme Court have made clear their beliefs on this issue. Dissenting in *McDonald v. City of Chicago,* Justice Stephen Breyer spoke for the other liberals on the court: "I can find nothing in the Second Amendment's text, history, or underlying rationale that could warrant characterizing it as 'fundamental' insofar as it seeks to protect the keeping and bearing of arms for private self-defense purposes."[4] These Justices are eager to reverse the court's previous rulings.

A Hillary Clinton presidency would most likely spell the end of the Second Amendment as we know it. In an off-the-record comment to donors in New York City in September 2015, she made it clear that she believes the government can ban guns.[5] She also has praised Australian and UK gun control laws (the UK prohibits all guns except for shotguns).[6]

Americans have seen this before. In June 2008, then Senator Barack Obama assured everyone, "I have said consistently that I believe that the Second Amendment is an individual right, and that was the essential decision that the Supreme Court came down on."[7] But just months earlier, in February 2008, Obama came out in support of D.C.'s handgun ban.[8] And in April of that year, Obama said of Americans, "they get bitter, they cling to guns or religion."[9]

I was at the University of Chicago Law School when Obama was a part-time lecturer. He told me in 1996, "I don't believe that people should be able to own guns." I am not surprised at many of the rules he's trying to implement, often in underhanded ways.

President Obama's latest Supreme Court nominee, Appeals Court Judge Merrick Garland, would undoubtedly vote to uphold gun bans. In *District of Columbia v. Heller*, a three-judge panel of the D.C. Circuit ruled against the city's handgun ban. In an unsuccessful move to overturn the ruling, Garland voted to have the panel's decision reconsidered. This is only one of several anti-gun votes that Garland has cast as a judge.[10]

But the Supreme Court battles are just one part of the war on guns. We are now facing proposals that would have seemed unthinkable just five or six years ago. Obama has even sought to prohibit gun purchases by Social Security recipients who have trouble managing their finances. The push is for these individuals to be classified as "mentally defective." Some 4.2 million Social Security recipients could be affected.[11] This is personal for me, as my elderly mother has given my sister power of attorney to handle her finances. Without a gun, my mother would have no realistic means of defending herself.

It is a real stretch to argue that those who can't manage their finances pose a physical threat to themselves and others. What is next? Are we going to deny people the right to self-defense if they can't drive or can't do math because they too are "mentally defective"?

Having a gun is by far the most effective way for people to protect themselves from criminals. Women and the elderly have the most to gain from owning a gun because they're likely to be at a major disadvantage in physical strength.

Americans sixty-five and over make up over 14 percent of the U.S. population, but they are responsible for only 3 percent of murders in which the age of the perpetrator is known. Because unsolved murders disproportionately tend to involve young gangs, the true percentage is probably significantly lower.

For several years, Obama has been requiring that veterans be reported to the NICS background check system if they need someone else to manage their Veterans Administration (VA) benefits. The only way out is to forfeit the benefits before the information is given to the background check system. According to the Congressional Research Service, 99.3 percent of all names reported to the NICS list's "mental defective" category were provided by the Veterans Administration (VA).[12] It's preposterous that veterans should be the ones who end up losing their right to own a gun.

Before throwing more names into the system, it might be time to correct some of the massive flaws in the National Instant Criminal Background Check System. The biggest problem is that virtually every-one who is stopped from buying a gun is a false-positive. This means that someone is stopped from buying a gun just because his name resembles that of someone who is on the government's list of prohibited peo-ple. Adding more names only makes it more likely that the system will stop people who *should* be able to buy a gun.

Ironically, Democrats such as President Obama would be quite upset if a literacy or intelligence test was required of voters. The right to self-defense is no less fundamental than the right to vote. Disarming veterans and the elderly is just a step in Obama's efforts to ban gun ownership.

We don't make the country safer by disarming its most vulnerable citizens. In fact, gun bans always result in higher crime rates. They just aren't effective in disarming criminals.

Although police are hugely important to fighting crime, they almost always arrive at the scene after the crime has been committed. What scares criminals most is the thought of their victims having guns. A gun response when confronted by a criminal is the safest, according to the Bureau of Justice Statistics' National Crime Victimization Survey.[13] Gun control advocates seem to think that waiting for police to arrive is a good enough option for poor Americans.

Prominent Chicago Democrat Rep. Luis Gutierrez keeps introducing legislation to ban the production of inexpensive guns in the United States.[14] While some criminals do use these smaller and lighter guns, they are also useful for self-defense. And, of course, they are the preferred choice of poorer potential victims who cannot afford more expensive guns.

In 2013, the Obama administration took the extremely unusual step of lobbying a state legislature. The administration wanted the Colorado State House to pass a bill that would impose both a tax and a background check on the private transfers of all guns.[15] All but two Democrats voted down a Republican amendment that would have exempted people below the poverty level from paying the new state tax.[16]

In 2013, Maryland Democrats passed legislation requiring the licensing and registration of handguns. Now getting a handgun requires $205 to $230 in fees and training expenses.[17] Republicans again tried to exempt poor individuals from paying the government fees, but the Democrat-controlled state legislature wouldn't even let the amendment come up for a vote. These rules seem designed to reduce gun ownership. Bleeding-heart liberal Democrats don't seem to care if the poor are dispropriotionately affected.

Democrats will do anything to stop people from exercising their Second Amendment rights. After *Heller* and *McDonald*, leaders in Washington, D.C. and Chicago created licensing processes that only two to three thousand people in each city have successfully navigated.[18]

D.C. has only one federally licensed gun dealer in the whole city. The prices are steep. If you buy a gun elsewhere and try to bring it to D.C., you will be charged $125 for a background check.[19] In 2011, a *Washington Post* reporter went through the process of getting a gun and found that the fees and training costs added up to $834.[20] Of course, it also took time to complete and notarize registration forms, take tests, and have fingerprints taken.[21] All of these costs dwarf the actual price of most guns. The *Washington Post* ran the fitting front-page headline: "Since D.C.'s handgun ban ended, well-heeled residents have become well armed."[22]

The fees in Chicago were not quite as extravagant. Immediately after the *McDonald* decision, the city imposed a one hundred dollar license fee plus another fee of fifteen dollars per gun.[23] Illinois requires a state license, though that only costs another ten dollars. The mandatory five hours of training classes typically came to about $150. However, there's nowhere in the city where these training hours can be fulfilled. And if you don't have access to a car, you won't have any way of legally transporting your gun to the firing range.[24]

Nationally, gun ownership varies very little with income, but there is a huge difference in Chicago. Zip codes with a median family income of $120,000 have twice the handgun ownership rate of areas with a median family income of $60,000, which in turn have twice the handgun ownership rate of zip codes with a median of $30,000.[25]

Illinois was the last state in the union to issue concealed handgun permits. And it only did so after being ordered to by a federal court. Unsurprisingly, Illinois made it as difficult as possible to get a permit, imposing fees and training requirements with a price tag of around $500.[26] Just the fee for the five-year permit itself is about three times higher than the average cost in the rest of the U.S.[27]

Nor is this a new phenomenon. Back in 1993, Hillary Clinton supported a 25 percent tax on handguns and raised the dealer license fee from thirty dollars to $2,500 (the equivalent of over $4,100 in 2016).[28]

It is clear that these costs make people less likely to obtain a permit. In 2015, Texas had four times the population of Indiana but only 40 percent more permits (840,000 versus 600,000).[29] It's not that Texans like guns less, it's just that they have to go through five hours of training and pay $140 in fees. In Indiana, the cost is only $49.95 and there are no training requirements.[30]

Democrats are unwilling to admit that their gun control regulations are disarming poor Americans. President Obama characterizes Voter ID laws that offer free IDs as "voter suppression laws,"[31] but sees no irony in imposing much greater inconveniences and costs on prospective gun owners.

DISARMING THE MOST VULNERABLE

Increasing the costs of gun ownership can have deadly consequences. Since a Massachusetts licensing law took effect in 1998, the number of registered gun owners in the state has plummeted from 1.5 million to just over 200,000.[32] During this time, Massachusetts' murder rate soared relative to neighboring states. We will explore this and other examples in the book.

In January 2016, President Obama held a town hall event on CNN to explain his newest push for gun control. Rape victim Kimberly Corban had this exchange with Obama:[33]

> Corban: As a survivor of rape, and now a mother to two small children—you know, it seems like being able to purchase a firearm of my choosing, and being able to carry that wherever my—me and my family are—it seems like my basic responsibility as a parent at this point.
>
> I have been unspeakably victimized once already, and I refuse to let that happen again to myself or my kids. So why can't your administration see that these restrictions that you're putting to make it harder for me to own a gun, or harder for me to take that where I need to be is actually just making my kids and I less safe?
>
> Obama:...I just want to repeat that there's nothing that we've proposed that would make it harder for you to purchase a firearm....

Obama's response was clearly false. Washington D.C.'s expanded background checks impose a $125 cost to privately transferring ownership of a gun.[34] These background checks cost less in some states, but even a sixty dollar fee can make the difference for less affluent Americans.

Hillary Clinton claims that guns "are the only business in America that is wholly protected from any kind of liability."[35] In fact, gun dealers can be sued for selling guns that they know will be used for criminal purposes. They can also be sued if someone is harmed as a result of them breaking a state or federal law. Gun manufacturers can be sued if a defect results in injury.

Just over a decade ago, gun makers and dealers were being sued even if they followed all the laws in selling a gun, but the gun ended up being used in a crime. Gun makers were also being sued on the basis that they "specifically geared" their products to gang members by offering guns that were powerful, inexpensive, easily concealed, and corrosion resistant. Suing an industry for offering conveniently-sized, affordable products, aspects of guns that the over 13 million concealed handgun permit holders in the U.S. value, shows how far the liability-litigation madness has gone.

Clinton wants to again make gun makers and sellers liable for any crimes committed with their guns. These were the rules prior to the 2005 Protection of Lawful Commerce in Arms Act, when gun control advocates thought that they could bring so many lawsuits they would simply overwhelm gun makers with legal costs. But it is one thing to sue a federally licensed dealer for selling a gun to someone who he knew was a criminal, or even to someone who didn't have the proper ID. It is quite another to hold a dealer responsible for what every customer does with his gun.

But beyond that, holding a licensed dealer responsible for any crime committed with a gun makes as much sense as holding a car dealership or running-shoe seller responsible for any crime committed with their products. Of course, faster cars or running shoes also make it easier for criminals to escape from the scene of the crime. Even Senator Bernie Sanders recognized the possible consequences of such action. "What you're really talking about is ending gun manufacturing in America," he said with some hyperbole in a presidential debate with Clinton.[36]

The amazing thing is how the vast majority of Democrats think Sanders's concern is unreasonable. Senator Chris Murphy (D-CT) is just one example. The terrible Sandy Hook shooting took place in his state, and everyone wants to help those families. But the gun used in the shooting was legally sold to the killer's mother, and the killer then stole the gun from her. Instead of proposing to eliminate "gun-free zones"—places this book will show are targets for these mass public shooters because victims aren't able to defend themselves—Murphy angrily attacked Sanders: "Right now, [Sanders] is standing in clear opposition to the families of Sandy Hook who want to be able to contest their case in court. He is saying they should be barred from making that case…you are not going to win Connecticut if you are not 100% in on the fight against the gun lobby. I don't think you'll win a primary in New York if you're not 100% in."[37]

These lawsuits would certainly raise the costs of doing business for gun dealers and manufacturers, and therefore raise the price of guns. Hillary and Senator Murphy may claim that they care about the poor, but poor people in the highest-crime areas are the most likely to be priced out of owning guns for protection.

Gun control advocates consistently push to make gun ownership more costly. But if they really believe that licensing and background checks work, why should gun owners bear the entire cost in taxes and fees? The reduction in crime is something that would benefit everyone, not just gun buyers. In fact, the law-abiding gun owners who pay these fees are the ones who are helping reduce crime. But as efforts in Colorado and Maryland reveal, gun control advocates are really just intent on discouraging gun ownership.

THE FLOOD OF MISINFORMATION

The debate isn't going away any time soon. When President Obama unveiled his newest gun control proposals in early January 2016, 85 percent of registered Democrats supported it.[38]

The war on guns doesn't just involve politicians. While people's views on guns have become much more supportive than fifteen years ago, Michael Bloomberg and other billionaires, large foundations, and the Obama administration have embarked on a campaign that covers all the bases: funding research, training reporters on how to cover guns, and advertising. Few people appreciate the massive tidal wave of research these groups have funded or the uncritical media coverage that they received.

As we will see later, even the FBI's data have been corrupted by the Obama administration. Polling data on gun ownership in the U.S. has been manipulated. Data on gun ownership across countries is no different. If you can manipulate the data on gun ownership and it is the only data available, you can greatly influence the debate on guns.

Misleading claims have been made about how frequently mass public shootings occur in the U.S. compared to Europe and the rest of the world (hint: they aren't more common in the U.S.); how frequently mass public shootings occur in places where civilians can protect themselves with guns (very rarely); whether large capacity magazines are associated with more fatalities (they aren't); if background checks on the private transfers of guns stop mass public shootings (they don't); or if countries with lower gun ownership rates have higher murder rates (yes). Those are just some of the issues that we will be exploring in this book.

Michael Bloomberg, George Soros, and others are not stupid. They are spending hundreds of millions of dollars on producing false and misleading information because they have seen from polls that it makes a difference. They know that if they are going to win the gun debate, they must change people's perceptions. For some hardcore supporters of the right to self-defense, these studies might not matter. But Bloomberg and others know that for the broad majority of Americans in the middle of the debate, bombarding them with false claims about guns can make a big difference.

If you want to make sure that Americans are as safe as possible, it is important to arm yourself with responses to these false claims. This book will help you do that.

CHAPTER 1

CHANGES IN PUBLIC PERCEPTION

INTRODUCTION

Something remarkable has been taking place: there has been a sea change in people's beliefs in whether gun ownership makes them safer. But gun control advocates have not given up and are redoubling their efforts by preparing massive funding for gun control research.

There are other signs that Americans are putting increased stock in self-defense. Since 2007, the number of concealed handgun permits has soared from 4.6 million to more than 13 million. A record 1.7 million additional permits were issued between 2014 and 2015—a 15.4 percent increase.

The Roper Center and Pew opinion polls show how the gun control debate has changed over the last couple of decades.[1] Their polls are fairly similar to ones by CNN and Gallup.[2] For Roper, during the 1990s, opposition to additional gun control was just 30 percent. After 2000, however, opposition has been on a fairly consistent rise, reaching 49 percent at the end of 2015. A dramatic 19 percent point rise occurred over just fifteen years.

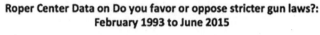

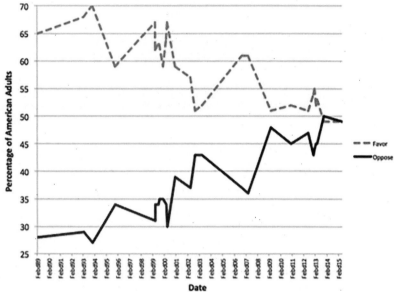

The Pew polling data also shows opposition to gun control rising by eighteen percentage points between 2000 and July 2015, though opposition had reached its peak of 52 percent in December 2014.

Again, this shift is all due to a massive transformation in people's views on the costs and benefits of gun ownership. In 2000, when Gallup began asking Americans whether they thought that they were safer with a gun in the home, only 35 percent of Americans answered *yes*. Fifty-one percent said that a gun would put them in *more* danger. By 2014, the numbers had flipped, with people saying, by a margin of 63 to 30 percent, that they are safer with a gun in the home. That is a twenty-eight percentage point shift, a change which roughly corresponds to the twenty-four percentage point increase in Americans who oppose more gun control.

Changing attitudes also explain the changing demographics of permit holders. Since 2012, the Pew Research Center has been asking this same question of different demographic groups. By 2015, a 25 percent

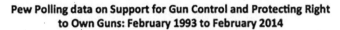

Pew Polling data on Support for Gun Control and Protecting Right to Own Guns: February 1993 to February 2014

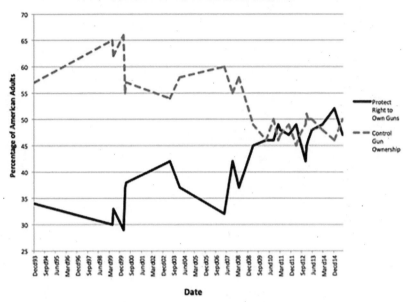

Date

greater proportion of blacks were answering that they thought owning a gun improves safety. There was an 11 percent increase among women— greater than the increase among men. Both blacks and women have seen the largest increase in concealed handgun permits. Blacks now make up 7 to 8 percent of permit holders. Women now hold over a quarter of concealed handgun permits. Between 2007 and 2015, the number of permits has grown by 156 percent among men and 270 percent among women.

Other polls confirm that people have this impression that guns make them safer. An October 2015 Gallup poll found that a 56 to 41 percent margin of Americans believe that increased concealed carry leads to improved safety.[3] The results are reversed only among Democrats and those with postgraduate degrees. This is quite a change from 2005, when 65 percent of Americans told Gallup that they felt less safe in places allowing concealed weapons. Only 25 percent said that they felt safer.[4] Even among gun owners, less than half (45 percent) said that they felt

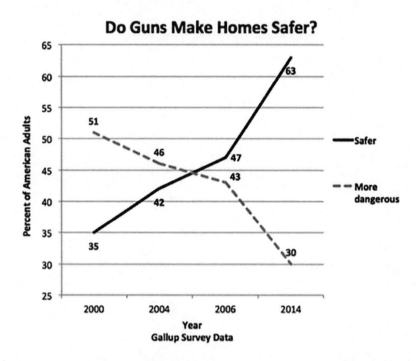

safer. Forty-four percent of Americans said then that only public safety officials should carry guns.

A January 2016 poll by Investor's Business Daily found that a 52 to 42 percent margin of Americans believe that gun ownership is more likely to increase public safety than gun control is to keep guns out of the hands of criminals.[5] In a June 2015 Rasmussen poll, 68 percent of Americans said that they would feel safer living in a neighborhood where guns are allowed.[6]

Gun control advocates are determined to reverse these trends by waging political war in Washington, D.C. and in state legislatures. They are pouring money into bogus research and training reporters on how to cover the issue of gun control. They care only about the conclusions, not the quality of the research. And the media is receptive to their research, failing to interview critics of gun control and not asking proponents the tough questions.

THE MEDIA PUZZLE'S MISSING PIECES

This sea change in American views about gun ownership is especially remarkable because it has come in the face of such heavily biased media coverage. We hear all the time about shootings and accidental gunshots, but there is very little mention of the defensive gun uses that happen every day across America.

Here is a list of some recent mass public shootings that were clearly prevented by concealed handgun permit holders. If the permit holders hadn't been there, these cases would have clearly gathered massive national news coverage. Instead, coverage was limited to one or two local news stories. None of the stories got national news coverage:

- Conyers, Georgia, May 31, 2015: A permit holder was walking by a store when he heard shots ring out. Two people had already been killed. The permit holder started firing, and the killer ran out of the store. Rockdale County Sheriff Eric Levett said of the incident: "I believe that if Mr. Scott did not return fire at the suspect, then more of those customers would have [been] hit by a gun[shot]. . . . So, in my opinion he saved other lives in that store."[7]
- New Holland, South Carolina, May 5, 2015: A man, firing his gun, approached a volunteer fire department with a "parking lot full of children and firefighters." Fortunately, two firefighters had permitted concealed handguns and confronted the man with weapons drawn. The assailant "pointed the firearm at individual firefighters for lengthy periods of time." Eventually, the man was persuaded to drop his gun.[8]
- Chicago, Illinois, April 2015: An Uber driver had just dropped off a passenger when he saw gunman Everardo Custodio open fire on a crowd of people. The Uber driver shot and wounded the gunman. Assistant State's Attorney,

Barry Quinn, praised the driver for "acting in self-defense and in the defense of others."

- Philadelphia, Pennsylvania, March 2015: A permit holder was walking by a barbershop when he heard shots fired. He quickly ran into the shop and shot the gunman to death. "I guess he saved a lot of people in there," said Police Captain Frank Llewellyn.[9]

- Darby, Pennsylvania, July 2014: Convicted felon Richard Plotts killed a hospital caseworker and shot his psychiatrist. Fortunately, the psychiatrist used his concealed handgun to critically wound Plotts, who was still carrying thirty-nine bullets.[10]

- Chicago, Illinois, July 2014: Three gang members fired on four people who had just left a party. Fortunately, one of these four individuals was a military serviceman with a concealed handgun permit. He was able to return fire and wound the main attacker. The other attackers were kept at bay. The UK's Daily Mail reported, "The night might have had a very different outcome had the incident occurred a year earlier [before Illinois's concealed-handgun law was passed]."[11]

- Plymouth, Pennsylvania, September 2012: William Allabaugh critically wounded one man inside a restaurant before fatally shooting a man on the street. A concealed-handgun permit holder then wounded Allabaugh. "We believe that it could have been much worse that night," said Luzerne County Assistant District Attorney Jarrett Ferentino.[12]

- Salt Lake City, Utah, April 27, 2012: A knife-wielding man started stabbing people and yelling, "You killed my people." Two of the victims were seriously injured. A store employee described the scene: "There is blood all over. One got stabbed in the stomach and got stabbed in the head and held his hands and got stabbed all over the arms." Police Lt. Brian Purvis noted, "This was a very volatile situation that could have gotten even worse. We can only assume, judging from what we saw, that it could have gotten a lot worse. So he [the permit holder] was definitely in the right place at the right time."[13]

- Spartanburg, South Carolina, March 2012: Armed with a shotgun, Jesse Gates kicked in a door to his church. Concealed-carry permit holder Aaron Guyton drew his gun and held Gates at gunpoint, enabling other parishioners to disarm Gates before anyone was harmed. Spartanburg County Sheriff Chuck Wright called the churchgoers heroes.[14]

I have tried to limit myself to cases where police, prosecutors, or media have claimed that permit holders saved multiple lives. Lives have been saved in countless other cases that would have turned into mass public shootings or single-victim crimes, but these occurrences did not have confirmation by law enforcement or prosecutors.[15] In addition, since most of these dramatic stories of self-defense generate only one or two local news stories, there may very well be a lot of cases that we don't know about due to lack of news coverage.

In a couple of these cases, I have tried reaching out to national media to cover them. But even in the Conyers, Georgia case, where the life-saving efforts of the permit holder were caught on film, I could not get cable news editors interested in the story. The lack of coverage given even these dramatic cases shows the risks of relying on media news stories to determine the number of defensive gun uses.

CHAPTER 2

ACADEMIC "EXPERTS" AND MEDIA BIAS

The media not only ignores positive examples of defensive gun use; news reports about the scientific side of the gun control debate are just as unbalanced. Coverage generally focuses on interviewing pro-gun control academics and questioning a gun shop owner or an NRA spokesperson for the other side of the argument. Of course, the *New York Times* will never run a news article on studies that find that guns save lives. Even when they write about studies supporting gun control, newspapers choose only to present comments by academics who support gun control. These articles give the impression that objective, qualified scientists are concerned about using gun control to save lives, while those with a profit or some other ulterior motive are willing to say anything to keep selling these lethal weapons. One of my books, *The Bias Against Guns* (2003), went through example after example of these one-sided reports in the media.

Unfortunately, little has changed. In January 2016, CNN ran a lengthy news story on studies that found gun control to be effective in preventing suicides.[1] It wasn't just my academic research that reporters ignored on this topic;[2] there was also no mention of the National Research Council's research showing that suicidal individuals had merely "substituted other methods of suicide."[3] Nor did the studies mentioned by CNN give any consideration to research which found that firearm suicides are not so much the product of higher gun ownership as factors related to rural areas (e.g., older men in rural areas are more likely to commit suicide because of the large male-to-female imbalance).[4]

Consider a December 2015 *Deseret News* article on how to curb mass shootings. The only academics interviewed were gun control advocates, namely Garen Wintemute of the UC-Davis Violence Prevention Research Program and Mark Rosenberg of the Task for Global Health. The only opposing perspective came from National Rifle Association spokeswoman Catherine Mortensen. Likewise, a January 2016 story in the *New York Times* on Obama's new proposed gun control regulations balanced discussions with a pro-gun control professor and Bloomberg's Everytown with some federally licensed gun dealers and gun owners.[5]

SURVEYING THE EXPERTS

If anything, the hard part should be finding academics who *advocate* gun control, not ones who oppose it. Economist Gary Mauser and I surveyed economists and criminologists who have published peer-reviewed, empirical research on the relationship between gun ownership, crime, and suicide.[6] Limiting our survey to those who had published between January 1997 and July 2013, we emailed the survey to fifty economists and eighty criminologists.

Of the fifty economists, there were forty-three Americans, four Canadians, two Australians, and one Swede. The response rate was 70 percent (thirty-five out of fifty). Among the eighty criminologists were sixty Americans, nine Canadians, two Australians, and one Frenchman. Thirty-nine of the eighty responded, for a 49 percent response rate.[7]

Economists and criminologists both study crime, but they look at the subject through different lenses. Gary Becker got economists started with his seminal contribution in the *Journal of Political Economy*.[8] Economics sees the world in terms of the "law of demand"—as something becomes more costly, people do less of it. For instance, economists believe that an increase in the risk of conviction or in the severity of punishment results in fewer crimes. Law enforcement is consistently a key factor behind crime rates. Criminologists tend to put less stock in the concept of deterrence.

Maybe this lack of a unifying theory is what causes a divide among criminologists. Gary Kleck of Florida State University even said that he doesn't know of any "credible criminologist" who believes that "with more guns there are less crimes."[9] The late James Q. Wilson, however, concluded in 2005: "I find that the evidence presented by Lott and his supporters suggests that [right-to-carry] laws do in fact help drive down the murder rate."[10]

These two groups of academics have different beliefs about politics and society. Taking the average of surveys on academic economists' political views, we find that Democrat economists outnumber their Republican colleagues by almost three to one.[11] The imbalance is even greater in sociology, of which criminology is a subfield. There are about thirty-seven Democrat faculty members for every Republican. Many sociology departments do not have even a single Republican.

Economists are also generally more skeptical of regulation. Knowing the unintended consequences of economic regulation, they are more likely to realize that regulations designed to save lives can actually result in more death.[12]

This survey is the first of its kind to compare the views of economists and criminologists on guns. We focus on researchers who have actually published empirical work on gun issues.[13] Our survey contains more than 4.2 times as many economists and 22 percent more criminologists than the only other survey, which included studies that merely mentioned the words "firearm" or "gun."[14] As we will see, economists and criminologists both still tend to hold favorable views of gun ownership.

There is a clear consensus among economists about self-defense, gun-free zones, firearms and suicide, and concealed handgun laws. Among North American economists:

- Eighty-eight percent say that guns are more frequently "used in self-defense than they are used in the commission of crime."
- Ninety-one percent believe that gun-free zones are "more likely to attract criminals than they are to deter them."
- Seventy-two percent do *not* agree that "a gun in the home causes an increase in the risk of suicide."
- Ninety-one percent say that "concealed handgun permit holders are much more law-abiding than the typical American."
- Eighty-one percent say that permitted concealed handguns lower the murder rate.

After including all those who have published worldwide, these percentages fall by between three and eight percentage points. But the numbers are still quite high, and largely mirror the literature surveys on concealed carry laws.[15] As discussed earlier, this survey also provides results consistent with Pew and Gallup surveys of the general U.S. adult population.

Criminologists were far more divided, being about equally split on three of the five questions.

Without question, most researchers believe that guns are used more often in self-defense than in the commission of a crime. They also believe that gun-free zones attract criminals; that guns in the home do not increase the risk of suicide; that concealed handgun permit holders are much more law-abiding than the typical American; and that permitted concealed handguns lower the murder rate. All of these results are statistically significant.

SURVEY RESULTS

FIGURE 1

Question 1: In the United States, are guns used in self-defense more often than they are used in the commission of crime?

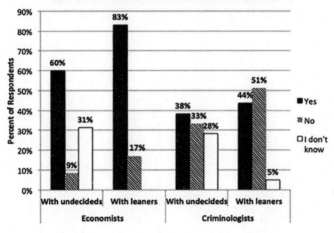

FIGURE 2

Question 2: Are gun-free zones, areas where civilians are banned from having guns, more likely to attract criminals than they are to deter them?

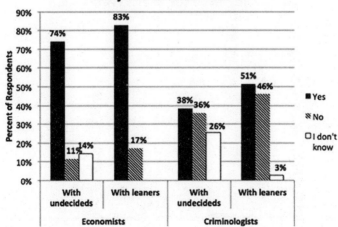

FIGURE 3

Question 3: Would you say that, in the United States, having a gun in the home causes an increase in the risk of suicide?

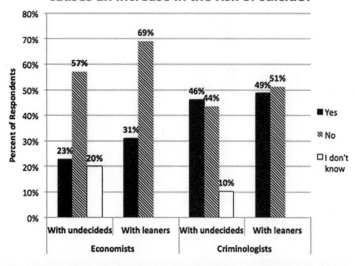

FIGURE 4

Question 4: Would you say that concealed handgun permit holders are much more law-abiding than the typical American?

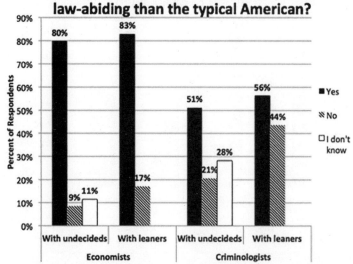

FIGURE 5

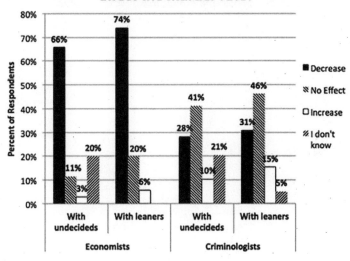

Question 5: How does allowing people to carry a permitted concealed handgun affect the murder rate?

FIGURE 6

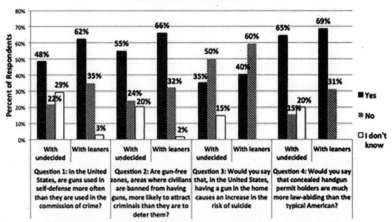

Combining Results for Economists and Criminologists from Entire World

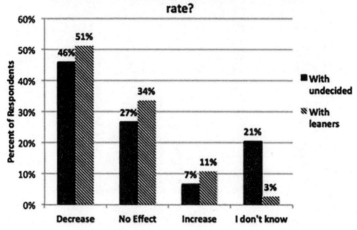

FIGURE 7

Combining Results for Economists and Criminologists
from Entire World
**Question 5: How does allowing people to carry a
permitted concealed handgun affect the murder
rate?**

COMPARING ECONOMISTS AND CRIMINOLOGISTS

The responses to questions one, two, and five clearly show that the notion of deterrence is much less widely accepted among criminologists than among economists (Graph 6).[16] Criminologists are only slightly more likely than not to say that gun-free zones attract criminals. Same with the question of whether guns are more likely to be used in self-defense than in the commission of a crime. The differences were not statistically significant (see Appendix Table 1.2a-c).

Both criminologists and economists, however, overwhelmingly believe that concealed handguns *reduce* rather than *increase* murders. Even when a decision is required of respondents who answered "I don't know," economists are twelve times as likely to answer that concealed handguns reduce murder than they are to answer that they cause an increase. Criminologists are twice as likely to believe this. However, the majority of criminologists think that concealed handguns have no effect.

The differences don't end there. Economists overwhelmingly believe that gun ownership does not increase the risk of suicide, whereas criminologists are very equally divided. Both economists and criminologists say that concealed permit holders are "much more law-abiding than the typical American," but again, criminologists are much more divided.

Overall, researchers strongly lean towards the view that guns are more often used in self-defense than in crime; that gun-free zones attract criminals; that guns in the home do not increase the risk of suicide; that concealed handgun permit holders are much more law-abiding than the typical American; and that permitted concealed handguns lower murder rates (Graph 6). Those answers are all given by margins of at least twenty percentage points (and as much as forty percentage points). The results are all statistically significant.

In other words, if the media wanted to, they could easily find academics on different sides of the gun debate.

COVERING ALL THE BASES

Michael Bloomberg would like the media's already skewed coverage of the effects of gun ownership to be even more unbalanced. His gun control group, Everytown, is funding two-day workshops at Columbia University's Dart Center for Journalism. For example, in May 2015, journalists came from around the country to learn about "covering guns." Needless to say, Columbia would never allow the National Rifle Association (NRA) to sponsor an event on this subject.

Bruce Shapiro, executive director of the Dart Center, claimed that there was "no party line" and called the workshop "very balanced."[17] In fact, gun control advocates made up fifteen of the panel's seventeen experts. Weren't journalism schools supposed to teach journalists to present both sides of a story? Only two law enforcement officers made presentations: Sheriff Clarence W. Dupnik of Pima County, Arizona, and Tucson Chief of Police Roberto A. Villaseñor. Both are proponents of stricter gun control. Dupnik, a liberal Democrat, has long attacked Arizona's concealed handgun laws for being too lax.[18] He described the move to eliminate gun-free zones as "insane." Villaseñor has been an outspoken supporter of President Obama's gun control proposals, even visiting the White House.[19]

But these officers represent a minority view. According to a 2013 survey of PoliceOne's 450,000 members (380,000 active duty and 70,000 retired), 91 percent of law enforcement officers *support* concealed carry laws.[20] Eighty percent believed that concealed carry permit holders could have prevented casualties in tragedies such as those in Newtown and Aurora. Ninety-two percent think that Obama's proposed assault weapon ban would either increase or have no effect on violent crime. Many other police surveys show similar results (e.g., Police Magazine and National Association of Chiefs of Police).[21] Indeed, police probably support private gun ownership more strongly than any other group. Columbia University could very easily have found officers who believe that people should be able to defend themselves.

All five of the workshop's academic researchers also happened to be proponents of more gun control. Roseanna Ander argues: "We absolutely have a sub-optimal federal policy right now on guns, and a lot of the things that [Obama] outlined are really important and promising."[22] Philip Cook maintains that the previous assault weapons ban just didn't go far enough.[23] Jim MacMillan claims that the solution is simple: "Fewer guns would equal fewer deaths." Garen Wintemute considers Obama's proposed assault weapons ban to be a "great idea" and states that "Gun policy in the US...reflects the priorities of a radical fringe of gun owners."[24] Finally, Jill Messing advocates stricter gun control as a means of reducing domestic violence.[25]

Despite all the academic research pointing in exactly the opposite direction, Columbia managed not to get a single researcher who is skeptical of gun control. Just two speakers actually supported gun ownership, and conservative commentator S.E. Cupp had no particular expertise on the issue. Conservative lawyer David Kopel spoke only about the history of the Second Amendment. Kopel's talk, however, was paired with one by Larry Rosenthal, a professor at the Chapman University Law School and a strong gun control advocate.[26] Cupp was up against Tim Evans of the *Indianapolis Star*, Mark Follman of *Mother Jones* magazine, and associate professor Marc Cooper of the University of Southern California Annenberg School for Communication and Journalism.[27]

Columbia's Dart Center treated Bloomberg and his various anti-gun groups as objective sources of information. "Nearly 12,000 murdered with guns each year," parroted Columbia in an online post announcing the workshop. In fact, the FBI reports that there were 8,124 murder victims in 2014. Since 2010, the number of victims has stayed below 9,000.[28] Columbia also repeated the absurd claim that the U.S. has a firearm murder rate "20 times higher than other developed countries." Chile has a murder rate very similar to that of the U.S. Brazil and Russia are both developed countries that have much higher firearm murder rates than the U.S.

The Dart Center reiterated Bloomberg's claim that "nearly 100 school shootings have occurred since the massacre at Sandy Hook Elementary only two years ago."[29] The *Washington Post* gave this claim "Four Pinocchios," the rating reserved for the most egregious falsehoods.[30] One would think that Columbia would set a good example for its students by doing some basic fact-checking and presenting both sides of the issue. Columbia ought to know that it is only hindering Americans from discerning the truth about guns.

Just look at the wall-to-wall coverage of a February 2014 report from Mayors Against Illegal Guns and Moms Demand Action. More than 2,000 news stories covered the report. It claimed that forty-four "Mini-Newtowns" had taken twenty-eight lives at schools and colleges since the Newtown, Connecticut massacre on December 14, 2012.[31] According to the report, these shootings have become so commonplace that the media no longer pays attention to them. This claim became an Obama talking point. "It happens now once a week. And it's a one-day story. There's no place else like this," said Obama in a June 2014 interview.

These "Mini-Newtowns" included lone, nighttime suicides that took place when no one else was around at school. They included cases of legitimate self-defense, as well as gang-related shootings that took place in the vicinity of school grounds. The only criteria for these

"Mini-Newtowns" was that a shot was fired. In some cases, no one was even hurt. About 40 percent of the deaths (eleven out of twenty-eight) were suicides. Probably a third of the remaining cases—and most of the remaining deaths—involved gang fights. Others involved crimes such as robbery.

Bloomberg's groups influence the media in other ways. For one thing, they have control over whom they debate on television and radio shows. I know this from personal experience. On a half dozen occasions, I have been asked to appear on CNN or elsewhere, only then to be told that I'm out because the representative from Bloomberg's group wouldn't appear with me on the show. I have even been told this as I was driving to the television studio. All the producers could give me was their sympathy. A couple producers even asked me if I could recommend a replacement who held my same views.

On two occasions, things haven't gone quite the way that the Bloomberg people intended. In April 2015, C-SPAN's *Washington Journal* invited me to participate in a one-hour debate with Ted Alcorn, research director at Everytown. Alcorn had already agreed to appear on the show. But when the C-SPAN producer told Alcorn that I would be on the other side, he informed her that he would no longer be able to participate, because something had come up. When the C-SPAN producer suggested that they might simply let me appear by myself, Alcorn suddenly realized that he could appear on the show. However, he was only available for the last half-hour of the segment after I had spoken, and insisted that he appear by himself.

I learned all of this from the C-SPAN producer, who was slightly miffed over the situation. She encouraged me to let viewers know about Alcorn's unwillingness to debate me. From the show transcript:[32]

> Lott: I wanted to mention one last thing. I was really disap-
> pointed that the people from Everytown, your producer said
> that I should mention this, weren't willing to go on with me
> right now to discuss this. I think that the audience would gain
> a lot more from the give and take, where someone could make

a claim, and the other person could rebut it. I am disappointed that they have continually refused to appear at the same time.

When Alcorn finally appeared on *Washington Journal*, the first caller asked him about his unwillingness to debate.

> Caller: Yes, I guess that my first comment is that I think it is quite telling that the people who are opposed to gun rights refuse to appear on screen with Dr. Lott or other economists or criminologists whose research has shown that expanding gun rights is strongly correlated with falling crime rates and with reducing violent crime. And I guess the question that I would have is: why is that?

After responding with a long discussion about how we "live in a moment when gun rights in the U.S. have an unprecedented level of protection," Alcorn eventually got to his main concern.

> Alcorn: When there's a credible scientist—somebody who wants to have a real constructive conversation about this, we're going to be there. But folks who seek to minimize the issue of gun violence, the grave issue of gun violence in this country or to draw attention away from the real issues to themselves—that's not a conversation that I think is productive to be a part of.

Apparently, in Alcorn's dictionary "credible scientist" means someone willing to agree with him. Of course, if he believed that I am wrong, he could use the debate as an opportunity to point out any errors on my part. The more likely explanation is that Everytown can play hardball and afford to lose these opportunities, because they have more mainstream media personnel who agree with their point of view and will push their agenda. They also likely know that most producers will let Everytown have its way about whom to debate.

Another instance occurred at Fox News. I was asked to appear on Stossel to discuss Bloomberg's claims regarding domestic violence and the risks of guns in the home.[33] Once more, Everytown refused to participate as soon as they learned that I would be appearing with them. The producer tried hard to accommodate Everytown's concerns. But he let them know that the segment would go forward with or without their participation. Everytown's PR people did send some statements that were read and discussed on the show, but a debate with a live person would have been much more enlightening.

CHAPTER 3

THE TIDAL WAVE
OF PUBLIC HEALTH
RESEARCH

It's actually kind of appalling. We're one of the richest nations in the world, and we aren't exactly forbidding scientists to look at this, but the federal government is strongly discouraging it.[1]
—Sherry Towers, professor at Arizona State University,
January 21, 2016

I t is an article of faith that the evil NRA has stopped research on gun violence and gun safety. News story after news story keeps pointing to the 1996 Dickey Amendment, which imposed restrictions on Centers for Disease Control funding of firearms research. They claim that this legislation "stopped" or imposed a "virtual ban" on such research. Take some headlines that appeared in 2013 and 2014:[2]

- The *Washington Post* proclaimed, "Federal scientists can again research gun violence" and, "Gun research is allowed again." It even claimed that "[Academics] were forced to stop their work at the point of a gun—or at least at the insistence of National Rifle Association."[3]
- Reuters: "Research restrictions pushed by the National Rifle Association have stopped the United States from finding solutions to firearms violence."[4]

- ABC News noted on January 31, 2014: "In 1996, the NRA successfully lobbied Congress to pull millions of dollars out of government-funded firearms research. This has resulted in essentially a 17-year moratorium on major studies about gun injuries."[5]
- When we previously discussed media bias, we noted how the media's notion of balance is to pair pro-gun control academics against an NRA spokesperson. As another example, the *New York Times* ran two stories by Michael Luo about the Dickey Amendment. Luo quotes seven academics who agreed that the amendment had stopped research, but for balance Luo only talked to the NRA and former Congressman Jay Dickey.[6]

According to a Bloomberg report in January 2013, the Dickey Amendment "has driven many experts to abandon the field and kept young researchers from taking it up.... [T]he decline in federal research has undermined overall knowledge-creation because scholars are highly dependent on federal grants to support their research."[7] Of course, academics were only too willing to claim that they need more funding. Professor Mark Rosenberg of Emory University, who used to head the CDC's National Center for Injury Prevention and Control, described how cutting federal grants cultivated an atmosphere of fear and "terrorized people."[8] Jens Ludwig of the University of Chicago said that it is "very difficult" to do research without federal money.[9] Susan Sorenson of the University of Pennsylvania believes that the loss of federal funding has "decimated the field."[10] A number of academics signed an open letter demanding more federal funding for their research.[11]

In April 2016, 141 medical organizations, from the American Academy of Pediatrics to the American Medical Association to the Washington State Public Health Association, sent a letter to Congress complaining that "[the Dickey amendment] has caused a dramatic chilling effect on federal research that has stalled and stymied progress on gathering critical data to inform prevention of gun violence for the past

20 years. Furthermore, it has discouraged the next generation of research-ers from entering the field."[12]

As a result of Obama's orders after the December 2012 Newtown shooting, the federal government started awarding more money to research institutions, though it takes a few years before the research is written and published. The National Institute of Justice awarded its first four awards totaling 2 million dollars in October 2013.[13] The National Institute of Health started awarding proposals in 2014.[14] Thus NBC News ran an article entitled: "Obama's unlocking of federal funding ban on gun research yields little upshot in first year."[15]

The first of these studies funded by the CDC came out in November 2015.[16] Using data for Wilmington, Delaware, it discovered that the majority of young men who were involved in firearm crime were also involved in crime as juveniles, got expelled from school, were abused as children, dropped out of high school prior to graduation, and were unemployed. Then the study simply asserts that government programs providing "life skills training," "individual placement and support" for jobs, "multi-dimensional treatment foster care," and something listed as "coping power" would solve the problem. Wilmington City Council-woman Hanifa Shabazz "called on state and city officials to move with the utmost speed to implement the CDC's recommendations."[17]

Of course, I could have asserted with equal validity that school vouchers, more police, and eliminating the minimum wage would help children become productive members of society and reduce crime. But it isn't too surprising that research funded by a Democratic administra-tion would reach these policy conclusions. After all, one big problem with government-funded research is that politicians and their appointees can't keep politics from influencing where they donate money.

Bloomberg had already been involved in funding research, but other private funding quickly gained traction. The Fund for a Safer Future, organized by George Soros's Open Society Foundation and the equally left wing Joyce and MacArthur Foundations, put together 16 million dollars by the fall of 2013.[18] Some of their money is going toward "shap-ing the media conversation around the need for stronger gun laws" and developing grassroots organizations "demanding stronger gun laws."[19] The Fund for a Safer Future by itself awarded more money for gun control research than did the National Institute of Justice and the National Institute of Health—and even more than the 10 million dollars that President Obama proposed for the CDC.[20]

Given the time required for conducting research, writing the papers, and receiving feedback, as well as delays in the journal process, the Fund for a Safer Future announced that published articles will start appearing "within three years."[21]

On January 8, 2013, President Obama met with twenty-three large foundations to organize a national push for gun control. They included such organizations as the McCormick Foundation, the Robert Wood Johnson Foundation, and the California Endowment.[22]

In 2016, with complaints about the 1996 federal budget amendment and concerns that the Republican-controlled Congress wasn't providing more funding, the California legislature moved forward with 5 million dollars in funding for public health research on firearms.[23] "Our researchers at the University of California are top in the nation, and if Congress refuses to act responsibly, we need to step up and fill the void," asserted California state senator Lois Wolk (D-Davis).

Research on gun control, however, did not decline, even after the 1996 Dickey Amendment. Federal funding declined, but research either remained constant or increased. After 2011, when the restriction on CDC funding was extended to all Health and Human Services agencies, firearms research has actually seen a steady increase. Because putting out these studies takes time, this increase could not have been affected by last year's changes in federal funding.

CHANGES IN FIREARM RESEARCH

Michael Bloomberg's Mayors Against Illegal Guns said in January, 2013, "Academic publishing on firearm violence fell by 60% between 1996 and 2010."[24] Despite this widely publicized claim,[25] no evidence was ever provided that firearms research actually declined in the wake

FIGURE 1

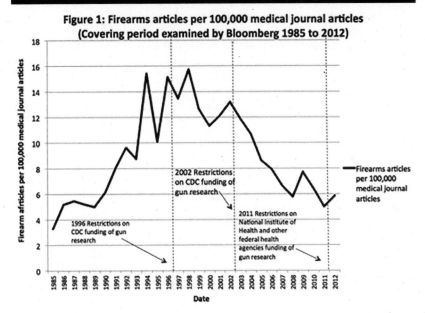

Figure 1: Firearms articles per 100,000 medical journal articles
(Covering period examined by Bloomberg 1985 to 2012)

of the Dickey Amendment. The same goes for the more extensive 2011 restrictions, which prevented the NIH and other federal health agencies from funding gun research.

What Bloomberg actually measured was firearms research *relative to all other research*. After 1996, firearms research in medical journals did in fact fall as a percentage of all research (see Figure 1). However, up through 2013, when the concerns over firearms research surfaced, there was clearly no decrease in either the total number of papers or pages devoted to firearms research. After that, well before even the smallest increase in federally funded studies, research had exploded.

Three amendments have been claimed to affect federal funding for firearms research. The funding restrictions are usually labeled depending on when the vote on the amendments took place—1996, 2002, and 2011. However, the funding changes took place respectively for the 1997, 2003, and 2012 federal government appropriation bills. This distinction differentiates between when the congressional votes occurred and when the actual funding changes took place.[26]

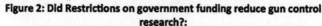

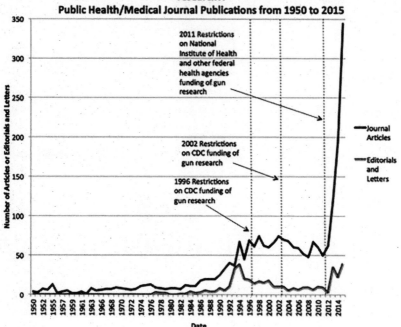

Figure 2: Did Restrictions on government funding reduce gun control research?:
Public Health/Medical Journal Publications from 1950 to 2015

In fact, the number of firearms journal articles published in medical journals was relatively flat between 1996 and 2012, before Obama's changes in research funding could have any effect. But at the same time, those changes were dwarfed by a 133 percent increase in all medical journal articles. By 2013 and 2014, still well before any publications, written or published, could be funded by the federal government, the number of articles had soared to 121 and 196, respectively.[27] In 2015, 229 articles were published through August that year, and 344 at an annual rate.

Another way to measure total research output is the number of pages written on firearms. A couple of very short papers involve less work than a longer one. Given that journal space is scarce, journals will also give more space to research that they regard as more significant. But looking at the number of pages also shows no decrease in research—rising from 459 pages in 1996 to 753 in 2002 and back down to 456 in 2012. After

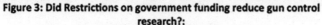

FIGURE 3

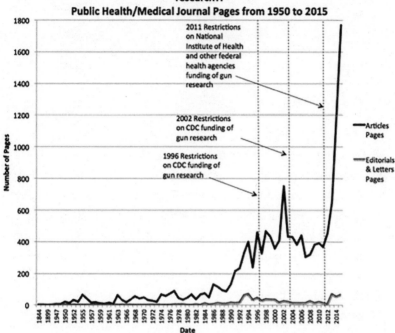

Figure 3: Did Restrictions on government funding reduce gun control research?:
Public Health/Medical Journal Pages from 1950 to 2015

that, it soared to 651 pages in 2013 and 1,202 in 2014. Again, through August 2015, there were 1,179 pages, and at an annual rate of 1,769.

Maybe additional government funding would have led to more research. However, neither Figures 2 nor 3 suggest that experts were driven to "abandon the field." And there certainly was no "virtual ban on basic federal research."

Medical journal articles are required to mention any outside funding sources that they received. I collected data on funding sources for papers published from 1992 to 2013, and only 15 percent of the papers mention a funding source. Such funding isn't really necessary for virtually all research. Part of academic salaries are explicitly designated to cover their research, and the vast majority of social science research isn't that costly—it just involves using data that has already been collected by organizations such as the FBI and Centers for Disease Control.

Table 1: Funding sources for firearms research: assuming a three year lag in impact on research (1992 to 2013)		
	Share of research funded	Share of research federally funded
Pre-2000	8.5%	2.9%
2000 and later	18.2%	3.3%
Average over entire period	14.7%	3.2%

Assume that research is published within about three years after it is funded. If so, both federal funding and funding generally increased after the 1996 Dickey Amendment. As Table 1 shows, just 8.5 percent of the pre-2000 papers mention any funding source. Among later firearm papers, 18.2 percent mention a funding source.[28] From 1992 to 2013, only about 3 percent of papers on gun control ever received U.S. government funding. Moreover, the growth in papers appears to have been driven entirely by private funding (e.g., Bloomberg and the Joyce Foundation).

During 2013 there was a big increase in published firearms research with twenty-three papers receiving private funding, the largest number during the period being studied. Still that increased private funding only supported about a quarter of the increase in the number of papers published between 2012 and 2013. Papers citing the federal government for funding their research only increased by one paper between 2012 and 2013.

BLOOMBERG'S NFL AD CAMPAIGN

Michael Bloomberg is overwhelming the gun debate by spending over 50 million dollars a year just on his Everytown organization. In 2013, Bloomberg alone outspent all self-defense rights groups (including the NRA) by 6.3 to 1 on television ads.[29] Even discounting Bloomberg's massive expenditures, other gun control groups still spent 10 percent more than self-defense rights groups.

Bloomberg has had other advantages. The NFL allowed Bloomberg to run Super Bowl ads in 2012 and 2013, but prohibited a commercial on "personal protection and fundamental rights."[30] In his 2012 ad, Bloomberg called for "common sense reforms that would save lives" and said that signing up for his group was "the patriotic thing to do."[31] In 2015, the NBA lent its name and star players to ads which were "timed to reach millions of basketball fans during a series of marquee games on Christmas Day."[32]

Bloomberg also got something that self-defense rights groups could never dream of—news stories that uncritically repeated the claims in his ads. Bloomberg's 2013 Super Bowl ad got favorable news coverage in such national media outlets as National Public Radio, *Politico*, *The New Yorker*, *Business Insider*, *Slate*, and *The Daily Caller*.[33]

In the 2012 Super Bowl ad, Michael Bloomberg banters with the mayor of Boston over their cities' sports teams. Bloomberg is shown boasting about the 600 mayors who support his position on gun control. But with around 35,000 mayors across the U.S., 600 is a tiny number, only 1.7 percent of the total. Almost all of the 600 mayors are from small towns.

Bloomberg's Super Bowl ad the next year in 2013 came just six weeks after the Newtown tragedy. This ad was much more heavy-handed. A child's voice pleaded for safety and background checks as pictures of five young children played on the screen. In fact, background checks would have had no effect in Newtown because the killer used guns that his mother had legally purchased. Economists and criminologists alike consistently find no benefit from background checks (a subject we will explore further later).

In 2014, the ad that the NFL turned down featured a former Marine talking about his responsibility for his family's safety. Unlike Bloomberg's ads, this ad never even mentions the word *gun*, just the concept of personal protection. The company even told the NFL that it would happily remove its logo, which features a gun, and replace it with a picture of an American flag. But apparently the stumbling block was the vague reference to someone being responsible for his family's safety. The NFL and NBA are private organizations that are free to support Bloomberg if they so choose. But right now, these organizations seem to be guided by political correctness rather than consistent rules or guiding principles.

Early in 2015, I was invited to testify before the state legislatures in Wyoming and Nevada about gun-free zones. I found that Bloomberg had gotten there first, renting out buses and hiring college students to pass out flyers. He was also running attack ads against the state legislators who were sponsoring legislation to eliminate gun-free zones. One thirty-second ad accused Nevada Assemblywoman Michele Fiore of wanting legislation "allowing criminals to carry hidden, loaded guns in our schools and college campuses."[34] This is an outrageous falsehood. Eliminating gun-free zones doesn't mean that just anyone can carry a gun. You still need to have a concealed handgun permit, which requires a criminal background check. And as we will see, permit holders are an incredibly law-abiding bunch.

Bloomberg's spending has weighed very heavily on local politics across the country. When Milwaukee Sheriff David Clarke ran for reelection in 2014, Bloomberg spent $151,000 just on ads attacking Clarke in the Democratic primary—more money than Clarke and his challenger spent on the entire race.[35] Bloomberg obviously targeted Clarke because he has been an outspoken advocate of using guns for self-protection.[36] Clarke narrowly won that election (52 percent to 48 percent).[37]

In two Virginia State Senate races in November 2014, Bloomberg spent a stunning total of over $2.2 million in just the last couple weeks before the vote.[38] By contrast, between the end of August and the November election in 2014, the NRA *nationwide* spent only $14.7 million.[39]

Bloomberg is smart and willing to spend whatever it takes to influence the gun debate. He isn't simply pouring money into political races. He is organizing people around the country, training the media, and spending the money necessary to produce research that supports his goals.

THE INCREDIBLY FLAWED PUBLIC HEALTH RESEARCH

Michael Bloomberg, George Soros, and numerous left-leaning foundations have been spending hundreds of millions of dollars on a huge push for "scholarly public health studies." In fact, these studies are mostly fearmongering. They exaggerate the threat that guns pose to children, to their owners, and to our country. And these researchers are getting paid quite well to do so. Their studies will be released in rapid succession in the months leading up to the 2016 general election. Anything seems fair game in this war on guns.

By creating the data used in the gun control debate, gun control adovcates hope to be able to control the debate itself. And they have already had success in doing so. These anti-gun studies will attempt to convince Americans that:

- They are actually too irresponsible to own and operate a gun.
- Gun ownership will lead to the death of their loved ones through accidental shootings and suicides.
- People who advocate gun ownership are dangerous.

The benefits of gun ownership have generally gone ignored in medical journals that have studied gun ownership, what is called *the public health literature*. There is no mention that widespread gun ownership deters criminals from breaking into homes. There is no mention that gun ownership helps protect residents from harm in the event of a break-in, or that mass public shooters consistently attack gun-free zones where they don't have to worry about victims being able to defend themselves. And gun owners—contrary to what the media advises—should not unquestioningly store their guns locked and unloaded. That defeats the purpose of being ready at a moment's notice.

The media is doing quite a job of scaring people. A recent 2014 study in the journal *Pediatrics* received massive media attention, including extensive coverage in *USA Today* and an entire hour on ABC News's *20/20*.[40] Here's how ABC's *World News Tonight* reported the findings:[41]

> Looking at children and guns, the most recent statistics from 2009. And take a look tonight, they are eye-opening. The new numbers are arresting.... 7,391 children rushed to the hospital every year because of those gun injuries, so often accidents in the home. Four hundred and fifty-three of those children die at the hospital.

The vast majority of these "children" are actually young adults. These are not little kids who accidentally hurt themselves by firing their parents' gun. Consider these facts:

- Seventy-six percent of these injured "children" were seventeen, eighteen, or nineteen years old.
- Sixty-two percent of injuries were the result of criminal assaults.
- The injuries are overwhelmingly concentrated in large, urban areas.

These deaths are clearly tragic. But they are largely a result of gang violence, a problem that won't be solved by scaring law-abiding Americans into not owning guns.

Then there was the media attention given in early 2014 to a study by Dan Webster of the Bloomberg School of Public Health. He claimed that closing the so-called "gun-show loophole" for background checks—as Missouri did for a while—was effective in reducing murder. The study received extensive coverage from the BBC, CBS, NBC, PBS, and newspapers across the country.

Between 1981 and 2007, Missouri had "universal background checks" in addition to the federal "Brady Law" background checks. The "universal" checks required that private sales of handguns—as opposed to sales done through stores—also be subject to such checks.

In the five years after 2007, when universal background checks were abandoned, Missouri's murder rate rose by 17 percent. However, in the five years *before* that change, it had actually *increased* by 32 percent. Missouri was already on an ominous path and the rate of increase slowed after the law was eliminated. More importantly, however, note the cherry-picking needed for Webster to obtain even a biased result. The problem isn't only ignoring other states. Even if you just take Missouri, why not examine the change in crime rates when the law was adopted? If Webster had looked at the same five years before and after the adoption of the law, he would have found no evidence that Missouri's crime rate fell relative to the rate in the rest of the U.S. Eighteen other states either currently have universal background checks or had them at some point during the past three decades. Nor was Missouri the only state that ended this law. When you examine all the states, there is no evidence to be found that these background checks affect murder rates.

Some think that government funding is the best way of ensuring that research is unbiased. But this book will show how politicians can't keep politics out of who they choose to fund or what "experts" they put on various committees. Academics, like any special interest group members, will always claim that they need more money.

Virtually all of the research showing that gun ownership endangers society comes from doctors and public health researchers. Here's what is hidden or left out of the following discussions.

GUNS IN THE HOME

At a town hall at George Mason University in January 2016, President Obama said, "If you look at the statistics, there's no doubt that there are times where somebody who has a weapon has been able to protect themselves and scare off an intruder or an assailant, but what is more often the case is that they may not have been able to protect themselves, but they end up being the victim of the weapon that they purchased themselves."[42] He was parroting one study: *keeping a gun in the home was strongly and independently associated with an increased risk of homicide.*[43] Its primary proponents are Arthur Kellermann and his many coauthors. A gun, they have argued, is less likely to be used in killing a criminal than it is to be used in killing someone the gun owner knows.

In his most well-known paper, Kellermann's "case sample" consists of 444 homicides that occurred in homes.[44] His control group is comprised of 388 individuals who lived within a mile of the deceased victims and were of the same sex, race, and age range. After learning about the homicide victims and control subjects—whether they owned a gun, had a drug or alcohol problem, etc.—these authors attempted to see if the probability of a homicide correlated with gun ownership.

But these studies make an amazing assumption. They assume that if someone died from a gun shot, and a gun was owned in the home, that it was the gun in the home that killed that person. The paper is clearly misleading, as it fails to report that *in only eight of these 444 homicide cases* was the gun that had been kept in the home the murder weapon.[45] Moreover, the number of criminals stopped with a gun is much higher than the number killed in defensive gun uses. In fact, the attacker is killed in fewer than one out of every 1,000 defensive gun uses. Fix either of these data errors and the results are reversed.

To demonstrate, suppose that we use the same statistical method—with a matching control group—to do a study on the efficacy of hospital care. Assume that we collect data just as these authors did, compiling a list of all the people who died in a particular county over the period of a year. Then we ask their relatives whether they had been admitted to the hospital during the previous year. We also put together a control sample consisting of neighbors who are part of the same sex, race, and age group. Then we ask these men and women whether they have been in a hospital during the past year. My bet is that those who spent time in hospitals are much more likely to have died.

Would we take that as evidence that hospitals kill people? I would hope not. We would understand that although we controlled for the variables of age, sex, race, and neighborhood, the people who had visited a hospital during the past year were really not the same as people in the "control" sample. Obviously, the hospitalized people were sick or injured and faced a higher risk of death. You don't want to compare a sick a person with a healthy person, but with other sick people to see what would happen if one went to the hospital and the other didn't.

Similarly, people who are at greater risk of being attacked are probably more likely to arm themselves. Even though they live within a mile of the deceased, they might still live in a more dangerous neighborhood or their homes might be more dangerous for another reason. Perhaps a small number of these people are involved in dangerous, illegal activities. Even with a gun, it might still be more likely for something bad to happen to them than to the comparison group, but less likely than the risk that they faced if they never got the gun.

The big problem for public health researchers is that they are trying to apply medicinal testing approaches to human behavior. In a drug test, some patients with a disease may be provided with the drug while others would be given a placebo. The drug and the placebo would be assigned randomly. A comparable approach for testing the link between homicide and gun ownership would be to randomly assign guns to some of the households. The remaining households would be gun-free if they wanted to have a gun. That way, gun ownership would not be affected by other factors that may be related to a person's probability of being killed. Of course, it would probably be impossible to actually carry out such a study.

Economists solve this problem by looking at costs or prices. So if a local hospital closes down or if the price of medical care goes up, some sick people who previously received medical care no longer received it, the question is what happens to the mortality rate. Or, for guns, if it is more costly for some people who would previously have owned guns not to own them, the question is what happens to the murder or accidental gun death rate.

While there are no official government statistics on people accidentally shooting people they know (having mistook them for intruders), we can use news searches to get a rough idea of the frequency of these cases. We used Nexis to search for news stories from 2011 to 2013. Though each incident garnered news stories in major U.S. media outlets (*USA*

Today, CNN, Fox News, *New York Daily News*), it is amazing how rare these cases are. Eight tragedies occurred in 2013, eleven in 2012, and only five in 2011.[46]

Gun uses in homes get news coverage at least a thousand times a year, but coverage of them is almost entirely limited to small stories in local media.

CHAPTER 4

WHY LICENSES, REGULATIONS, AND BACKGROUND CHECKS DON'T HELP

Whether in Canada, Hawaii, Chicago, or Washington, D.C., police are unable to point to a single instance of gun registration aiding the investigation of a violent crime. In a 2013 deposition, D.C. Police Chief Cathy Lanier said that the department could not "recall any specific instance where registration records were used to determine who committed a crime."[1]

The idea behind a registry is that guns left at a crime scene can be used to trace back to the criminals. Unfortunately, guns are very rarely left at the scene of the crime. Those that are left behind are virtually never registered—criminals are not stupid enough to leave behind guns registered to them. In the few cases where registered guns were left at the scene, the criminal had usually been killed or seriously injured.

Canada keeps some of the most thorough data on gun registration. From 2003 to 2009, a weapon was identified in fewer than a third of the country's 1,314 firearm homicides. Of these identified weapons, only about a quarter were registered. Roughly half of these registered guns were registered to someone other than the person accused of the homicide. In just sixty-two cases—4.7 percent of all firearm homicides—was the gun identified as being registered to the accused. Since most Canadian homicides are not committed with a gun, these sixty-two cases correspond to only about 1 percent of all homicides.

From 2003 to 2009, there were only sixty-two cases—just nine a year—where registration made any conceivable difference. But apparently, the registry was not important even in those cases. Despite a handgun registry in effect since 1934, the Royal Canadian Mounted Police and the Chiefs of Police have not yet provided a single example in which tracing was of more than peripheral importance in solving a case. No more successful was the long-gun registry that started in 1997 and cost Canadians $2.7 billion before being scrapped.

In February 2000, I testified before the Hawaii State Senate joint hearing between the Judiciary and Transportation committees on changes that were being proposed to the state gun registration laws.[2] I suggested two questions to the state senators: (1) how many crimes had been solved by their current registration and licensing system, and (2) how much time did it currently take police to register guns? The Honolulu police chief was notified in advance about those questions to give him time to research them. He told the committee that he could not point to any crimes that had been solved by registration, and he estimated that his officers spent over 50,000 hours each year on registering guns.

But those aren't the only failings of gun registration. Ballistic fingerprinting was all the rage fifteen years ago. This process requires keeping a database of the markings that a particular gun makes on a bullet—its unique fingerprint, so to speak. Maryland led the way in ballistic investigation, and New York soon followed. The days of criminal gun use were supposedly numbered. It didn't work.[3] Registering guns' ballistic fingerprints never solved a single crime. New York scrapped its program in 2012.[4] In November 2015, Maryland announced it would be doing the same.[5]

But the programs were costly. Between 2000 and 2004, Maryland spent at least $2.5 million setting up and operating its computer database.[6] In New York, the total cost of the program was about $40 million.[7]

Whether one is talking about D.C., Canada, or these other jurisdictions, think of all the other police activities that this money could have funded. How many more police officers could have been hired? How many more crimes could have been solved? A 2005 Maryland State Police report labeled the operation "ineffective and expensive."[8] These programs didn't work.

RETHINKING IN LIGHT OF REALITY

Gun-control advocates have long predicted the success of ballistic fingerprinting. Dan Webster of Johns Hopkins' Bloomberg School of Public Health argued that the program would work because the vast majority of criminals obtain their guns legally. Authorities, he predicted, would be able to establish matches between firearms in the database and spent rounds found at crime scenes.[9] Bloomberg might have felt that he got his money's worth from Webster's claims, but Webster was wrong on both counts. Very *few* criminals legally purchase guns themselves. Recording the markings on guns was a waste of time and money.

Gun-control advocates ignored simple physics. When a bullet travels through the gun barrel, friction creates markings on the bullet. Imperfections in the way the barrel was drilled can produce different markings on the bullet; such imperfections are most noticeable in older or inexpensive guns. Many other factors influence the particular markings left on the bullets—for instance, how often the gun is cleaned and what brand of cartridge is used.

Unlike human fingerprints and DNA, a gun's ballistic fingerprint changes over time because of wear.[10] A child's fingerprint can still be used much later in life. A ballistic fingerprint, on the other hand, is more like the tread on a car tire. New tires of the same model and brand, with some minor exceptions, are essentially identical. Over time, though, friction causes the tread on tires to wear. The more the car is driven after the crime, the harder it is to match the tire tracks left at the scene to the tires when they are eventually found. The same holds true for guns. The greatest friction on a gun occurs when the gun is first fired—and that dramatically and quickly reduces the usefulness of recording the gun's ballistic fingerprint when it is purchased. Moreover, criminals can thwart ballistic fingerprinting by replacing the barrel of a gun. Still easier, they can alter the ballistic fingerprint by just scratching the inside of the barrel.

The response from gun-control advocates is that fifteen years and at least 10 million dollars wasn't enough. They simply need more time because the science is valid. They claim that, on average, most guns used in crimes were bought nearly fifteen years prior. But even if that were accurate, it doesn't explain why the systems in Maryland and New York haven't solved a single crime.

It is shocking what lengths public health researchers have gone to in order to justify gun registration. It is bad statistics to only analyze data from one state or from a particular set of years. Since most readers are not familiar with the data, researchers need to be very clear as to why they are only examining a small portion of the total sample. Otherwise, they may just be using whatever data happens to support their conclusions.

In 2015, researchers from the Johns Hopkins Center for Gun Policy and Research, part of the Johns Hopkins Bloomberg School of Public Health, claimed that "a 1995 Connecticut law requiring a permit or license—contingent on passing a background check—in order to purchase a handgun was associated with a 40% reduction in the state's firearm-related homicide rate."[11]

But looking at only Connecticut makes no more sense than our previous discussion of looking at only Missouri. Ten states have required licensing (Hawaii, Illinois, Iowa, Missouri, Massachusetts, Michigan, Nebraska, New Jersey, New York, North Carolina, and the District of Columbia). Suppose for a second that the Connecticut law really did reduce firearm homicides; looking at just the one state makes it impossible to discern whether the drop was due to licensing, registration, or background checks. The authors just claim that the change is due to all three laws, but the only way that you would know if that were true would be to take states that had adopted different combinations of those three laws. When you are looking at one state, you can't even know if something else unique to Connecticut might be changing.

As the authors of the study note, from 1995 to 2005, the firearm homicide rate in Connecticut indeed fell from 3.13 to 1.88 per 100,000 people. This amounts to a 40 percent drop over a ten-year period ("We estimate that the law was associated with a 40% reduction in Connecticut's firearm homicide rates during the first 10 years that the law was in place"). But there are two problems with this conclusion. First, homicide rates fell by 32 percent across the whole country over those same years. Possibly, they could argue that homicide rates had fallen 8 percent faster in Connecticut, but there is no way they can assume that the entire 40 percent drop was due to the laws that they wanted to focus on.

A second problem is that the firearms homicide rate was falling even faster immediately prior to the licensing law's enactment in 1995. From 1993 to 1995, the Connecticut firearms homicide rate fell from 4.5 to 3.13 per 100,000 residents. This is a drop of more than 30 percent in just two years. The national decline over those two years was 17 percent. The Bloomberg School of Public Health researchers do not address this inconvenient fact that firearm homicides were falling even faster *before* Connecticut adopted its laws (though the preceding drop is clearly visible in Figure 1, on page three of their study).

For a study published in 2015, with much more recent data abounding, 2005 was also an extremely convenient and arbitrary end year to pick.[12] Everything changes if 2006 is picked as the end year. Connecticut's firearm homicide rate fell by only 16 percent between 1995 and 2006. Meanwhile, the U.S. and the rest of the Northeast experienced much greater drops of 27 percent and 22 percent, respectively. When we extend the period from 1995 to 2010, we again find that Connecticut experienced a smaller than average drop in firearm homicides.

The Bloomberg School of Public Health researchers would also have run into problems if they had examined a shorter period of time. In three of the four years immediately after the law was passed in 1995,

FIGURE 1

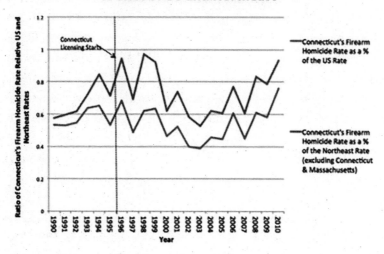

Connecticut's Firearm Homicide Rate Relative to Rest of US and Northeast

Connecticut's firearm homicide rate rose relative to the firearm homicides in the rest of the U.S. and other Northeastern states (Figure 1). But there is no theory offered for why Connecticut's firearm homicide rate would first rise relative to other Northeastern states, then fall relative to them for six years, and then rise relative to them for four of the next five years.

The same graph for next-door Massachusetts—which had all the same licensing, registration, and background checks as Connecticut—shows how bad things were after the state's 1998 gun licensing law went into effect (Figure 2). No wonder why gun-control advocates pick Connecticut.

The Bloomberg School of Public Health researchers not only cherry-pick the years and states to look at, but also what crime rates they examine. In 1995, Connecticut's overall violent crime rate stopped falling and then flattened relative to the rest of the U.S (Figure 3). There is no clear overall change in murder rates before and after the licensing law went into effect (Figure 4). Robbery and aggravated assaults rates were falling

FIGURE 2

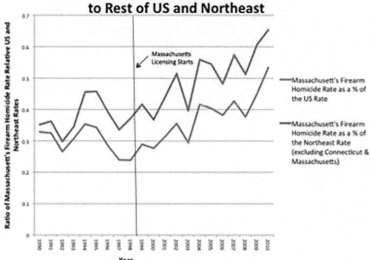

Massachusetts' Firearm Homicide Rate Relative to Rest of US and Northeast

FIGURE 3

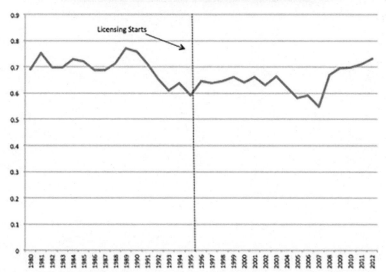

Connecticut's Violent Crime Rate Relative to Rest of US

FIGURE 4

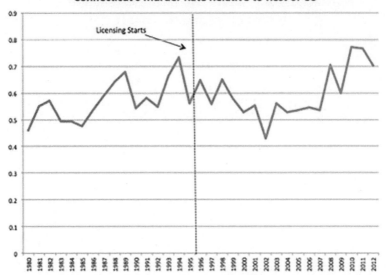

Connecticut's Murder Rate Relative to Rest of US

FIGURE 5

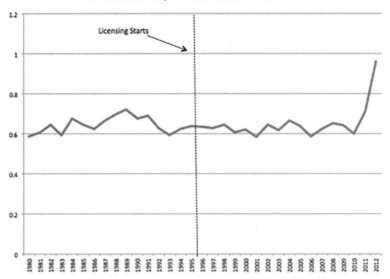

Connecticut's Rape Rate Relative to Rest of US

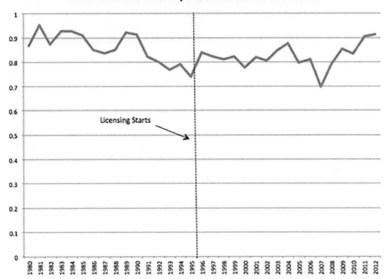

FIGURE 6

Connecticut's Robbery Rate Relative to Rest of US

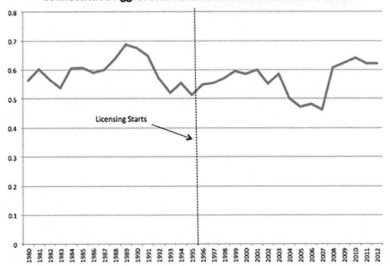

FIGURE 7

Connecticut's Aggravated Assault Rate Relative to Rest of US

prior to 1995 and then rose for a while afterward (Figures 6 and 7). Why not mention any of these other crime rates?[13]

Reporters may not have a good grasp of science, but they ought to start wondering when only one state is studied. It doesn't take much research to learn that many other states have adopted the same types of laws. Yet, despite all the cherry picking and distortions, the media gave the study massive amounts of uncritical news coverage. Apparently it was too good of a story to bother with journalistic concerns like getting both sides of the story. Among the media there was the Associated Press (with newspapers across the country carrying their story), *Washington Post, Newsweek, US News World Report, Philadelphia Inquirer, Newser, Baltimore Sun, Arstechnica,* and Huffington Post.[14] The notion that they might want to ask other academics if they had any concerns about the study never seems to have crossed these reporters' minds.

Here is a simple rule for journalists to follow: if a study doesn't have a really good reason to exclude or omit data, it shouldn't be taken seriously. At least Michael Bloomberg got his money's worth for funding this "study."

ARE BACKGROUND CHECKS EFFECTIVE?

You know that the case for background checks on the private transfers of guns is weak by realizing how far academic gun control advocates are willing to go to manipulate the data. With a 2016 study released by the prestigious medical journal, the *Lancet*, it seems that no medical journal is above publishing junk science to push gun control.[15] Yet, the study got massive news coverage including: PBS *Newshour*, CNN, Reuters, and the *Los Angeles Times*.[16]

"Expanded" background checks apply the current background checks on the purchase of guns from a dealer to cover the private transfers of guns, as well. The studies that we just discussed on Missouri and Connecticut have been pointed out to me by a number of reporters as proof that these types of checks can save lives. The *Lancet* study claims that these background checks on private transfers of guns will reduce state firearms deaths (homicides plus suicides) by 57 percent. But few researchers would look at firearm deaths across states in one year.

Consider a common comparison of different countries. As many people point out, the UK has both lower gun ownership rates and lower homicide rates than the U.S. Yet, it does not logically follow that reducing gun ownership leads to a reduction in crime. In fact, as discussed in more detail in the next chapter, after the UK's 1997 nationwide handgun ban, their homicide rate actually *increased by 50 percent over the next eight years*. The UK still had a lower homicide rate than the U.S., but this wasn't because of the handgun ban. Other factors must have played a role. The ban itself raised their homicide rate, but simply comparing countries' numbers made it look like the opposite was happening.

The point is that homicide or suicide rates can differ for lots of reasons that have nothing to do with gun control. Simply glancing across countries or states can be quite misleading. What most researchers would do is see how a location's crime rate changed after its laws change and how that change compares to places that didn't change their laws.

There are many other problems with this study, such as looking at different gun control laws in completely separate estimates. When I did research for the 2010 edition of *More Guns, Less Crime* (University of Chicago Press), using data from all the states from 1977 to 2005, I found that these expanded background checks produced a very small and statistically insignificant 2 percent increase in murder rates.

The cherry picking is outrageous. Gun laws for 2009 are used to evaluate firearms deaths in 2010 and firearm ownership for 2013. No explanation is offered for why different years are used for these different variables. Again, the preferred approach by researchers is to use all the crime or suicide data that is available for all the years. There must be a very good reason to selectively throw out data, and it is pretty hard to think what that would be. In a debate on Public Radio with the lead author of this study, Bindu Kalesan, I made these points. When the radio show host asked her about my concern with looking at data for only one year, Kalesan responded that "we intended this study to be the preliminary evidence to show that at least one of these laws can be implemented on the Federal level to reduce gun deaths."[17] But that claim makes no sense. As is true for so many of these public health studies, the data for her study might have taken at most a couple weeks to put together. It doesn't help to do a "preliminary" study if that study doesn't measure what you want it to measure.

In the debate, I said that Bindu's study showed laziness. After all, the gun laws her study used were already compiled for them by the gun control group, the Brady Center. The data on firearm suicides and homicides as well as non-firearm homicides are easily obtained from the U.S. Centers for Disease Control website.[18] The same is true of the data on state unemployment rates, firearm ownership, and firearm exports. But I have since realized I was wrong about laziness. The goal doesn't appear to be to get the studies right, but to produce lots of—poorly done—studies quickly so that they can get lots of media attention. They know that no matter how flawed the studies are, tens of millions of people will hear the claim that academics believe that gun control works.

There are other, more sophisticated ways that academics can selectively pick what data to use in their estimates. One common way is to change how variables are measured. Take a well-cited paper by Jens Ludwig and Phil Cook in the *Journal of the American Medical Association*.[19] Like others, they weren't able to find any evidence that the Brady Act had reduced homicide rates, but they claimed that it reduced suicides among those fifty-five and older.

But why use age fifty-five as the cutoff? If you are going to pick just one year, wouldn't a more natural one be age sixty-five? If you use the data the way that it is provided by the government in ten-year intervals, it quickly becomes obvious why Ludwig and Cook did what they did.[20] The data reveal that the reduced incidence of firearm suicides for persons older than fifty-four years is primarily affected by the group aged fifty-five to sixty-four years; however, this subcategory has by far the biggest drop in suicide rate for those fifty-five and older. The different age groups experienced apparently random increases and decreases in firearm suicides after enactment of the law: the groups aged thirty-five to forty-four years, forty-five to fifty-four years, and older than age eighty-five, for instance, all show significant increase in firearm suicide rates. Those from sixty-five to seventy-four show a small increase.

What theory could anyone have for why the Brady Act would lower the suicide rate for those who are fifty-five to sixty-four but raise the rate for those who are forty-five to fifty-four and sixty-five to seventy-four? What is clear is that the Brady Act had no consistent effect on suicide rates.

Just as academics need a good explanation before they throw out data, they also need to justify why they don't use the raw data in its original form.

CHAPTER 5

POLICE AND GUN OWNERSHIP

n the first two months of 2016, criminals have murdered ten police officers in the line of duty. The number might have been twelve if not for the actions of two concealed handgun permit holders:

- On January 16, a drunk man attacked a deputy sheriff near Austin, Texas. As the deputy relates what happened, "I remember thinking, stay in the fight. Just keep fighting, keep fighting. Do whatever you can do; just stay alive. You need to go home."[1] The deputy ended up having his gun taken away from him. Fortunately, a concealed handgun permit holder pointed his gun at the attacker and ordered him to "freeze!" "I'm alive today because of [the permit holder]," said the deputy. "There are no words to explain it. He's such an outstanding citizen."

- On February 5, in Upper Darby, Pennsylvania, a police officer tried to break up a fight between two teenagers who had just gotten out of school.[2] Two other students then jumped on the officer. A crowd of another forty to fifty students had been watching the fight and "all [started to] move in towards the officer." At that point, a permit holder stepped forward and told everyone to get away from the cop. As the Upper Darby Police Superintendent Michael Chitwood described it: "He had the gun in his hand, but he didn't point it at the kids, he just told them to back off. If this guy didn't come out and come to the aid of the officer, this officer would have had significant problems." Fortunately, the officer only suffered "significant hand injuries." The permit holder kept the mob at bay until other officers arrived. But that wasn't the end of it. Even one of the responding officers was hospitalized after suffering a "major injury to a leg."

One thousand and eighty-nine police officers have been killed in the line of duty between 1996 and 2015, an average of fifty-four killed per year. These public servants put their lives on the line to protect Americans. Their deaths should concern everyone, including public health researchers. But public health researchers' dislike of guns may be clouding their judgment. A study in 2015 in the *American Journal of Public Health*, again funded by Bloomberg, claims that more police were feloniously killed in states with more guns.[3] They mistakenly conclude that private gun ownership causes police deaths.

It is yet another study from which Bloomberg has gotten his money's worth. The study received extensive uncritical news coverage at TV networks such as NBC News, newspapers such as the *Chicago Sun-Times*, and international coverage such as the UK *Guardian*.[4] But if the researchers hadn't left out controls used by everyone else for this type of empirical work, they would have gotten very different results.

Previous research by Professor David Mustard at the University of Georgia has done just that. It found that concealed handgun permits tend to lead to fewer police deaths.[5] The authors of the new Bloomberg-funded study offered no explanation for their unorthodox approach.

Let me explain what happened. There is a big benefit to using what is called "panel data," following changes in crime rates across many different states over a number of years. Doing that allows researchers to have many different experiments and makes it possible to more accurately explain differences in crime rates across states or over time.

In discussing background checks, we examined the case of the homicide rate in the UK after the handgun ban in 1997. We found that crime rates can vary from country to country for lots of reasons that have nothing to do with gun control. A similar point applies over time. Suppose a state passes a gun control law at the same time that crime rates are falling nationally. It would be a mistake to attribute the overall drop in national crime rates to the law that got passed. To account for that concern, researchers normally see whether the drop in a state's crime rate is greater or less than the overall national change.

Looking at data by state over many years allows researchers to account for both of these potential biases, but the *American Journal of Public Health* study doesn't account for this bias over time, and the authors offer no explanation for this lapse. If they had done what professionals do and how they know research is supposed to be done, their results would have been reversed. Instead of validating their claim that a one-percentage point increase in the percent of suicides committed with guns increases the total number of police killed by 3.5 percent, they would have found that police killings are *reduc*ed by 3.6 percent.[6]

Previous work has shown that letting law-abiding citizens carry guns reduces the rate that criminals carry guns, thus making it safer for both civilians and police alike.[7] But perhaps the craziest thing about this study is how it measures gun ownership. While the media talks about gun ownership being related to police deaths, what they are actually measuring is the percentage of suicides committed with guns. While this may have some relationship to gun ownership, this much more likely picks up whether the population is relatively more male—as men are more likely to use guns for suicide—as well as other demographic and geographical differences. For example, even when women own guns, they are more likely than men to use other methods of committing suicide. Despite all the extensive news coverage of the *American Journal of Public Health* study, there were no interviews with anyone who might have been critical of the controversial study.

In reality, criminals have ways of getting guns even when guns are banned. For example, drug gangs will get their guns to protect their drugs just as easily as they get their drugs to sell. Thus gun control primarily disarms the citizens who obey the laws. There are lots of good, law-abiding citizens who not only protect themselves and their fellow citizens, but even help protect the police.

NRA ACADEMIC RESEARCH FUNDING DEBUNKED

On *Piers Morgan Tonight*, Alan Dershowitz claimed, "[W]hat's happening is the NRA is buying their data. They're buying their facts. They're hiring and commissioning so-called scholars to come up with the kinds of lies."[8] In another appearance he declared, "Your [John Lott's] conclusions are paid for and financed by the National Rifle Association…This [Lott's research] is junk science at its worst. Paid for and financed by the National Rifle Association … It [the NRA] only funds research that will lead to these conclusions."[9]

But the NRA doesn't fund empirical research for a simple reason—the media would ignore it. Talk about a double standard. Even hopelessly flawed, Bloomberg-funded studies are covered in thousands of uncritical news stories. And there does not seem to be any stigma to academic researchers accepting funding from Bloomberg. But that is the way the world works.

Still, this hasn't stopped gun control advocates from suggesting that researchers who find benefits of self defense are in the NRA's pocket. We aren't usually mentioned by name, although James Q. Wilson and myself are exceptions. John Donohue of Stanford Law School attacked Wilson in 2008 for having "testified as an expert witness on behalf of the execrable NRA."[10] His real crime, however, was that he had written approvingly of my research. Unable to debate on the merits, tying a researcher to the NRA is seen as one way of convincing others that the researcher is not objective. Wilson wrote me: "[Donohue] was lying.... I have never been hired by the NRA and I disagree with some of its views."[11]

Dershowitz has claimed that the NRA funded the research in my 1998 book *More Guns, Less Crime*. This myth has been debunked time and again, including in a long letter in the *Wall Street Journal*.[12] The bottom line is that I was a scholar at the University of Chicago Law School, which does not take gun-lobby contributions. Each of the three editions of my book was published by the University of Chicago Press and peer-reviewed by academics from across a range of specialties. The University of Chicago Press would not have published my research if it thought these claims against my research were true.

The claim is especially ludicrous, since the NRA doesn't seem to fund any statistical research at all. When I appeared on CNN with Dershowitz in July 2012, I forcefully responded, "Take that back. The NRA hasn't paid for my research. That's simply ridiculous."[13] When asked about these claims, the NRA told Cybercast News Service: "The NRA has never funded John Lott's research."[14] Dershowitz declined to provide any support for his charges when Cybercast asked him for evidence.

I currently run the Crime Prevention Research Center, which has a clear policy that it "does not accept donations from gun or ammunition makers or organizations such as the NRA or any other organizations involved in the gun control debate on either side of the issue."[15] The only academic I know of who gets money from the NRA is David Kopel, an adjunct professor at the Denver University Law School. Between 2004 and 2012, Kopel received $1.42 million from the NRA Civil Rights Defense Fund, apparently for doing legal work and law review research.[16] Kopel's behavior has helped create the stigma around NRA funding. He has gotten into trouble for not acknowledging in either his op-eds or testimony that the NRA has been a major funding source.[17] But these grants are public information, and they won't be hidden for long.

In Republican and Democratic administrations alike, conservative researchers have missed out on public funding. Republicans have simply not been as ruthlessly partisan as Democrats have been when it comes to allocating research dollars. George W. Bush's first director of the National Institute of Justice was Sarah Hart, a Democrat, who didn't share the Bush administration's views on gun control or the death penalty.[18] She used federal funding to support liberal positions on both issues. Bush's director of the Bureau of Justice Statistics was Larry Greenfeld.[19] Besides being a Democrat, Greenfeld's background should have raised a red flag, as he was the deputy director of the Bureau of Justice Statistics under the Clinton administration.[20] He was eventually demoted and moved to another agency in 2005 after pushing poorly done research on traffic stops and racial profiling.[21]

Democrats, by contrast, make sure to appoint fellow Democrats to these important positions. They make sure to fund studies that will support their positions. The point isn't that Republicans should be as ruthless as Democrats, but simply to acknowledge that government can't keep politics out of whose research is funded and question whether the government should be involved at all.

CHAPTER 6

DOCTORING THE POLLS AND FUDGING THE DATA

G un control advocates are trying to portray gun owners as freaks and social misfits. Michael Bloomberg's Everytown has released one ad that features an awkward, paranoid gun owner trying to pick up a woman at a bar.[1] The man, who shows off that he is carrying three handguns, says, "These guns are the only things standing between us and tyranny." The lady works for the government and asks him if he views her as the threat. The ad is filled with stupid statements from the man, such as warning about the much bigger danger posed by hammers than guns. He assures her that the police won't accidentally shoot him if he tries to stop a crime, because he is wearing a button saying he is "A good guy with a gun." Apparently the Bloomberg people were not satisfied with the heavy-handedness of the ad; it ends with a written statement: "Don't date a #gunsplainer."

Despite surging gun sales, opponents of the Second Amendment like to give the impression that gun owners are a dwindling minority. According to Hollye Dexter, cochair of Women Against Gun Violence:

FIGURE 1

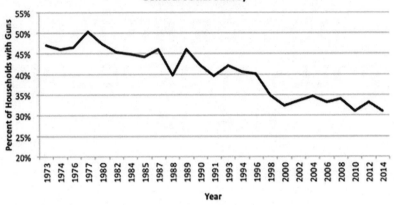

Do you happen to have in your home any guns or revolvers?
General Social Survey

The amount of households that own guns is like under 30%, or around 30%, and it's not as high as it used to be. What is happening is that those people are creating arsenals, and that is also disconcerting to me. That there are fewer households with guns, but they have a lot more of them. That freaks me out a little bit.[2]

So is gun ownership falling? It depends on which poll you look at. The answer is *yes*, according to a new General Social Survey (GSS) by the National Opinion Research Center (NORC). According to the GSS, approximately 32 percent of homes have guns, down from 50 percent in the late 1970s.[3] "The number of Americans who live in a household with at least one gun is lower than it's ever been," reported Emily Swanson of the Associated Press.[4]

A couple of much more limited Pew Research surveys have suggested a similar drop in gun ownership.[5] Surely, gun control advocates such as GSS director Tom Smith view this decline as a good thing. In a 2003 book of mine, I quoted Smith saying that the large drop in gun ownership would "make it easier for politicians to do the right thing on guns."[6]

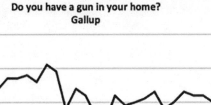

FIGURE 2

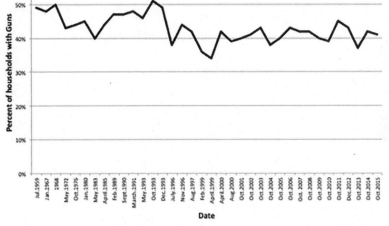

Do you have a gun in your home?
Gallup

Gun control advocates are already trying to decrease gun ownership by dramatically exaggerating the risks of having guns in the home.[7] Now they are hoping that believing gun ownership is falling will cause people to think twice before buying a gun. That is not mere speculation—gun control advocates have told me this themselves.

Gallup and ABC News/*Washington Post* polls show that gun ownership rates have been relatively flat over the same period. According to Gallup, household gun ownership has ranged from 51 percent in 1994 to 34 percent in 1999. In 2014, the figure was 42 percent—comparable to the 43–45 percent figures during the 1970s.[8] A January 2016 CNN poll showed that 40 percent of Americans lived in households with guns.[9] Another 9 percent were unwilling to say, implying that the true rate is above 40 percent.

The ABC News/*Washington Post*, CNN, and Gallup polls show that in 2015 somewhere between 132 and 136 million Americans lived in homes with guns, with 30 million or so being under age eighteen.

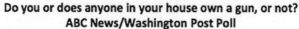

FIGURE 3

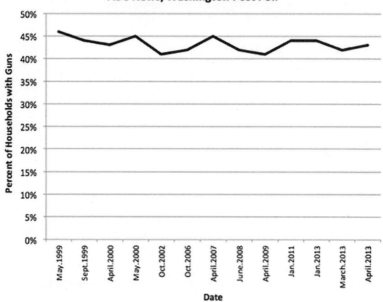

Do you or does anyone in your house own a gun, or not?
ABC News/Washington Post Poll

In 2011, Gallup published a poll with the headline, "Self-Reported Gun Ownership in U.S. Is Highest Since 1993."[10] How much news coverage did this get? None, as far as I can see. The ABC News/*Washington Post* poll shows an even more stable pattern. In 1999, the household ownership rate was between 44 and 46 percent.[11] In 2013, the rate was 43 percent.

In late 2013 and early 2014, I witnessed another example of media bias on this issue. Lauren Pearle, a producer with ABC News, contacted me about a special that Diane Sawyer was going to do on kids and guns.[12] Referring to the GSS survey, Pearle pointed to the dramatic fall in gun ownership and wondered whether gun owners would someday be only a "fringe" group. But I pointed out to her how strange it is that ABC News wouldn't use its own survey, which shows that gun ownership hasn't been falling. Pearle was skeptical that such a poll existed until I sent her the links to ABC's polling data. Needless to say, Diane Sawyer's report, which was covered on everything from *ABC Evening News* to *Good Morning America* to *20/20*, never mentioned the ABC survey and instead focused solely on the General Social Survey.[13]

There are other hard measures that suggest that we should be very careful of relying too heavily on polling to gauge the level of gun ownership. For example, the number of concealed handgun permits has soared nationwide from about 4.6 million in 2007 to over 13 million by the beginning of 2016.[14] The National Instant Criminal Background Check System (NICS) shows that the number of gun purchases has exploded over time—doubling from 11.2 million in 2007 to 23.1 million in 2015.[15] In Illinois, people are required to obtain a Firearm Owner Identification (FOID) card to own a gun. The number of people with those cards has soared from a little over 1.3 million in 2010 to 1.9 million in December 2015.

There are also some other problems with using polling to measure gun ownership. As touched on earlier, some people don't feel comfortable saying whether they own guns. A recent Zogby Analytics survey asked, "If a national pollster asked you if you owned a firearm, would you determine to tell him or her the truth or would you feel it was none of their business?"[16] Thirty-five percent of current gun owners said it was none of the pollster's business. This answer is slightly more common among those who claim not to be gun owners.

The same GSS poll—the one that finds gun ownership to be at a record low—also finds that "confidence in all three branches of government is at or near record lows."[17] Perhaps increasing distrust of the government is making people less likely to admit to owning a gun.

We also know that recent events influence people's willingness to acknowledge gun ownership. After mass shootings, the polls suddenly find fewer people saying that they own guns. In the 1990s, mass public shootings such as Columbine probably made people reticent to acknowledge to pollsters that they owned guns. After all, it's not very plausible that gun ownership could have fallen by seventeen percentage points between 1994 and 1999 (as Gallup polling shows), even though gun sales soared during the early to mid-1990s.

But this isn't the only limitation of gun ownership polls. Married men are much more likely than married women to say that they have a gun in the home. Either the men are hiding guns from their wives or, more likely, women are more reticent to admit to a pollster that they own a gun. If it is the latter, that fact would cause an eight percentage point increase in the GSS poll's reported gun ownership rate.

There is a reason why websites such as RealClearPolitics.com have become popular with people who follow elections. They offer an average of all available polls. While any one poll might have errors in it or may be purposefully skewed to obtain a particular result, the average of polls is likely to give us a much more accurate picture. The point is no different for polls on gun ownership, though it is likely that all polls underestimate the true rate that people own guns, and that gap may have been increasing in recent years.

The selective use of polls might provide gun control advocates with a momentary talking point. But what is beyond dispute is that hard numbers show a huge increase in gun sales and in the percentage of Americans who carry guns.

BLOOMBERG'S ALARMIST TACTICS: SCHOOL SHOOTINGS

Are schools and colleges dangerous places with lots of gun violence? Some gun control groups give the impression that firearm murders and suicides are very common at educational institutions. Bloomberg's Everytown claims that 170 school shootings occurred between January 1, 2013 and March 10, 2016. This covers everthing from kindergarten through college. "It is difficult to see how many of the incidents included in Everytown's list...would be considered a 'school shooting' in the context of Sandy Hook," said Michelle Ye Hee Lee, a fact checker at the *Washington Post*.[18] Suicides are included in their numbers. Also included are late night shootings taking place in school parking lots, on their grounds, or even off school property, often involving gangs. As "shootings,"

Bloomberg also includes any incident where shots were fired, even when nobody was injured.

Here are some of the cases included in the misleading statistics:[19]

- June 2015: A man and a woman at South Macon Elementary School shot a cat to death.[20]
- April 2015: A student at a community college in Beaver Falls, Pennsylvania, accidentally shot himself in his leg in the school parking lot. "The [police] chief said the man was clearing his gun of any bullets before he entered the school for classes, and the gun went off. The man told police he was going to leave his gun in his car and wanted to empty it of ammunition."[21]
- April 2014: In front of the Detroit-based East English Village Preparatory Academy, "Two people inside the car began shouting gang affiliations and opened fire."[22] They shot a nineteen-year-old who later died.
- January 2014: A student at Eastern Florida State College retrieved his gun from his car after two men started attacking him. The student fired his gun after being struck with a pool cue. The gun was legally stored in the car, and police found that the student had acted in self-defense.[23]
- November 2013: A professor at the South Dakota School of Mines Technology committed suicide in an empty classroom.[24]
- November 2013: A twenty-three-year-old man committed suicide late at night on the grounds of Algona High/Middle School in Iowa. His body was found at 1:20 a.m.[25]
- September 2013: A nineteen-year-old man committed suicide in the parking lot of a Portland, Maine high school. No one at the school was threatened.[26]
- February 2013: A nineteen-year-old college student was killed at 9:00 PM in a field near the Hillside Elementary

School in San Leandro, California.[27] The gunfire apparently erupted during a game of dice.

The list goes on. So why does Bloomberg find it necessary to pad his numbers and equate these shootings with the Sandy Hook tragedy? Out of the 170 shootings, no one was killed in almost three-quarters of them—125.[28] Out of forty-five school shootings where someone was killed, gangs were involved in at least thirteen cases (and possibly as many as sixteen).[29] Some schools happen to be located in high-crime areas, so gang activity sometimes spills over onto school grounds. It is highly misleading to link such violence to the Newtown tragedy.

One of the supposed motivations behind the report put out by the gun control groups was that the media was ignoring these so-called "mini-Newtowns." Yet, all of these cases received extensive coverage. A gun at a school (or even near a school) is considered newsworthy. For example, *USA Today* ran at least one story on twenty-six of the forty-five cases with at least one fatality.

Some perspective is needed. Contrary to the image that Bloomberg is pushing, high school shootings have actually been *decreasing* over the last two decades. To illustrate, let's compare the five school years from 1992–93 to 1996–97 with the five school years from 2009–10 to 2013–14 (Figure 4).[30] During the first period, the number of non-gang, non-suicide shooting deaths averaged twenty-five per year in kindergarten through college. During the recent five year period, it averaged less than half that, only twelve per year—and that figure includes the horrific Newtown massacre.

To put these numbers in perspective, in 2014 there were about 50 million young people between the ages of six and seventeen.[31] Another 25 million people were enrolled in colleges.[32]

These statistics in no way diminish the devastation that has been caused by school shootings. But scaring Americans seems to be Bloomberg's only tool for drumming up support for gun control laws. The need for massive exaggerations suggests that gun control advocates realize the numbers aren't really on their side.

FIGURE 4

Non-gang, Non-suicide On School Firearm Deaths (K-12 Schools and Universities)

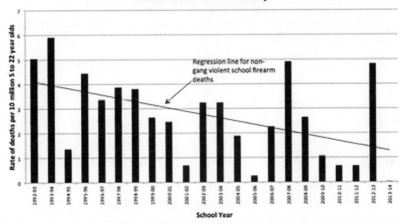

BLOOMBERG'S TACTICS ON MASS SHOOTINGS

In a July 2014 report, Everytown looked at shootings since 2009 where four or more people were killed. Everytown found 110 shootings, but the vast majority of these were gang-related. Many also occurred in residences, not public areas.

The FBI definition of mass public shootings excludes "shootings that resulted from gang or drug violence" or that were part of some other crime.[33] The FBI also defines "public" places as "includ[ing] commercial areas (divided into malls, businesses open to pedestrian traffic, and businesses closed to pedestrian traffic), educational environments (divided into schools [pre-kindergarten through twelfth grade] and IHEs), open spaces, government properties (divided into military and other government properties), houses of worship, and healthcare facilities."[34]

Mass public shootings rivet our attention on the news. In most cases, they are carried out for the purpose of attracting media attention. They occur in areas where it is relatively easy to kill a lot of people—places like schools, malls, and movie theaters.

Gang-related shootings, by contrast, are not designed to attract media attention. They are, of course, intertwined with the issue of illegal drugs. Absent legalization, drug gangs will keep fighting over turf. Gun laws, or a lack thereof, cannot be blamed for these shootings.

There is another reason that the FBI definition excludes gang fights. Unlike mass public shooters who attack defenseless crowds of people, gang members often intentionally go up against armed opponents. There is a lot at stake fighting over valuable drugs.

In another chapter, we will look more closely at mass public shootings and what distinguishes them from other kinds of shootings. For now, we can focus on the massive mathematical and recording errors in the Everytown report. Of course, these "errors" consistently work in favor of the desired conclusions. Even using their own definitions, Everytown gets some of the numbers wrong. The Bloomberg group misstates the average age of the shooters and the average number of people killed *each year* by assault weapons (7.7 versus the actual figure of 7.3). Much more importantly, however, the report incorrectly claims that mass public shooters don't target gun-free zones and rarely have histories of mental illness.

The Everytown report claims that 86 percent of mass shootings occur in places where civilians are allowed to carry guns (as opposed to gun-free zones). But they're talking about all mass shootings, not just those that occurred in public. With no regard for why the FBI makes the distinctions that it does, Everytown lumps mass public shootings together with gang shootings and shootings in residences.

There are other problems with the report. In many states, private businesses can choose to post signs forbidding permitted, concealed handguns. But Everytown just assumes that guns must have been allowed if no signs were mentioned in media reports. In fact, the media virtually never reports this information. When these attacks have occurred, I have had to either search online, call up the businesses, or get people in the area to go and see if signs are posted.

Everytown claims that guns are allowed on military bases such as Fort Hood. In fact, only military police officers can carry on base. If Bloomberg's people had ever been to a major military base, they'd know that Fort Hood is the size of a small city. The military police are no more likely than their civilian counterparts to instantly be at the scene of a shooting.

Everytown seems to assume that places with concealed carry laws are actually always issuing permits. Although most states will issue a permit if you meet certain objective criteria, other states allow discretion to decide whether or not you have good reason for getting a permit. On this basis, Boston doesn't even issue any permits at all. Los Angeles County has issued only 240 concealed handgun permits. All of these have gone to judges, reserve deputies, and very wealthy donors to the Los Angeles Sheriff's campaign fund.[35] Clearly, this isn't the same thing as letting civilians defend themselves.

Everytown reports that mental illness was noted in only 10 percent of mass shooters. This number is ridiculously low and doesn't count many cases where mental health was an obvious factor. It is also the result of including residential and gang shootings, as opposed to just mass public shootings.

Here are some examples of mental illness in mass public shootings that Everytown failed to mention in its report.

- Ka Pasasouk murdered four people in Northridge, California, on December 2, 2012: "In March 2011, while in prison for the methamphetamine conviction, Pasasouk underwent a psychiatric evaluation because of concerns regarding his behavior."[36]
- Wade Michael Page murdered six people in Oak Creek, Wisconsin, on August, 5, 2012: "'The suicide scare of 1997 would have been enough to alert Army doctors that Page had mental illness and was unfit for duty,' said John Liebert, a psychiatrist who does fitness exams for the military and has written an academic text on suicidal mass murderers."[37]
- Maurice Clemmons murdered four people in Lakewood, Washington, on November 29, 2009: Five weeks before

these murders, a court-ordered mental health evaluation was completed. It reported that Clemmons hallucinated about "people drinking blood and people eating babies and lawlessness on the streets, like people were cannibals."[38]

- Robert Stewart murdered eight people in Carthage, North Carolina, on March 29, 2009: "They also argued that Stewart suffered from mental illness including depression and borderline personality disorder, and that he had been taking regular doses of the prescription sleep aid Ambien far in excess of the recommended limit. Combined with *prescriptions for an antidepressant and anti-anxiety drug....*"[39]

- Major Nidal Malik Hasan, an Army psychiatrist, murdered thirteen people at Fort Hood on November 5, 2009: Hasan exhibited many strange behaviors, but nothing was done for fear of being seen as discriminating against a Muslim. "He also told colleagues at America's top military hospital that non-Muslims were infidels condemned to hell who should be set on fire. The outburst came during an hour-long talk Hasan...gave on the Koran in front of dozens of other doctors at Walter Reed Army Medical Centre in Washington DC, where he worked for six years before arriving at Fort Hood in July.... One Army doctor who knew him said a fear of appearing discriminatory against a Muslim soldier had stopped fellow officers from filing formal complaints."[40]

There are several other cases in which mental illness was noted, albeit not by mental health professionals. One such case was that of Jeong Soo Paek. Six years before the attack, his sister described her brother as suicidal and said that his mental health was deteriorating.[41] Jiverly A. Wong, who killed thirteen people in Binghamton, New York, sent a "two-page delusional rant to a Syracuse television station saying the police were spying on him, sneaking into his home, and trying to get into car

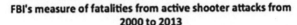

FIGURE 5

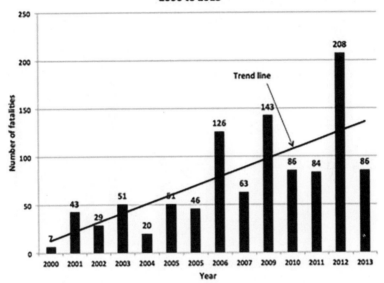

FBI's measure of fatalities from active shooter attacks from 2000 to 2013

accidents with him."[42] Overall, it is abundantly clear that Everytown did a very sloppy and incomplete job of identifying cases of mental illness.

It is amazing that anyone takes Bloomberg's reports seriously.

EVEN FBI CRIME DATA ISN'T SAFE

Unfortunately, the Obama administration is now using the FBI as a propaganda tool. Just weeks before the November 2014 election, the FBI released a report claiming that public shootings had skyrocketed since 2000.[43] Supposedly, 160 "mass" or "active" shootings had occurred in public places from 2000 to 2013, increasing from just one in 2000 to seventeen in 2013.

Typical newspaper headlines were "F.B.I. Confirms a Sharp Rise in Mass Shootings Since 2000" (*New York Times*); "Mass Shootings on the Rise, FBI says" (*Wall Street Journal*); "FBI: Mass shooting incidents

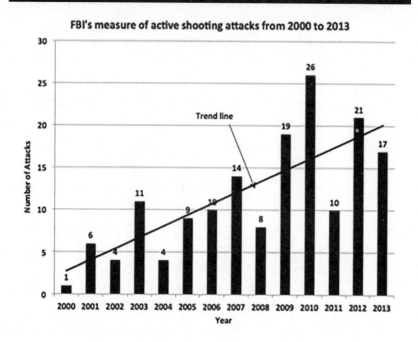

FIGURE 6

FBI's measure of active shooting attacks from 2000 to 2013

occurring more frequently" (CNN); and "Mass shootings in U.S. have tripled in recent years, FBI says" (*Los Angeles Times*).[44]

In a study recently published in the *Academy of Criminal Justice Sciences Today*, I show that the FBI data were remarkably dishonest. Crimes were undercounted at the beginning of the period and over-counted toward the end.[45] In fact, mass public shootings have only increased slightly over the last four decades. The change isn't even sta-tistically significant. Out of the 160 cases the FBI report counts from 2000 to 2013, thirty-two instances involved a gun being fired with no one killed (see Appendix Table 1.3). And eleven of those have either zero or just one person wounded. Another thirty-five cases involved one single person murdered. The increase in attacks is an illusion resulting from how the data was put together.

These so-called "active" shooters drive much of the purported increase in attacks. An "active" shooter case occurs any time a gun is fired, even if no one is injured or killed. Such cases involving one or no deaths have allegedly increased considerably. Seventeen cases occurred during the seven-year period from 2000–2006. The next seven years saw fifty cases, with most of those in the last few years.

The problem here is that the authors used Google news searches to compile these cases. Google is good for finding recent stories, but articles become more scarce as one looks further back in time. That isn't a problem for finding mass public shootings, where large numbers of people are killed. Suppose there are 800 news stories within the first week after an attack. Five years later a Google news search might show only 400 stories. After ten years, maybe just a couple hundred will show. But it will always find some news articles about the event. However, when no one was wounded or killed in a shooting, you might be lucky to find one news story even a week after the event. After a few years, a Google news search might find no evidence that the shooting ever took place.

There are other ways of searching for these news stories that don't suffer from this problem—computer databases that permanently save all the news stories that they collect. A couple of the best known databases are Nexis and Westlaw, but those weren't used in collecting these cases, so the drop off in these "active" shooter cases is very likely just a result of how the data is collected. In any case, there is no reliable way to find cases where guns are fired and no one is actually shot.

Amazingly, the FBI report also manages to miss twenty multiple victim shootings in which at least two people were killed. Among them was a 2001 Chicago bar shooting that left two dead and twenty-one wounded. Another missed shooting left four dead at a concert in Columbus, Ohio in 2004. Worst of all, the FBI missed a school shooting that left nine people dead. The missing cases were three times more likely to have occurred from 2000–2006 than from 2007–2013, thus making the earlier years look safer than they actually were.

THE FBI'S MISSING CASES

Year	Mo.	Day	City	State	Attacker Name	Killed in public	Wounded	Location
2000	3	2	Pittsburgh	Pennsylvania	Ronald Taylor	2	3	Restaurant
2000	3	10	Savannah	Georgia	Darrel Ingram	2	1	School
2000	4	28	Mount Lebanon	Pennsylvania	Richard Baumhammers	5	1	Neighborhood
2001	1	11	Nevada County	Nevada	Scott Thorpe	3	2	County mental health office / Restaurant
2001	4	13	Chicago	Illinois	Luther Casteel	2	21	Bar
2002	4	6	Tacoma	Washington	Felise Kaio, Jr.	2	1	Bar
2002	5	31	Long Beach	California	Antonio Pineiro	2	4	Supermarket
2002	6	11	Kearney	Missouri	Lloyd Robert Jeffress	2	2	Monastery
2002	10	29	Tucson	Arizona	Robert S. Flores	3	0	School
2004	12	8	Columbus	Ohio	Nathan Gale	4	7	Concert
2005	2	24	Smith County	Texas	David Hernandez Arroyo, Sr.	2	4	Tyler Courthouse
2005	4	8	Eastern Shore	Maryland	Allison Lamont Norman	9	5	School and multiple public locations
2005	12	4	Fort Lauderdale	Florida	Ralston Davis, Jr.	2	1	Multiple locations (apartment/gas station)
2006	4	19	St. Louis	Missouri	Herbert Chalmers, Jr.	2	1	Home and Workplace
2006	9	3	Shepherdstown	West Virginia	Douglas W. Pennington	2	0	University
2007	8	6	Newark	New Jersey	Melvin Jovel	3	1	School
2008	10	26	Conway	Arkansas	Kawin Brockton, 19, Kelsey Perry, 19, Mario Tony, 20, Brandon Wade, 20	2	1	School
2012	2	21	Norcross	Georgia	Jeong Soo Paek	3	0	At the spa
2013	6	12	St. Louis	Missouri	Ahmed Dirir	3	0	Office (in a Missouri office at AK Home Health Care LLC)
2013	6	20	West Palm Beach	Florida	Javier Burgo	2	0	Alexander W. Dreyfoos School of the Arts

FIGURE 7

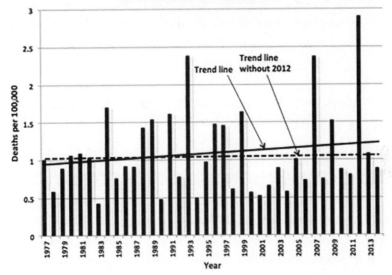

Deaths per 10,000,000 Americans from Mass Public Shootings, at least 2 people killed per attack

Another slight of hand involves choosing 2000 as the starting date for the analysis. It is widely known that 2000 and 2001 were unusually quiet years with few mass shootings. The authors probably knew perfectly well that they could get the desired results by starting with those years, omitting some of the early shootings, and finally padding later years by counting non-mass shootings.

Let's look at the numbers from before 2000. In 2000, University of Chicago economist Bill Landes and I analyzed data on mass public shootings from 1977 to 1999. Exactly like the later work by the FBI, we limited our study to non-gang attacks that resulted in two or more fatalities in a public place. We also excluded shootings if they occurred in connection with some other crime, such as a robbery.

The attached graph shows the rate of death from mass public shootings. There has only been a slight, statistically insignificant upward trend over the thirty-eight years from 1977 through 2014. Even then, the trend entirely depends on a single year—2012 —when there were ninety-one deaths (Figure 7).

The problem with the Obama administration's false numbers goes much farther than the influence that they may have had on the 2014 election. These numbers may be used in academic research, leading to flawed results. And they are also used in the gun control debate. I have run into gun control advocates who use these flawed numbers many times. Remember George Orwell's famous quote from *1984*: "He who controls the past controls the future." Those who control the data control future debates.

But how far does this corruption go? For example, can we trust the data in the FBI report on the Ferguson police department?

THE CONSEQUENCES OF THESE STUDIES

Excessive and uncritical media coverage isn't the only result of these studies. They provide talking points for politicians. When President Obama addressed the country on January 5, 2016, about his latest push for gun control, Bloomberg-funded research provided the "facts" that Obama cited:

- "Congress actually voted to make it harder for public health experts to conduct research into gun violence; made it harder to collect data and facts and develop strategies to reduce gun violence."
- "After Connecticut passed a law requiring background checks and gun safety courses, gun deaths decreased by 40%. Forty percent."
- "Since Missouri repealed a law requiring comprehensive background checks and purchase permits, gun deaths have increased to almost 50% higher than the national average."
- "A violent felon can buy the exact same weapon over the internet with no background check, no questions asked. A recent study found that about 1-in-30 people looking to buy guns on one website had criminal records—one

out of 30 had a criminal record. We're talking about individuals convicted of serious crimes—aggravated assault, domestic violence, robbery, illegal gun possession. People with lengthy criminal histories buying deadly weapons all too easily."

Astute readers will note that the first three quotes originated from Bloomberg-funded studies that we have already discussed. The same is true for the fourth quote, and it too is misleading. Here is how they came up with it: Michael Bloomberg's Everytown organization set up a website pretending to sell guns, but *no guns were sold*. Criminal background checks were done on the people's names for those who visited the site and people who might have criminal backgrounds were identified: however, there were all kinds of false positives. Someone might not have a criminal record, but someone else with a similar name might.

And so the crusaders for gun control march on, with botched research, muddy numbers, and assumptions presented as facts.

CHAPTER 7

HOW DOES THE U.S. COMPARE TO OTHER COUNTRIES?

But we are the only advanced country on Earth that sees this kind of mass violence erupt with this kind of frequency. It doesn't happen in other advanced countries. It's not even close.[1]
–President Obama, announcing his new executive orders on guns, January 7, 2016

We have a pattern now of mass shootings in this country that has no parallel anywhere else in the world.[2]
—President Obama, interview that aired on CBS Evening News, December 2, 2015

I say this every time we've got one of these mass shootings: This just doesn't happen in other countries.[3]
—President Obama, news conference at COP21 climate conference in Paris, December 1, 2015

You don't see murder on this kind of scale, with this kind of frequency, in any other advanced nation on Earth.[4]
—President Obama, speech at U.S. Conference of Mayors, June 19, 2015

We are the only developed country on earth where [mass public shooting] happens.[5]
—President Obama, Tumblr Q&A, June 11, 2014

Obama has continually repeated the claim above in various forms over the years.[6] Tell it to the French, who witnessed three mass public shootings last year. January 2015 saw two attacks, one on the *Charlie Hebdo* magazine and another on a Paris supermarket. In the November attacks, 130 people were killed and 368 were injured. Although 2015 was certainly an anomaly, the fact remains that in one year France suffered more mass public shooting casualties—killings and injuries—than the U.S. experienced from the beginning of Obama's presidency until the end of 2015 (532 to 396).

Obama also overlooks Norway, where Anders Behring Breivik used a gun to kill sixty-seven people and wound 110 others. Still others were killed by bombs that Breivik detonated. Of the four worst K-12 school shootings in history, three have occurred in Europe. Germany was host to two of these—one in 2002 at Erfut and another in 2009 at Winnenden. These two attacks claimed a total of thirty-four lives.

Sometimes Obama limits his comparison to other "advanced" countries. But he has gone still further, claiming that there is "no parallel anywhere else in the world." In fact, mass public shootings are a lot more common and a lot more deadly outside of Europe and the U.S.

We collected a list of the worst mass public shootings in the world from 1970 to March 2016. Though most lists look at shootings where four or more people have been killed, these lists undoubtedly miss many shootings in Africa, Southern Asia, and South America. These places can have murder rates eight or ten times higher than the rate in the U.S. Some of these large mass shootings in Africa only received a couple news stories (e.g., four of the shootings in Nigeria appear to have been discussed in only four contemporary news stories: Kaduna [thirty-eight killed], Kabamu [thirty-six killed], Dogon-Daji [twenty-one killed], and Naidu [sixteen killed]).[7] A number of these news stories did not even mention the number of people wounded and were not always clear about the number killed. In the United States, an attack that killed so many people would have follow-up stories until those details were provided.

My list only includes mass public shootings where at least fifteen people were killed. Since 1970, all of the twenty-five worst mass public shootings occurred *outside* the U.S. Muslims also committed twenty-two of the worst twenty-five mass public shootings in the world. If we are still missing any large mass public shootings, they surely occured outside of Europe, the U.S., and the Commonwealth countries.

The ISIS attacks in France were no different from the attacks by Al-Shabaab in Kenya, Boko Haram in Nigeria, Lashkar-e-Taiba in India, and Lashkar-e-Jhangvi in Pakistan. Similar targets were attacked using similar weapons. All of the countries defined them as Islamic terrorist attacks, not battles over national sovereignty.

Thus far, the U.S. has been lucky. The San Bernardino, Fort Hood, and Chattanooga, Tennessee terrorist attacks haven't been on the same scale as the shootings seen elsewhere in the world. Fortunately, the attackers did not use machine guns, as have commonly been used in attacks abroad.

Mass shootings were excluded if they were part of a war over sovereignty. If one were to include these cases, the list would include many more attacks in such places as the UK, Israel, the Phillippines, and Russia. In the case of Russia, I excluded five shootings that were part of the Russian-Chechen conflict.[8] The most deadly was the Besian School siege of September 1, 2004, which left 385 dead and another 783 wounded. Some evidence indicates that "the terrorists' real aim was not to kill the hostages but to negotiate a political settlement of the Chechen conflict."[9] I also did not count the October 19, 2010 attack on the Chechen Parliament (six killed, seventeen wounded), even though the Russian government had declared it to be a terrorist attack.[10]

Table 1. Deaths from mass public shootings where at least fifteen people have been killed (1970 through March 20, 2016)			
	Number murdered	Deaths per 1 million people	Percent higher or lower per capita rate than U.S. rate
Africa	1324	1.192	277%
Australia	35	1.513	379%
Europe	312	0.52	65%
India/Pakistan	421	0.294	-7%
Israel	55	6.825	2060%
Philippines	180	1.829	479%
USA	102	0.316	

Compared to Africa, Australia, Europe, and Israel, the U.S. has a relatively low per capita death rate from large mass public shootings. Indeed, among countries whose borders are primarily in Europe, the rate is 65 percent higher than that of the U.S. The U.S. makes up about 4.4 percent of the world population (322.8 million/7.411 billion) and accounts for 4.2 percent of the deaths from these attacks. When we just factor in the sovereignty-related Russian mass public shootings, the U.S. share of total deaths falls to 3.4 percent.

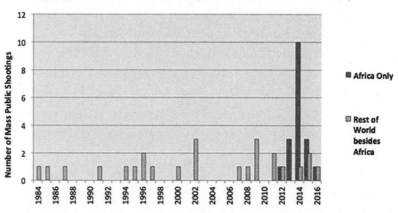

Number of Mass Public Shootings where at least 15 people have been killed (1984 to March 15, 2016)

Table 2: The worst mass public shootings in the world from 1970 to March 15, 2016: worst attacks listed first

	Country	Location	Target	Year	Month	Date	Killed	Wounded	Who did the attack?
1	Nigeria[11]	Gamboru and Ngala	Village	2014	May	5 & 6	300		Boko Haram, Islamic
2	Nigeria[12]	Konduga	Village	2014	May	7	>200		Boko Haram, Islamic
3	Pakistan[13]	Peshawar	School	2014	Dec.	16	148	114	Tehrik-i-Taliban (TTP or the "Pakistani Taliban"), an Islamic group
4	Kenya[14]	Garissa	University	2015	Apr.	2	147		Al-Shabaab, an Al-Qaeda offshoot
5	France[15]	Paris	Concert, Restaurant, Other	2015	Nov.	14	130	352	ISIS, Islamic
6	Nigeria[16]	Konduga	Village	2014	Feb.	14	121		Boko Haram, Islamic
7	Nigeria[17]	Izghe	Village	2014	Feb.	15	106		Boko Haram, Islamic
8	India[18]	Mumbai	Rail Terminus, Cafe	2008	Nov.	26	68*		Lashkar-e-Taiba, Islamic
9	Philippines[19]	Manili	Mosque	1971	June	19	70	Unknown number	Christians in retaliation for Muslim attack
10	Norway[20]	Utoya	Summer Camp	2011	July	22	67	110	Anders Behring Breivik, National Socialist Underground
11	Kenya[21]	Nairobi	Shopping Mall	2013	Sept.	21	63	175	Al-Shabaab, Islamic
12	Nigeria[22]	Yobe	College	2014	Feb.	25	59		Boko Haram, Islamic
13	Philippines[23]	Maguindanao	Attacked a group of people while traveling	2009	Nov.	23	57	>4	Muslim political clan
14	Philippines[24]	Ipil	Village	1995	April	3	53		Islamic Command Council

	Country	Location	Target	Year	Month	Date	Killed	Wounded	Who did the attack?
15	Nigeria[25]	Gujba	College	2013	Sept.	29	50		Boko Haram, Islamic
16	Pakistan[26]	Karachi	Bus	2015	May	13	>45	About 36	Jundallah, Islamic
17	Nigeria[27]	Mamudo	School	2013	July	6	42		Boko Haram, Islamic
18	Pakistan[28]	Rawalpindi	Mosque	2009	Dec.	4	>40	80	Muslim gunmen
19	Tunisia[29]	Sousse	Beach Resort	2015	June	26	39		Seifeddine Rezgui, college student who followed ISIS
20	Nigeria[30]	Kobin	Village	2014	June	23	39		Boko Haram, Islamic
21	Nigeria[31]	Kaduna	Two Neighboring Villages	2014	June	23	38		Boko Haram, Islamic
22	India[32]	Chittisinghpura	Village	2000	Mar.	18	36		Lashkar-e-Taiba, Islamic
23	Nigeria[33]	Kabamu	Village	2014	June	23	36		Boko Haram, Islamic
24	Australia[34]	Port Arthur	Tourist Site	1996	Apr.	28 & 29	35	23	Martin Bryant
25	Italy[35]	Rome	Airport	1973	Dec.	17	33	>20	Black September, Islamic
26	USA[36]	Blacksburg	School	2007	Apr.	16	32	17	Seung-Hui Cho
27	India[37]	Gujarat	Temple	2002	Sept.	24 & 25	31	80	Lashkar-e-Taiba, Jaish-e-Mohammed, Islamic
28	Israel[38]	Hebron	Subterranean Chambers	1994	Feb.	25	29	125	Baruch Goldstein, Jewish
29	India[39]	Jammu	Slum	2002	July	13	29	>=30	Islamic
30	Israel[40]	Tel Aviv	Airport	1972	May	30	26	80	Japanese Red Army, recruited and assisted by Palestinian Liberation Army
31	Pakistan[41]	Ganjidori	Bus	2011	Sept.	20	26	3	The Lashkar-e-Jhangvi

	Country	Location	Type	Year	Month				Perpetrator
32	USA[42]	Newtown	School	2012	Dec.	14	26	2	Adam Lanza
33	USA[43]	Killeen	Cafeteria	1991	Oct.	16	23	27	George Hennard
34	Nigeria[44]	Dogon-Daji	Village	2014	June	23	21		Boko Haram, Islamic
35	USA[45]	San Ysidro	Restaurant	1984	July	18	21	19	James Huberty
36	Mali[46]	Bamako	Hotel	2015	Nov.	20	20	7	Al-Mourabitoun, Al-Qaeda in the Islamic Maghreb
37	Nigeria[47]	Otite	Church	2012	Aug.	7	19		Boko Haram, Islamic
38	Germany[48]	Erfurt	School	2002	Apr.	26	18		Robert Steinhäuser
39	UK[49]	Stirling	School	1996	Mar.	13	17	15	Thomas Hamilton
40	Italy[50]	Rome	Airport	1985	Dec.	27	16	99	Abu Nidal Organization
41	Africa[51]	Ivory Coast	Beach Resort	2016	Mar.	13	16	33	Al-Qaeda in the Islamic Maghreb, Al-Mourabitoun
42	Yemen[52]	Adan	Retirement home	2016	Mar.	5	16		Islamic State group and Yemen's al-Qaeda affiliate suspected, attacked a Christian facility
43	UK[53]	Hungerford	Forest, Petrol Station, School	1987	Aug.	19	16	15	Michael Robert Ryan
44	Nigeria[54]	Naidu	Village	2014	June	23	16		Boko Haram, Islamic
45	Brazil[55]	São Gonçalo do Amarante	Town	1997	May	21	15	3	Genildo Ferreira Do Francais
46	Germany[56]	Winnenden	School	2009	Mar.	11	15	9	Tim Kretschmer

* The Islamic terror group based in Pakistan named Lashkar-e-Taiba (Army of the Pure) killed 164 and wounded 308. Yet, many of these casualties were due to bombs. It is hard to separate out how many of the deaths were due to shootings and bombs and also determine whether the deaths were due to fighting with the Indian military, but on the first day where just deaths by shooting occurred, there were at least sixty-eight people killed in two of the targets—the Rail Terminus (fifty-eight) and the Leopold Cafe (at least ten). Those deaths would by themselves rank this as the seventh worst attack.

Africa has experienced an explosion in large mass public shootings. Since 2012, Africa has been host to 78 percent of all such shootings which claimed fifteen or more lives. Supposedly, Africa didn't have any of these attacks from 1984 to 2011. Given the scant news coverage given to recent mass shootings in Africa, it is very possible that we are simply lacking news reports of earlier attacks.

No matter how you look at it, Obama is wrong in saying that America leads the world in mass public shootings. It is wrong even when we look at mass public shootings as they are traditionally defined: four or more deaths in a public place. Many European countries actually have higher rates of death from mass public shootings. It is simply a matter of adjusting for America's much larger population. Norway, after all, only has a population of 5 million people.

Table 3: The frequency of mass public shootings with four or more people killed (comparing European countries, Canada, and the United States from January 2009 to December 2015)		
Rank	Country	Frequency per million people
1	Macedonia	0.471
2	Albania	0.360
3	Serbia	0.281
4	Switzerland	0.249
5	Norway	0.197
6	Slovakia	0.185
7	Finland	0.184
8	Belgium	0.179
9	Austria	0.119
10	Czech Republic	0.096
11	France	0.092
12	UNITED STATES	0.078
13	Canada	0.056
14	Netherlands	0.059
15	Italy	0.017
16	England	0.015
17	Russia	0.014
18	Germany	0.013

During the first seven years of Obama's presidency (January 2009 to December 2015), twenty-five mass public shootings occurred in Europe and the United States. The United States had the twelfth highest frequency of attacks, with 0.078 attacks per million people. Switzerland, Norway, Finland, Belgium, Austria, the Czech Republic, and France all had higher rates.

Table 4: Comparing annual death rate from mass public shootings with four or more people killed (comparing European countries, Canada, and the United States from January 2009 to December 2015)		
Rank	Country	Death rate per million people
1	Norway	1.888
2	Serbia	0.381
3	France	0.347
4	Macedonia	0.337
5	Albania	0.206
6	Slovakia	0.185
7	Switzerland	0.142
8	Finland	0.132
9	Belgium	0.128
10	Czech Republic	0.123
11	UNITED STATES	0.089
12	Austria	0.068
13	Netherlands	0.051
14	Canada	0.032
15	England	0.027
16	Germany	0.023
17	Russia	0.012
18	Italy	0.009

In terms of mass public shooting fatalities, the U.S. came in eleventh with an annual rate of 0.09 deaths per million people. Norway had by far the highest rate, 1.9 fatalities per million people. But other "advanced" countries such as France, Switzerland, Finland, Belgium, and the Czech Republic had much higher rates.

Table 5: Mass public shootings in Europe and the EU (January 2009 through December 2015, EU countries are shown in bold)						
Year	Month	Day	Location	Country	Fatalities (not including shooters)	Non-fatal Injuries
2009	3	11	Winnenden	Germany	13	7
2009	12	31	Espoo	Finland	5	0
2010	6	2	Cumbria	England	12	11
2010	8	30	Devinska Nova Ves	Slovakia	7	15
2011	4	9	Alphen aan den Rijn	Netherlands	6	17
2011	7	22	Oslo and Utoya	Norway	67	110
2011	12	13	Liege	Belgium	6	125
2012	3	19	Toulouse	France	4	0
2012	4	12	Smilkovci	Macedonia	5	0
2012	9	5	Chevaline	France	4	0
2012	11	5	Moscow	Russia	6	1
2013	2	27	Menznau	Switzerland	4	5
2013	4	9	Velika Ivanca	Serbia	13	1
2013	4	22	Belgorod	Russia	6	1
2013	9	16	Annaberg	Austria	4	1
2014	5	24	Brussels	Belgium	4	0
2014	11	3	Tirana	Albania	4	2
2015	1	7	Paris	France	12	11
2015	1	9	Paris	France	4	0
2015	2	24	Uhersky Brod	Czech Republic	9	1
2015	5	10	Wurenlingen	Switzerland	4	0
2015	5	15	Naples	Italy	4	6
2015	5	17	Kanjiza	Serbia	6	0
2015	8	25	Roye	France	4	3
2015	11	13	Paris	France	130	368
				Total Europe	343	685
				European Union Total*	295	675
				United States	199	197

* Some countries in Europe are not part of the European Union.

Table 6: Mass public shootings in U.S. from January 2009 through December 31, 2015						
Year	Month	Day	City	State	Fatalities (not including shooters)	Non-fatal injuries
2015	11	2	San Bernardino	CA	14	21
2015	10	1	Umpqua Community College	OR	9	9
2015	7	16	Chattanooga	TN	5	3
2015	6	17	Charleston	SC	9	1
2014	11	15	Springfield	MO	4	0
2014	10	24	Marysville	WA	4	1
2014	2	20	Alturras	CA	4	2
2013	9	16	Washington	DC	12	8
2013	5	4	Aguas Buenas	Puerto Rico	4	6
2013	3	13	Herkimer	NY	4	2
2012	12	14	Newtown	CT	26	2
2012	9	27	Minneapolis	MN	6	3
2012	8	5	Oak Creek	WI	6	3
2012	7	20	Aurora	CO	12	70
2012	5	30	Seattle	WA	5	1
2012	4	2	Oakland	CA	7	3
2011	10	12	Seal Beach	CA	8	1
2011	9	6	Carson City	NV	4	7
2011	1	8	Tucson	AZ	6	13
2010	8	3	Manchester	CT	8	2
2010	6	6	Hialeah	FL	4	3
2009	11	5	Fort Hood	TX	13	30
2009	11	29	Parkland	WA	4	0
2009	4	3	Binghamton	NY	13	4
2009	3	29	Carthage	NC	8	2
				Total	199	197
						396

The EU and the U.S. share extremely similar annual fatality rates (0.083 to 0.088), but the EU's annual injury rate is more than twice as high (1.33 to 0.61). In fact, *total annual casualties per million people are 56 percent higher in the EU than in the U.S.*

There are lots of other countries around the world that clearly have higher death rates from mass public shootings. But these cases are very hard to find for countries outside of Europe, especially during earlier years. Take the Solomon Islands, for example. Despite the Islands' 1999 ban on handguns and virtually all rifles, twenty people died in three mass public shootings from 2000 to 2002.[57] There may have been other mass public shootings, but the Islands' "Truth and Reconciliation Commission" report only provides details from 1998 to 2003. Even if these were the only mass public shootings from 1998 through 2015, the annual death rate would come to 2.27 per million people (given an average population of 490,000 over those eighteen years). *This is twenty-six times higher than the U.S. rate.*

A couple of other studies have also, to significant media fanfare, compared mass public shooting fatality rates. One was by Jaclyn Schildkraut of the State University of New York-Oswego and Texas State University researcher, H. Jaymi Elsass.[58] That study looked at shootings from 2000 to 2014, but left out a large number of cases from other countries. They missed three mass public shootings in France alone:

- Tours, France, October 29, 2001: Four people are killed and ten are wounded when a French railway worker opens fire on a busy city intersection.
- Nanterre, France, March 27, 2002: A man kills eight city councilors after a city council meeting.
- Toulouse and Montauban, France, March 11–22, 2012: Mohammed Merah kills seven people and injures five in a series of three attacks and then a final, thirty-hour police siege.

Other cases were missed in such countries as Austria, Belgium, Finland, the Netherlands, Italy, Macedonia, Spain, Switzerland, and

Slovakia. By contrast, the authors seem to have found all the attacks in the U.S. As a result, the U.S. is made to look a lot worse compared to the rest of the world.

In December 2015, *Washington Post* "Fact Checker" reporter Michelle Lee wrote me: "[Schilkraut] said they are still adding cases, and that it's not a complete database." However, Schilkraut and Elsass had already gone public with their findings about how the U.S. compared to other countries. They did so with full knowledge that they were missing many shootings in foreign countries

A new study by Adam Lankford reportedly covers the years 1966 to 2012. It claims of the U.S., "Despite having less than 5% of the global population (World Factbook, 2014), it had 31% of global public mass shooters."[59] Headlines in major media gave the claims massive uncritical coverage.

- *Wall Street Journal*: "U.S. Leads World in Mass Shootings"[60]
- *Los Angeles Times*: "Why the U.S. is No. 1—in mass shootings"[61]
- *Time* magazine: "Why the US has 31% of the World's Mass Shootings"[62]
- *Washington Post*: "American exceptionalism and the 'exceptionally American' problem of mass shootings"[63]
- CNN: "Why the U.S. has the most mass shootings"[64]

Similar coverage was given by *USA Today*, Associated Press, *PBS Newshour*, NPR, ABC Evening News, Fox News, and many hundreds of other outlets.[65] Many prominent outlets have covered the claim repeatedly. It has received coverage in countries such as Australia, Argentina, Armenia, Brazil, Canada, China, Denmark, Germany, Ireland, India, Iran, Mexico, Peru, Sweden, Turkey, UK, Vietnam, and Cuba.[66]

But while Lankford shared his study with reporters, he required that they didn't share it with researchers. Despite the wide publicity given to his findings, he repeatedly turned down my requests to see his paper. On

December 1, 2015, the *Washington Post*'s Michelle Lee wrote me: "I do
have a copy but [Lankford] asked that I not distribute it or post it online
before it's formally published. You can contact him and request, maybe
now that his study is being discussed he might be more open to share?"
But I had contacted Lankford both before and after Lee's email—he
declined to provide either the paper or his data.

Reporters might not appreciate how incredibly unusual it is for academics not to share their papers with other academics. There are many
websites set up to facilitate doing just that (e.g., the Social Science
Research Network and Researchgate.com). Academics not only benefit
from feedback, they desperately want other academics to read their
papers. After all, they want to get cited in papers written by other
researchers. More citations help people earn tenure and get promoted.
They get you better positions. In decades of being in academia, I have
never seen an academic refuse to hand out a paper that was already
accepted for publication.

I finally obtained a copy of Lankford's paper when it was published
at the end of January 2016 —more than five months after it originally
started getting news attention. Incredibly, even after his paper was published, Lankford still refused to let me look at his list of mass public
shootings from other countries. All I wanted was a list similar to what I
have just provided in the preceding tables.

Indeed, he won't even give journalists any specific details on how he
collected his sample. There is no information on his use of different
databases, foreign languages, or search terms. In his paper, he claims to
have a "complete" collection of foreign cases from the 1960s, 1970s,
1980s, and 1990s that involved as few as four deaths. As mentioned
earlier, this seems like an impossible task for many places in Africa and
South America.

The U.S. at least has computerized databases of news stories, but even
these are greatly limited prior to 1991. For 1991, there are at least 389
newspapers included in the Nexis/Lexus database.[67] Just prior to 1991, there
are only thirty-one newspapers. This number quickly gets smaller and
smaller as one goes further back in time. And, of course, the

English-language news media of decades ago couldn't be counted on to cover mass public shootings in Europe, let alone Africa or other parts of the world.

At first, I simply hoped that Lankford had discovered some previously unknown way of collecting these cases. But his paper provides very little specific information, not even telling us the number of shootings in more than four foreign countries. No breakdown is provided by continent. It is hard to believe that Lankford even has such information, but there is no way of checking his data and seeing what cases he has missed.

People shouldn't trust a researcher who refuses to share even the most basic information behind his research.

Finally, we must bear in mind that guns are not the only tools of mass killing. In America, by far the worst mass murder at a school was carried out with dynamite in 1927.[68] That attack left forty-five dead and fifty-eight injured. The 1985 Oklahoma City Bombing and the 2013 Boston Marathon bombings were other rare exceptions in the United States, but bombs are much more commonly used in countries such as Russia. From 2009 to July 2014, Russia saw 0.24 annual deaths per million from bombings with four or more fatalities.[69] That rate is almost 2.7 times higher than the death rate from mass public shootings in the U.S.

Obama could have looked at his own State Department's annual terrorism reports. Between 2007 and 2011, an average of 6,282 terrorist attacks per year occurred outside of Iraq, Afghanistan, and the U.S. On average, more than 27,000 people were killed, injured, or kidnapped each year.

Table 7: U.S. State Department counting of terrorist attacks around the world						
	2007	2008	2009	2010	2011	Average
Attacks worldwide removing war zones	14,415	11,663	10,968	11,641	10,283	11,794
Attacks worldwide minus Iraq and Afghanistan	7,083	7,189	6,386	5,608	5,146	6,282
People killed, injured, or kidnapped excluding Iraq and Afghanistan	23,142	29,725	34,263	25,785	22,627	27,108

Source for data for 2011: http://www.state.gov/documents/organization/195768.pdf

CHAPTER 8

DO COUNTRIES WITH MORE GUNS HAVE HIGHER HOMICIDE RATES?

What we also have to recognize is, is that our homicide rates are so much higher than other industrialized countries. I mean by like a mile. And most of that is attributable to the easy, ready availability of firearms, particularly handguns.[1]
—President Obama, remarks at a town hall at Benedict College, Columbia, SC, March 6, 2015

The first myth is that the United States is the most violent industrialized nation in the world.... Not only is the current Russian homicide victimization rate more than 3 times higher than in the United States, but it has been comparable to or higher than the U.S. rate for at least the past 35 years.[2]
—William Pridemore, Homicide Studies, 2000

"America has the highest gun homicide rate, the highest number of guns per capita," recites Charles Blow of the *New York Times*.[3] In another story, the *New York Times* quotes researcher David Hemenway as saying: "Generally, if you live in a civilized society, more guns mean more death."[4] Bloomberg's *Businessweek* also makes similar claims.[5] Like most international comparisons of gun ownership rates, all of these claims make use of something called the 2007 Small Arms Survey, a group that receives funding from and often works closely with George Soros's Open Society Institute.[6]

The UN provides homicide data for 192 countries, but the Small Arms Survey only lists gun ownership and homicide data for 116. All of the countries that are missing are countries that have homicide rates higher than the U.S. rate. The Small Arms Survey makes it look as though there are only twenty-five countries with higher homicide rates than the U.S. In fact, there are 101 countries with higher rates.

So how do homicide rates compare across all 192 countries for which the UN provides data?[7] For 2008, the U.S. rate was slightly less than 5.4 homicides per 100,000 people. The worldwide rate was 10.5 (about twice the U.S. rate), and the median was six per 100,000. Yet there is one important caveat to realize when looking at these numbers—they are provided by the countries themselves, and you can't always trust their numbers. Politicians and dictators like to give the impression that they are doing a better job than they actually are. This is a problem in some United States jurisdictions such as Chicago, where what look like murders are reclassified as "noncriminal death investigations."[8]

The homicide rates of many other countries are clearly grossly underestimated. During the 1990s, the Russian Ministry of the Interior reported an annual rate that was at least 25 percent less than the actual figure.[9] The Russian government has again become less transparent in recent years, so this problem has undoubtedly gotten worse. In 2012, the Venezuelan government claimed that the homicide rate was thirty-nine per 100,000 people, but the Venezuelan Violence Observatory put the rate at seventy-three per 100,000.[10] Argentina has a Chicago-like problem, with at least 15 percent of murders being classified as "unknown intent."[11] China's crime numbers are probably no more believable than its economic numbers.[12]

There are other real problems with the Small Arms Survey. For example, it claims that there are only seven guns per one hundred people in Israel and supposedly forty-seven guns per one hundred people in Switzerland. Anyone who has ever been to Israel knows that this estimate is ridiculously low. Indeed, about 12 to 15 percent of the adult Jewish population in Israel is allowed to carry handguns in public.[13]

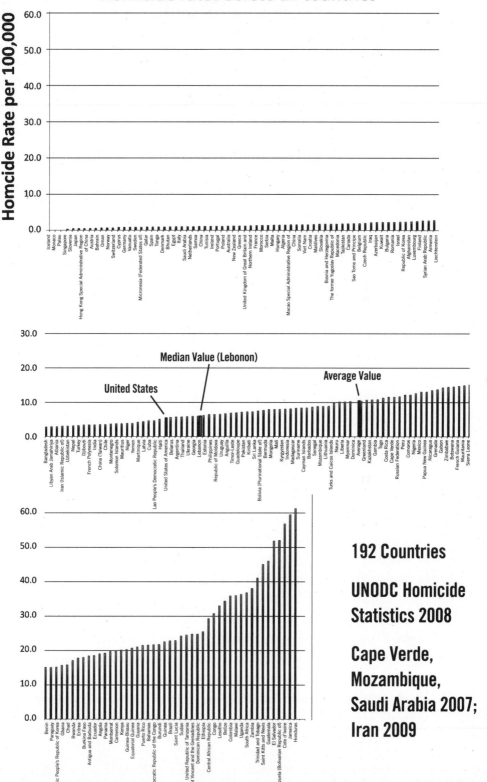

Homicide rates across all countries

192 Countries

UNODC Homicide Statistics 2008

Cape Verde, Mozambique, Saudi Arabia 2007; Iran 2009

The vast majority of guns in Israel are technically owned by the government, but the debate seems to be more about the claimed dangers of people possessing guns than whether they own them. In Israel, the government may own almost all the guns, but citizens can possess them for many decades. Similarly, when the Small Arms Survey was done in 2007, able-bodied Swiss males between the ages of eighteen and thirty-four were conscripted, with women allowed to voluntarily serve.[14] About two-thirds of males are conscripted.[15] Their military weapons are kept in their homes. After conscription ends, these individuals can apply for permission to continue to keep their military weapons. After age sixty-five, people are given the option of buying their guns. But in both countries—even if the gun is in your home, or you carry it around with you all day—if the government officially owns the gun, the Small Arms Survey acts as if it doesn't exist.

The Small Arms Survey claims that the United States has by far the highest level of gun ownership, with 88.8 guns per one hundred people. Both Israel and Switzerland probably have much higher gun ownership rates, contrary to the Small Arms Survey's data.[16]

There are also other problems with the survey. For example, a much better measure of gun ownership would be the percentage of the population owning guns and not the number of guns per one hundred people, as used by the Small Arms Survey. Presumably, the issue is whether people have access to guns, not the number of guns that an individual has access to.

But still, despite all those problems, higher gun ownership, as measured by the Small Arms Survey, is actually associated with *fewer total* homicides.

Gun control advocates tend to focus only on firearm homicides. That seems pretty arbitrary. A stabbing death is just as horrible as a shooting death. Reduced gun ownership could reduce gun murders, but increase other kinds of murders by making it easier for strong male criminals to prey on those who are weaker physically. But, as Figures 2 and 3 show, it still turns out that the relationship between either firearm homicides or total homicides and the Small Arms Survey is very similar.

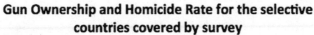

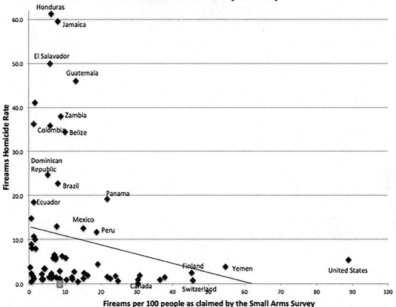

Gun Ownership and Homicide Rate for the selective countries covered by survey

People frequently use the terms "homicide" and "murder" interchangeably, but they aren't the same. The big difference is justifiable homicides—in other words, self-defense. For most countries there isn't a big difference between homicides and murders, though in the U.S. this difference is quite significant. In 2014, there were 8,124 firearm murders and 10,945 firearm homicides—a 2,821 or 35 percent difference in deaths.[17] Using the murder numbers would reduce the U.S. death rate relative to that in other countries.

Usually, when gun control researchers do a study, only a small set of countries are used in any comparison, typically limited to so-called "civilized," as David Hemenway or Piers Morgan calls them, or "developed" countries.[18] It isn't clear what is meant by "civilized" countries, so what can Americans learn from these other "developed" nations?

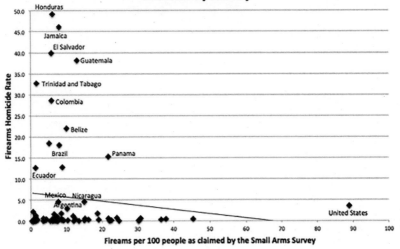

Small Arms Survey measure of Gun Ownership and Firearm Homicide Rate for the selective countries covered by survey

First, here is how homicide rates vary across developed countries. Currently, thirty-four countries are in the OECD, though the agency also includes Brazil and Russia in its statistical data, as they meet the definition of "developed."[19] (Both countries have been negotiating for membership, but Russia has had talks suspended because of the Crimea crisis.)

Among only developed countries, there is still a correlation between fewer homicides and increased gun ownership (as measured by the obviously biased Small Arms Survey). The relationship, however, is not statistically significant.

Even limiting oneself to industrialized countries and using the measure of gun ownership supplied by gun control advocates, the cross-country data continues to imply that more guns equals fewer homicides.[20] Still, this type of comparison isn't very convincing. There is a real problem in using data from only one particular point in time.

My book *The Bias Against Guns* also provided a simple example of the basic problem with this kind of "cross-sectional" analysis:

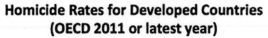

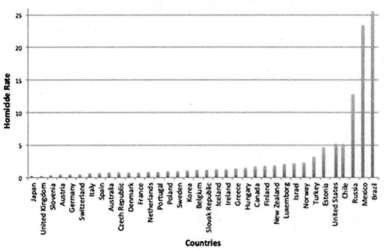

The *New York Times* recently conducted a cross-sectional study of murder rates in states with and without the death penalty and found that "Indeed, 10 of the 12 states without capital punishment have homicide rates below the national average, Federal Bureau of Investigation data shows, while half the states with the death penalty have homicide rates above the national average." However, they erroneously concluded that the death penalty did not deter murder. The problem is that the states without the death penalty (Alaska, Hawaii, Iowa, Maine, Massachusetts, Michigan, Minnesota, North Dakota, Rhode Island, West Virginia, Wisconsin, and Vermont) have long enjoyed relatively low murder rates, something that might well have more to do with other factors than the death penalty. Instead one must compare, over time, how murder rates change in the two groups—those adopting the death penalty and those that did not.

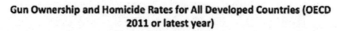

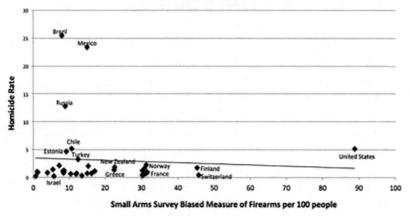

To resolve this issue, one must examine how the high-crime areas that chose to adopt the controls changed over time—not only relative to their own past levels, but also relative to areas that did not institute such controls.

GUN BANS: BEFORE AND AFTER

Every place that has banned guns (either all guns or all handguns) has seen murder rates go up. You cannot point to one place where murder rates have fallen, whether Chicago or D.C. or even island nations such as England, Jamaica, and Ireland, or obscure places such as the Solomon Islands.

Take the handgun ban in England and Wales in January 1997.[21] Homicide rates were in flux after the ban, but only one year (2010) had a homicide rate lower than the rate in 1996. The immediate effect was about a 50 percent increase in homicide rates. Firearm homicide rates almost doubled between 1996 and 2002. The homicide and firearm homicide rates only began falling after a large 8 percent increase in the number of police officers during just 2003 and 2004. Despite the increase in the number of police, the murder rate still remained similar to the immediate pre-ban rate.[22]

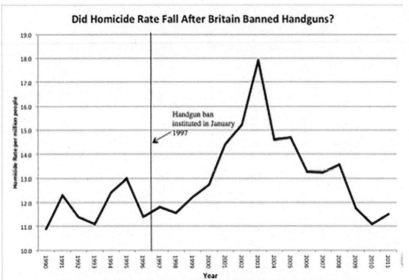

Did Homicide Rate Fall After Britain Banned Handguns?

Homicides, Firearm Offences and Intimate Violence 2010/11: Supplementary Volume 2 to Crime in England & Wales 2010/11 (http://www.homeoffice.gov.uk/publications/science-research-statistics/research-statistics/crime-research/hosb0212/hosb0212?view=Bin

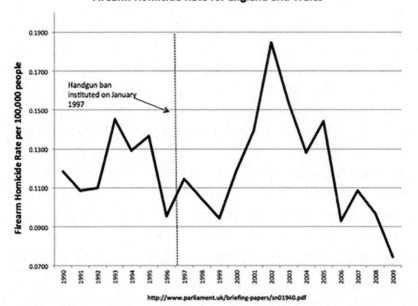

Firearm Homicide Rate for England and Wales

http://www.parliament.uk/briefing-papers/sn01940.pdf

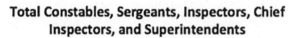

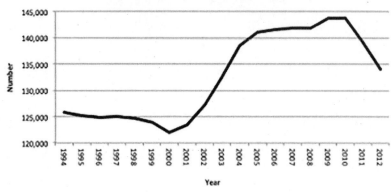

Police Service Strength England and Wales,
Home Office Statistical Bulletin, 2007 and 2012

Since we are talking about changes within a country, how different countries measure homicide and murder is not relevant to the discussion here.

While they haven't gotten the same attention as the UK's handgun ban, other countries have tried banning guns. In order to make useful comparisons, we limit ourselves to countries that have crime data both before and after the bans were implemented. My previous work has dealt extensively with the dramatic increases in murder rates in Chicago and Washington, D.C. after their handgun bans went into effect respectively in November 1982 and February 1977.

By August 5, 1972, Ireland required that all privately held pistols, revolvers, and all rifles over .22 caliber be surrendered to local police stations.[23] Jamaica's Gun Court Act of 1974 virtually eliminated the issuing of handgun licenses to civilians.[24] In 2012, Venezuela banned guns in an "attempt by the government to improve security and cut crime."[25] The Solomon Islands banned guns in 1999.[26]

The Republic of Ireland and Jamaica both experienced large increases in homicide rates after enacting handgun bans.[27] From 1945 through 1971, Ireland's homicide rates stayed in the relatively narrow

Ireland's Homicide Rate

Jamaica's Homicide Rate

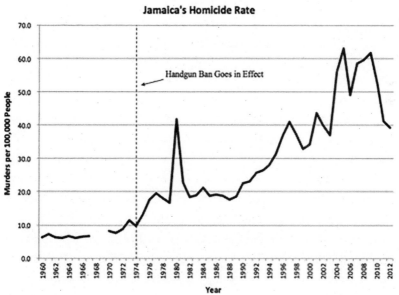

range from 0.1 to 0.6 per 100,000 people, with an average of 0.3. After the ban, the homicide rates from 1972 to 2012 rarely overlapped with the rates before the ban (ranging from 0.4 to 1.8 per 100,000 people),

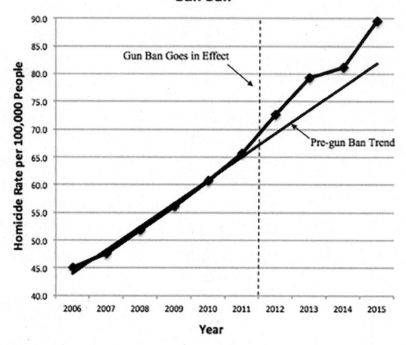

with an average of 0.9. Ireland's 1974 homicide rate spike was quite high even with terrorist attacks subtracted from the total.[28] The big increase starting in the 1990s was largely due to a rise in drug gangs as recreational drug use soared.[29]

Jamaica's increase in homicides was even more dramatic than the increase in Ireland. The homicide rate is always higher after the ban than it was before, with the average homicide rate going from 7.3 per 100,000 during 1967 to 1973 to 31.5 per 100,000 in 1995. Jamaica's explosion in homicides during the 1990s is also directly blamed on drug gangs.[30]

Even before the rise in drug gang problems, the homicide rates in Ireland and Jamaica were dramatically higher than they were prior to the gun bans. But one thing is clear: despite gun bans and island nations with relatively easy-to-control borders, drug gangs seemed to have no more problem obtaining guns than they had getting the illegal drugs that they sold.[31] And given how valuable drugs are, gangs have an incentive to smuggle in guns at the same time they smuggle in drugs. After all, if a gang has its drugs stolen, it can't go to the police to ask for help.

The post-ban change in Venezuela's homicide rate isn't as pronounced as the large, sudden increases seen in both Ireland and Jamaica. Venezuela's homicide rate was already rising dramatically before the gun ban was enacted in June 2012. The amnesty for people who turned in guns meant that many law-abiding citizens had already turned in their guns in the months leading up to the ban. The socialist government's policies undoubtedly also contributed to the country's deteriorating economy, and that probably played a role in the increase in homicides. But again, the evidence is that the ban made things worse rather than better.

The data for the Solomon Islands is far from complete, but we do have data for one year prior to the 1999 gun ban. We know that the 1997 homicide rate was just 40 percent of the average rate for the years after the ban.[32] In 2002, the Deputy Police Commissioner for the islands testified:[33]

> **Question:** Would it be fair to say that there are more guns here now than there were at the time of the signing of the Townsville Peace Agreement?
>
> **Joseph Baetolongia, Deputy Police Commissioner:** I would think so. I would think we, we have a lot more guns here now.

This quote by Baetolongia was featured in an article titled: "Guns and Money: Solomon Islands, a one-time South Pacific idyll, is on the brink of collapse." In fact, it is now common for tourists to be warned of gun violence (emphasis added):

> Foreign governments also warn their yacht-based citizens to take care in Honiara harbor where there have been reports of criminals boarding yachts at night and stealing valuables. They are *usually armed* and are not deterred if confronted.

It's best to let them take what they want and live to tell the tale.[34]

The Solomon Island gun ban came before the rise in murder rates and prior to the mass public shootings discussed in Chapter Seven.

CHAPTER 9

DOES AUSTRALIA SHOW THAT GUN CONTROL WORKS?

AUDIENCE MEMBER: *Recently, Australia managed to get away, or take away, tens of thousands, millions of handguns, and in one year, they were all gone. Can we do that? And why, if we can't, why can't we?*

CLINTON: *Australia is a good example… Why?…Australia had a huge mass killing about 20-25 years ago. Canada did as well, so did the U.K. And in reaction, they passed much stricter gun laws. In the Australian example, as I recall, that was a buyback program. The Australian government, as part of trying to clamp down on the availability of automatic weapons, offered a good price for buying hundreds of thousands of guns. Then, they basically clamped down going forward in terms of having more of a background check approach, more of a permitting approach, but they believed, and I think the evidence supports them, that by offering to buy back the guns, they were able to curtail the supply, and set a different standard for gun purchases in the future.… certainly the Australian example is worth looking at. Thank you.*[1]
—Hillary Clinton, October 15, 2015, New Hampshire

The above quotation is from a campaign speech that Hillary Clinton gave at Keene State College in New Hampshire during October 2015. Clinton was asked if the U.S. should try to take away everyone's handguns, as Australia once did. Clinton responded by praising Australia's gun buyback in 1996 and 1997, when the government used registration lists to identify who owned these newly prohibited weapons. Clinton also praised Canada and the UK, which used similar registration laws to confiscate guns. President Obama has also praised those laws.

Clinton made fun of those worried about confiscation. She said people get scared into thinking that "a black helicopter is going to land in the front yard, and somebody is going to take your guns."

But why should gun owners trust her when she praises other country's confiscation efforts? Is she right that the evidence shows that gun control made Australia safer?

Democrats keep telling people that they don't want to confiscate their guns. At the same time, they praise laws in countries that have confiscated people's guns. But Hillary Clinton is completely wrong in claiming that confiscation made these countries safer.

HOW THE NUMBER OF GUNS IN AUSTRALIA HAS CHANGED OVER TIME

Former Prime Minister of Australia John Howard wrote in the *New York Times* in 2013, "[T]here is a wide consensus that our 1996 reforms not only reduced the gun-related homicide rate, but also the suicide rate. The Australian Institute of Criminology found that gun-related murders and suicides fell sharply after 1996."[2] But the impact of Australia's gun buyback in 1996–97 is a lot less obvious than most might think. The buyback resulted in more than 1 million firearms being handed in and destroyed, reducing gun ownership from 3.2 to 2.2 million guns. But since then there has been a steady increase in the number of privately owned guns. By 2010, the total number of privately owned guns was back to the 1996 level.[3]

FIGURE 1

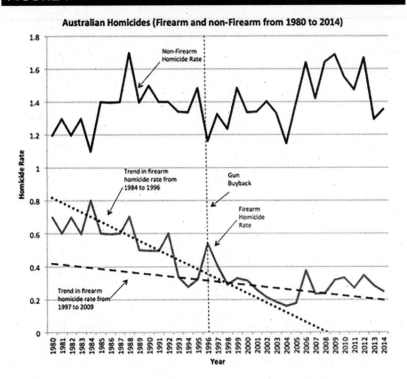

Australian Homicides (Firearm and non-Firearm from 1980 to 2014)

While Australia's population grew by 19 percent between 1997 and 2010, the total number of guns soared by 45 percent. If gun control advocates are correct, gun crimes or suicides should have plunged in 1997, gradually increasing after that. But that is not the pattern we observe.

When former Australian Prime Minister John Howard claims that homicide and suicide rates fell after Australia's 1996 law, what he ignores is that these rates were falling even before the law. Looking at simple before and after averages is extremely misleading. Firearm homicides and suicides were falling from the mid-1980s on, so you could pick any year from the mid-1980s on, not just 1996–97, and the average firearm homicide and suicide rates after the year you picked would always be lower than the average before it. The question is *whether the rate of decline changed* after the law went into effect.

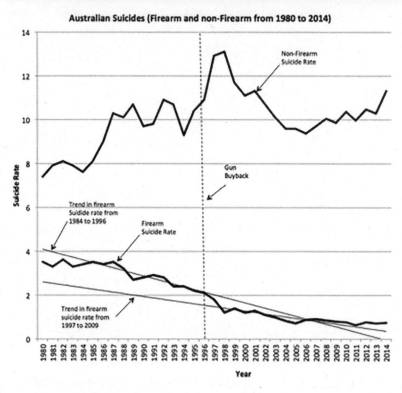

FIGURE 2

Australian Suicides (Firearm and non-Firearm from 1980 to 2014)

Prior to 1996, there was already a clear downward trend in the firearm homicide rate for at least thirteen years (Figure 1). This pattern continued at a slower rate after the buyback. The trend line is much flatter in the thirteen or more years after the buyback. The change after the buyback would also have been much flatter if one believes that 1996 was an aberration or that the impact of the 1996–1997 buyback wasn't instantaneous and started looking at years after 1997. There is certainly no sudden drop in firearm homicides after the gun buyback. The firearm homicide rates from 1998 to 2000 are virtually the same as the rates from 1993 to 1995. Hence, it is difficult to link the decline to the buyback.

The pattern from firearm suicides can be seen in Figure 2.[4] Compared to homicides, there is relatively little variability from year to year. And again, while it is true that firearm suicides fell after the buyback, they had been falling for more than a decade prior to the buyback. Indeed, the rate of firearm suicides was falling at a similar, if slightly slower, rate after the buyback as it was beforehand. Again, the trend line after the buyback is flatter whether one looks from 1997–2009 or at any year up through 2014. The buyback was not followed by any sudden drop. All of this data fits with the existing economic research and implies that something other than the availability of guns is driving down suicides.[5]

Before the buyback, firearm suicides were falling despite a very large increase in non-firearm suicides, and the upward trend in non-firearm suicides continued for another year after the buyback began. And yet after the buyback, between the years 1997 and 2004 to 2007, the drop in non-firearm suicides was larger than for firearm suicides. If the buyback reduced firearm suicides, why were firearm suicides falling faster than non-firearm suicides before the buyback and then falling more slowly than non-firearm suicides after the buyback?

The reason that some people who look at this data for firearm suicides and homicides conclude that the buyback was beneficial comes from a simple specification error. They look at the average firearm suicide and homicide rates before and after the buyback, but don't look carefully at the how these rates were declining before the buyback occurred.

Figure 3 illustrates Australia's armed robbery rates before and after the 1996 gun buyback.[6] If more guns really means more armed robberies, robbery should have quickly fallen after the buyback and then gradually increased. Just the opposite happened: the armed robbery rate soared right after the buyback and then gradually declined. Indeed, it took about ten years for armed robbery rates to fall back to the level of 1995, the year immediately before the buyback.

But just as we cannot credit the buyback with lowering firearm homicide or suicide rates, it is also hard to blame the buyback for the increase in armed robberies. After all, the armed and unarmed robbery rates mostly fluctuate in synchrony with each other. However, the post-buyback increase in the armed robbery rate was significantly sharper than the increase in the unarmed robbery rate. This could be a detrimental consequence of the buyback.

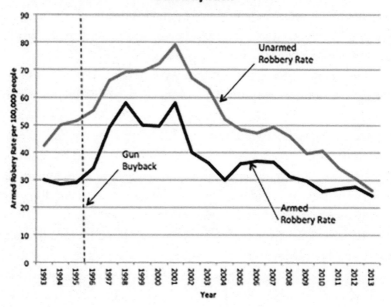

FIGURE 3

Australian Robbery Rate Before and After 1996-97
Gun Buyback

Despite all the wondrous benefits supposedly produced by the Australian gun buyback, any honest reading of the evidence shows no benefit from the law. The reason that these laws didn't produce much of a buyback seems obvious—the buyback only took guns away from law-abiding citizens. The reason the buyback did not produce higher crime rates is simple: self-defense use was already illegal and leads to extreme penalties if detected.

AUSTRALIA VS. NEW ZEALAND

Australia is frequently compared to the United States when it comes to mass public shootings. European countries such as France, Belgium, and Germany have even stricter gun control laws than Australia. They all have mass public shooting rates equal to or higher than those in the United States. With respect to mass public shootings, one could manage to find a country that "proves" what you want it to prove. It makes as much sense to pick one state from the United States as it does to pick one country.

The solution to this problem is to look at a lot of similar places and see what gun control measures actually made a difference. To do just that, Bill Landes (University of Chicago Law School) and I collected data on all multiple victim public shootings in all the United States from 1977 to 1999.[7] We examined thirteen different gun control policies including: waiting periods, registration, background checks, bans on assault weapons and other guns, the death penalty, and harsher penalties for committing a crime with a firearm. But only one policy reduced the number and severity of mass public shootings: allowing victims to defend themselves with permitted concealed handguns.

Since at least 1950, all but two U.S. mass public shootings have taken place in areas where guns are banned. And in Europe, every single mass public shooting has taken place where guns are banned.[8]

New Zealand provides a useful comparison to Australia.[9] In addition to being socioeconomically and demographically similar, they are both isolated island nations. Their mass murder rates were nearly identical prior to Australia's gun buyback. From 1980 to 1996, Australia's mass murder rate was 0.0042 incidents per 100,000 people. New Zealand's was 0.0050 incidents per 100,000 people. Post-1997, New Zealand experienced a similar drop without having altered its gun control laws.

It would be just as inappropriate for gun control critics to cite New Zealand as it is for gun control advocates to cite Australia. There are limits to picking one country and trying to infer what policies work to reduce public shootings. At least the U.S. affords the opportunity to look at many different, yet comparable, places that are all experimenting with various gun control laws.

CONCLUSION

It is very hard to look at the raw data on firearm suicides and homicides and see any benefits from Australia's gun buyback. In 2004, the

U.S. National Research Council released a report reaching this same conclusion: "It is the committee's view that the theory underlying gun buy-back programs is badly flawed and the empirical evidence demonstrates the ineffectiveness of these programs."[10]

Australia's buyback program was only one experiment, and we can't account for all of the other factors that may have come into play. The solution is then to look across many different states or countries and try to discern overall patterns.

The U.S. data is clear: laws that restrict gun ownership adversely affect people's safety. Police are extremely important in reducing crime—my research indicates that they are the single most important factor. But police themselves understand that they almost always arrive on the crime scene after the crime has occurred. Behaving passively is definitely not the safest course of action to take.

CHAPTER 10

MASS PUBLIC SHOOTINGS: THE MYTHS DEBUNKED

*The world recoiled in horror in 2012 when 20 Connecticut school-children and six adults were killed at Sandy Hook Elementary School.... The weapon was a Bushmaster AR-15 semiautomatic rifle adapted from its original role as a battlefield weapon. The AR-15, which is designed to inflict maximum casualties with **rapid bursts**, should never have been available for purchase by civilians (emphasis added).[1]*
—New York Times *editorial, March 4, 2016*

*Assault weapons were banned for 10 years until Congress, in bipartisan obeisance to the gun lobby, let the law lapse in 2004. As a result, gun manufacturers have been allowed to sell all manner of **war weaponry** to civilians, including the **super destructive .50-caliber sniper rifle**....(emphasis added)[2]*
—New York Times *editorial, December 11, 2015*

[James Holmes the Aurora, Colorado Batman Movie The-
*ater Shooter] also bought **bulletproof vests** and other tactical*
gear"(emphasis added).[3]
—*New York Times*, July 22, 2012

It is hard to debate guns if you don't know much about the subject. But it is probably not too surprising that gun control advocates who live in New York City know very little about guns. Semi-automatic guns don't fire "rapid bursts" of bullets. The *New York Times* might be fearful of .50-caliber sniper rifles, but these bolt-action .50-caliber rifles were never covered by the federal assault weapons ban. "Urban assault vests" may sound like they are bulletproof, but they are made of nylon.

These are just a few of the many errors that the *New York Times* made.[4] If it really believes that it has a strong case, it wouldn't feel the need to constantly hype its claims. What distinguishes the *New York Times* is that it doesn't bother running corrections for these errors.

A lot of people would assume that the worst attacks are perpetrated with "military-style" assault weapons. But the key word is "style." The civilian versions of the AR-15 and AK-47 are similar to military guns in their cosmetics, but not in the way that they operate. The original federal assault weapons ban did not cover the fully automatic machine guns used by the military, but rather the semi-automatic versions of those guns.

The civilian version of the AR-15 is essentially the same as a small game-hunting rifle in the bullets that it uses, the rapidity at which bullets are fired (one bullet per pull of the trigger), and the overall damage that can be inflicted. The civilian version of the AK-47 is similar, though it fires a much larger bullet. But these aren't the "machine guns" used by militaries, which do fire a burst of bullets. Unlike a semi-automatic, one pull of the trigger will continuously fire bullets as long as the trigger is depressed.

Given how frequently the media covers guns, it is amazing how little they know about them. In the first quote above, the *New York Times* seems confused about the differences between semi-automatic and machine guns. The *New York Times* is hardly alone in this. Shortly after the Sandy Hook attack, Wolf Blitzer interviewed me on CNN's *State of the Union* where he angrily asked me: "Why do people need a semi-automatic Bushmaster to go out and kill deer?"[5] The answer was simple: it is still a hunting rifle that has been made to look like a military weapon.

The real irony is that the .223-caliber bullets used in the Bushmasters or AR-15s are so small that many states ban them from being used to hunt deer.[6] The fear is that these relatively small bullets will not kill the animals but merely wound them, causing them to suffer. But .223-caliber bullets are best for hunting small-game animals.

As to the "super destructive .50-caliber sniper rifle," not only does the *New York Times* editorial get the law wrong, but it somehow neglects to mention that these guns have never been used to murder anyone, let alone used in the mass shootings that the editorial was discussing.[7] Part of the reason for them not being used in crimes is that these guns are extremely expensive (at least $4,000), big, and very heavy (nearly four feet long and weighing twenty-seven pounds).[8]

Numerous stories in the *New York Times* also referred to the Batman movie theater killer as wearing a bulletproof vest.[9] But if they had actually looked up "urban assault vest" on Amazon.com, they would have realized that the vest's nylon wouldn't have stopped any of the bullets fired at the killer.[10] What made the vest unique was all of its pockets, specifically designed to hold multiple magazines for bullets and other equipment.

So are there more fatalities when "assault weapons" are used? In the 2009 Fort Hood attack, Major Nidal Malik Hasan managed to fire a record of at least 220 shots using just a revolver and a semi-automatic handgun. The average number of rounds fired by those using high-capacity magazines was actually very similar to the number fired without them (seventy-one to sixty-five). That fact is apparently not too surprising given that the average time between shots tends to be much longer than the time that it takes to change a magazine.[11]

High-capacity magazines also have a greater chance of jamming. The attackers' guns jammed in both the Batman movie theater shooting and the Gabbie Giffords shooting in Tucson, Arizona.[12] Large magazines require exceptionally strong springs, and sometimes the last few bullets don't get loaded properly if the spring has lost even a little strength (this can happen as a result of people leaving bullets stored in the magazines).

Large capacity magazines do not appear to add to the deadliness of attacks. Overall, fourteen mass public shootings involved multiple guns and six involved large capacity magazines. The average number of people killed per attack in the two cases was very similar (10.1 where multiple guns were used and 11.5 with large capacity magazines), and even that small numerical difference was reversed by removing the one extreme case, the Newtown shooting (8.9 where multiple guns were used and 8.4 with large capacity magazines). If you look at only those cases with multiple guns and no large capacity magazines versus large capacity magazines and just a single gun, more people were actually killed in attacks with multiple guns (8.5 versus 6).

These numbers are not surprising. Shooters can fire many rounds simply by switching between loaded guns. Or they can bring extra magazines and change them in as little as a couple of seconds.

In Figure 1, while the differences between large capacity magazines and multiple guns suggest that multiple guns result in more fatalities, none of the differences are statistically significant.[13] But the results do indicate that banning large capacity magazines will do nothing to reduce fatalities.

Even if magazines could somehow be banned, how are you going to effectively stop people from obtaining multiple guns? It is one thing to completely ban a particular item. It is a much more difficult task to stop people from obtaining multiple copies of an item that is legal. And the numbers show that attackers are able to kill at least as many people by simply using multiple guns.

But the fact is that it's virtually impossible to stop criminals from obtaining the magazines they want. Magazines, large or small, are trivially easy to make. They are just boxes with springs, and can be made with the most simple tools. The advent of 3D printers has made them even easier to make.

There's no evidence that crime rates were affected by the 1994 federal ban on magazines holding more than ten bullets. Even the left-leaning

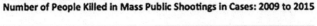

FIGURE 1

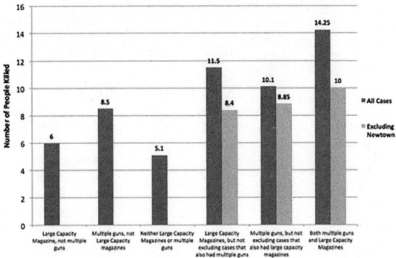

Number of People Killed in Mass Public Shootings in Cases: 2009 to 2015

Urban Institute, with funding from the Bill Clinton administration, was unable to find any such evidence.[14]

All this raises another irony. Large capacity magazine bans are only obeyed by law-abiding citizens.[15] This will prevent concealed handgun permit holders from carrying many bullets in their guns. Concealed handgun permit holders who carry in public usually just carry the magazine that is in their gun and don't carry multiple guns. Attackers, on the other hand, can prepare by bringing multiple guns and magazines. They can wear an "urban assault vest," like the one James Holmes wore, with pockets for the magazines. Even if they somehow can't get large magazines, they will be able to take a lot of smaller magazines with them.

For all the emphasis on assault weapons, 68 percent of mass public shootings did not involve any long guns (Figure 2). Eighty-four percent of shootings involved handguns, 24 percent rifles, and 20 percent shotguns (more than one type of weapon can be used in an attack).

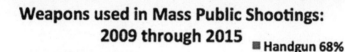

FIGURE 2

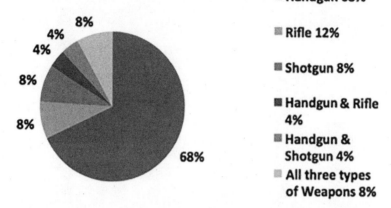

Weapons used in Mass Public Shootings:
2009 through 2015

■ Handgun 68%

■ Rifle 12%

■ Shotgun 8%

■ Handgun & Rifle 4%

■ Handgun & Shotgun 4%

■ All three types of Weapons 8%

8%
4%
4%
8%
8%
68%

KILLERS CHOOSE GUN-FREE ZONES

I do not recommend that [the policy banning soldiers from car-rying guns on military bases] be changed. We have adequate law enforcement on those bases to respond. ... You take the Fort Hood incident number two, the one where I was the commander of Third Corps, those police responded within eight minutes and that guy was dead. So that is pretty quick.... [16]
—General Mark Milley, U.S. Army Chief of Staff, April 7, 2016

Many shooters don't really care whether it is a gun-free zone or not, they are just there to kill people and they expect to die in their event...so I don't think that mass shooters are to be as respon-sive...as a careful calculating rational person might be.[17]
—Adam Winkler, UCLA Law Professor, 2014

What might be an "adequate" and "pretty quick" response time to General Milley may seem like an eternity to those present at these attacks. During the second Fort Hood attack in April 2014, eight minutes was long enough for Ivan Lopez to fire at least thirty-five shots with a semi-automatic pistol and leave three dead and fourteen injured.[18] That was only one shot every fourteen seconds. In the first Fort Hood shooting in November 2009, Major Nidal Malik Hasan took ten minutes to kill thirteen people and wound another thirty-two.[19] With his two handguns, he fired about 220 shots (approximately one shot every 2.7 seconds).[20] Lopez's and Hasan's attacks came to an abrupt end once police arrived, but the shootings could have been stopped so much sooner if someone with a gun had been there to begin with. These attacks aren't unusual in terms of their duration or the rapidity of fire.[21]

Since 2011, there have been only three mass public shootings in areas where concealed carry was allowed: the IHOP restaurant in Carson City, Nevada on September 6, 2011; the Gabrielle Giffords shooting in Tucson, Arizona on January 8, 2011; and the Kalamazoo shooting on February 20, 2016 at a Cracker Barrel restaurant. (This last case is a little complicated. Uber bans guns in its cars and the killer fired the gun from his car, but the shooter shot at another car and guns were allowed in the restaurant parking lot.) But these cases are very rare. From 1950–2010, not a single mass public shooting occurred in an area where general civilians are allowed to carry guns. Over the entire period from 1950 through February 2016, just over 1 percent of mass public shootings occurred in such places. If you look at only the period that we have been examining for the other data, 8 percent of mass public shootings have occurred in places where civilians are allowed to defend themselves.

Mass killers have even explicitly talked about their desire to attack places where civilians can't defend themselves. One need only listen to the February 2016 wiretap of an ISIS supporter who was planning an attack on one of the biggest churches in Detroit. Khalil Abu-Rayyan explained his choice of target this way: "A lot of people go there. Plus, people are not allowed to carry guns in church. Plus, it would make the news. Everybody would've heard."[22] Fortunately, Abu-Rayyan's father alerted the FBI.

The infamous 2015 Charleston, South Carolina church shooting was originally going to be a college shooting. But Dylann Roof changed plans after realizing that the College of Charleston had armed guards.

FIGURE 3

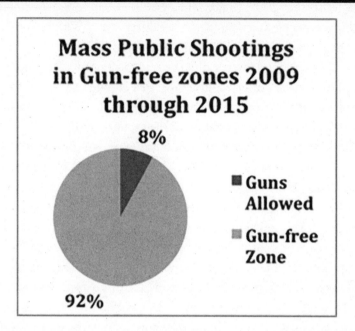

Mass Public Shootings
in Gun-free zones 2009
through 2015

8%

■ Guns
   Allowed

■ Gun-free
   Zone

92%

The Batman movie theater killer, James Holmes, initially considered attacking an airport. In his diary, which was released in 2015, he explained his decision against targeting the airport because of "substantial security."[23] He then selected the only theater within twenty minutes of his apartment that banned permitted concealed handguns.[24] There were six other theaters he could have gone to. The one he picked wasn't even the one with the largest auditorium or the one that was closest to his home.[25]

Or take Elliot Rodger, who fatally shot three people in 2014 near the campus of UC Santa Barbara. Rodger ruled out various targets where he thought someone with a gun would be able to stop his killing spree.[26] Justin Bourque, who shot to death three people in Canada in 2014, even posted to Facebook a cartoon of a defenseless victim explaining to his killer that guns are prohibited.[27]

As claimed in the above quote by Adam Winkler, it is often suggested that mentally ill killers are unlikely to be careful planners. Some people have a hard time imagining deranged individuals considering such issues as gun-free zones. Yet, many of these mentally ill people have left documents laying out their intentions.

Adam Lanza, the Newtown killer, spent two-and-a-half years putting together a report on mass public shootings. Law enforcement described, "A sickeningly thorough 7-foot-long, 4-foot-wide spreadsheet with names, body counts, and weapons from previous mass murders and even attempted killings. 'It sounded like a doctoral thesis, that was the quality of the research,' an anonymous law enforcement veteran said."[28] Lanza also collected information on media coverage for each killing. He observed that attacks with more deaths received greater media coverage.

Lanza may have been mentally ill, but he clearly knew what he wanted to accomplish and how he was going to do it. Take this report from *CBS Evening News*:

> Sources say Lanza saw himself as being in direct competition with Anders Breivik, a Norwegian man who killed 77 people in July 2011....
>
> Two officials who have been briefed on the Newtown, Conn., investigation say Lanza wanted to top Breivik's death toll and targeted nearby Sandy Hook Elementary School because it was the "easiest target" with the "largest cluster of people."[29]

James Holmes was also mentally ill, but Dr. William Reid, a state-appointed psychiatrist who performed Holmes's sanity evaluation, testified that Holmes carefully planned not only the theater to attack but also other minute details to maximize the number of possible victims.[30] Over and over again, mentally ill killers invest a lot of time and energy into planning their attacks. Many start thinking about their attacks a year or two in advance. Mass public shootings rarely involved less than six months of planning.

In a 2013 interview with academics who do research on gun control and gun-free zones, Jake Berry, a reporter with the *Nashua Telegraph*

(New Hampshire) found: "On the whole, Lott's colleagues—both in the media and academia—don't dispute his findings."[31] The dispute is over why these attacks keep occurring where guns are banned:

- David Hemenway, a public health researcher at Harvard, explained: "I suspect that most places that mass public shootings could logically occur are 'gun-free zones' either determined by the government (schools) or by private businesses and institutions."
- Similarly, Dan Webster, a public health researcher at Johns Hopkins, said: "Schools might be a likely target because that is where a mass of people congregate and those people involve a lot of troubled adolescents who may harbor bad feelings toward the people there who bullied them, were unfair to them, etc. The shooters in these instances didn't say, 'Hey, I'll find a gun-free zone where I can shoot a lot of people.' No, they went to a place for reasons wholly unrelated to gun-free zones."

Obviously, some killers do intentionally avoid attacking gun-free zones. They know what they are doing: they want to kill as many people as possible so that they can get more media attention. While the vast majority of schools are gun-free zones, a number of large public universities as well as some K-12 schools do not ban guns. Most movie theaters and malls don't ban guns. Indeed, in some states it isn't even possible for businesses to ban customers from carrying guns. Yet, we haven't been seeing attacks in those schools or businesses that allow people to carry.

It is not just James Holmes in Colorado picking the one movie theater where permitted concealed handguns weren't allowed. In Lafayette, Louisiana in 2015, John Houser attacked one of only two movie theaters in his area that banned permitted concealed handguns.[32] Likewise, the Westroads Mall in Omaha, Nebraska and the Trolley Square Mall in Salt Lake City, Utah were attacks where only the indoor malls that banned permitted concealed handguns were targets.[33] These killers had the choice of attacking theaters or malls where guns were allowed, but they consistently went out of their way to attack those rare places where guns weren't allowed.

Then there are the other gun-free zone businesses where these types of attacks occurred: a Korean spa in Norcross, Georgia (February 22, 2012); a nursing home in Carthage, North Carolina (March 29, 2009); the Tacoma Coffee Shop in Lakewood, Washington (November 29, 2009); and the Yoyito Cafe restaurant in Hialeah, Florida (June 6, 2010). Several of these cases surely had individuals motivated by hatred against someone in these businesses, but presumably there were those in other businesses who also faced angry people. Why is it only in these gun-free zones that we see so many people killed?

Attackers have good reason to target gun-free zones. As shown earlier, concealed carry permit holders have stopped many mass public shootings. In addition to the cases listed earlier, mass public shootings have been stopped in Pearl, Mississippi; Edinboro, Pennsylvania; Grundy, Virginia; Memphis, Tennessee; Colorado Springs, Colorado; Portland, Oregon; and Salt Lake City, Utah. It has happened at colleges, in busy downtowns, in churches, in malls, and outside apartment buildings. Concealed carry saves lives everywhere.

Mass public shooters avoid places where victims can defend themselves. After all, how quickly people can arrive with a gun to stop the attack reduces the number of likely victims and the publicity that the killer will be able to get.

MENTAL ILLNESS

Major Garrett: Do you believe the [mental health] legislation the Senate did not pass would have made any difference in this case [Elliot Rodger's Santa Barbara attack]? …

Senator Richard Blumenthal: I am going to urge that we bring back those bills, maybe reconfigure them to center on mental

health, which is a point where we can agree that we need more
resources to make the country healthier and to make sure that
these kinds of horrific, insane, mad occurrences are stopped
and the Congress will be complicit if we fail to act.[34]

More than half of mass public shooters (60 percent) were brought
to the attention of a medical practitioner, school official, or legal author-
ity *prior* to the shooting. That rate is slightly higher than the one the
New York Times came up with from analyzing mass public shootings
from 1949 to 1999.[35] The result also confirms something that we have
known for a long time—it is very difficult for psychiatric professionals
to know who will actually commit mass murder.

The issue of mental health was brought back into central focus by
the Santa Barbara killings of May 23, 2014. But there is a certain irony
here. This was the attack which spurred Sen. Richard Blumenthal
(D-CT) to push for more resources on mental health.[36] However, Elliot
Rodger, the killer, had already been receiving top-quality mental-health
counseling for years. One of his psychiatrists, Dr. Charles Sophy, is
nationally known and serves as medical director of the Los Angeles
County Department of Children and Family Services.[37] But Rodger's
141-page manifesto shows a real pride in being able to deceive these
experts.[38]

Santa Barbara County deputies visited Rodger's home on April 30
to investigate a complaint. Sheriff Bill Brown says the deputies described
Rodger as "quiet and timid...polite and courteous.... [T]here was no
problem, that he wasn't going to hurt himself or anyone else, and he just
didn't meet the criteria for any further intervention at that point."

Some blame the sheriff's deputies for not doing more to investigate
the initial complaint, but the psychiatrists were ultimately responsible
for ensuring that Rodger received proper treatment.[39] Even Rodger's
father said, "There is no way I thought that this boy could hurt a
flea.... [W]e didn't see this coming at all."[40]

Many other mass killers were already seeing psychiatrists before their
attacks. This includes Ivan Lopez (the recent 2014 Fort Hood shooter),

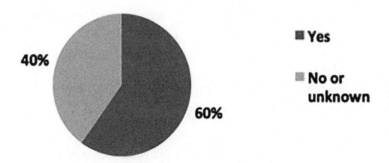

FIGURE 4

Mental illness diagnosed before Mass Public Shootings: 2009 through 2015

40%

60%

■ Yes

▨ No or unknown

Adam Lanza (Sandy Hook Elementary), James Holmes (Dark Knight movie theater), and Seung-Hui Cho (Virginia Tech).[41]

The Army psychiatrist who last saw Ivan Lopez found no "sign of likely violence, either to himself or to others."[42] James Holmes's psychiatrist warned the University of Colorado officials about her patient's violent fantasies, but she "rejected the idea" that the threat was sufficiently serious for him to be taken into custody.[43]

Seung-Hui Cho, the Virginia Tech killer, was subject to a commitment hearing.[44] However, licensed psychologist Roy Crouse performed an independent evaluation and found Cho to be "mentally ill" but concluded, "he does not present an imminent danger to (himself/others) ... he does not require involuntary hospitalization." A staff psychiatrist at Carilion St. Albans Psychiatric Hospital recommended outpatient counseling and determined that Cho "is not a danger to himself or others." The judge accepted these findings and determined not to have Cho involuntarily committed.[45]

These mass killers certainly didn't lack mental health care. The problem was that even top psychiatrists failed to identify them as real threats. And it's not as though psychiatrists lack incentives to get the diagnosis right. Beyond their reputation, professional pride, and desire to help, psychiatrists also have a legal obligation to inform authorities of threats. Families of the Aurora movie theater victims sued Holmes' psychiatrist for not recommending that his patient be confined.[46]

Psychiatrists frequently underestimate threats to safety, sometimes struggling to accept that their own patients could actually pose a serious violent threat. The problem is well known in the psychiatric profession, and an entire body of academic literature is devoted to the subject. Some people suggest that it's simply hard to predict these extremely rare mass shootings. Others argue that psychiatrists are trying to prove their fearlessness.

The rarity of these attacks certainly makes the first explanation plausible. There are roughly 1.6 million people with schizophrenia alone. From 2009 through 2015, mentally ill individuals caused fifteen of the twenty-five mass public shootings. Even if all fifteen individuals had schizophrenia (and that is clearly not the case), this comes to one mass public shooting for every 100,000 schizophrenics. To stop one person who is truly going to do something terrible, you may have to confine thousands of people who seem dangerous.

There is another real cost to linking gun violence with mental illness. Dr. Renee Binder, President of the American Psychiatric Association and herself a strong gun control advocate, rightly points out that, "People with mental illness are far more likely to be victims of violence...the majority of individuals with mental illness will never be violent toward others."[47] The mentally ill already have a hard enough time in our society, and treating them as potential murderers will not help matters.

However, if we really believe that a mentally ill individual poses a danger to others, simply prohibiting that person from buying a gun isn't likely to solve anything. If someone can get his hands on illegal drugs, he can also get his hands on illegal guns. Indeed, drug gangs usually sell both.

If someone is really a danger to others, the most effective solution is to send him to a secure mental health facility.

FIGURE 5

Victims from Mass Public Shootings: 2009 to 2015

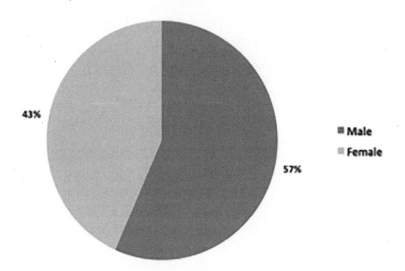

43%

■ Male
▤ Female

57%

A CLOSER LOOK AT MASS PUBLIC SHOOTERS

Data on mass public shootings allow us to examine both the victims and what happens to the killers themselves. Male victims were somewhat more common than female victims in mass public shootings (57 percent to 43 percent).

Perpetrators of mass public shootings died during their attack 69 percent of the time (38 percent of killers committed suicide and 31 percent were killed by others). The true suicide rate is higher, however, because some attackers chose what amounted to "police-assisted suicide." These killers planned on committing suicide, but found that they just couldn't carry through with killing themselves. So they put the police in the position of having to use lethal force.

When Obama and Hillary Clinton ran for president in 2008, gun control was largely a non-issue.[48] Clinton ran to the right of Obama on the gun issue, and Obama disowned his own past history when he

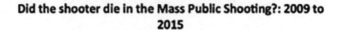

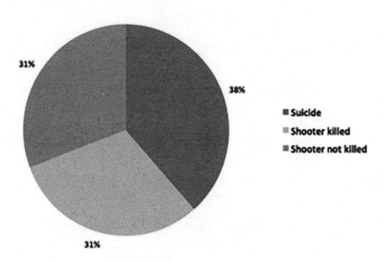

Did the shooter die in the Mass Public Shooting?: 2009 to
2015

31%

38%

■ Suicide
▓ Shooter killed
▓ Shooter not killed

31%

supported bans on guns. Instead, Obama promised to be a strong supporter of the Second Amendment.[49] Nor were guns really an issue during
the 2012 presidential election. The political climate had changed dramatically by 2016.

Mass public shootings have been the central focus of much of that
change. As we showed earlier, there hasn't been a significant increase in
occurrences since the late 1970s. These are indeed horrible attacks, and
something needs to be done to stop them, but the frequency and severity
of these attacks hasn't changed during the Obama administration. By
themselves, these attacks can't explain the change in the political atmosphere. What might explain the difference is President Obama's relentless
war on guns during his second term. Presidents have a huge megaphone,
and gun control is an issue that has resonated with the media.

In summary, mass public shooters differ from other mass killers in
many systematic ways. They usually die at the scene of the crime. And
over half are known to have suffered from mental illness prior to the

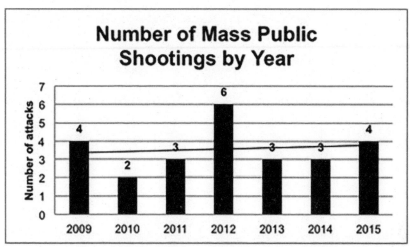

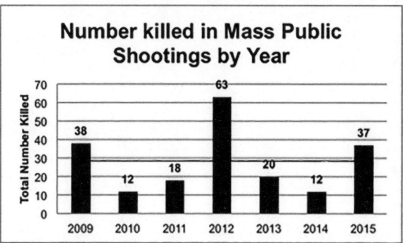

attack. The killers also carefully plan out their attacks: almost all take place where civilians are not allowed to defend themselves. The typical attack involving so-called "assault weapons" is no deadlier than those involving other types of weapons.

CHAPTER 11

BATHTUBS AND MOTOR VEHICLE REGULATIONS

D ebbie is a mom from Uxbridge, Massachusetts. She was in the examination room when the pediatrician asked her five-year-old, "Does Daddy own a gun?"[1]

When the little girl said *yes*, the doctor began grilling her and her mom about the number and types of guns, how they are stored, etc. If the incident had ended there, it would have merely been annoying. But Debbie got mad when a friend in law enforcement told her that the doctor had filed a report with the police (about her family's [entirely legal] gun ownership).

Maybe this doctor should have asked about the family bathtubs instead of the family guns. Because, according to the U.S. Consumer Product Safety Commission (CPSC), 346 children under age five drowned in bathtubs between 2006 and 2010.[2] By contrast, only ninety-four children under five died from accidental gunshots over the same period.[3] That is a difference of nearly a factor of four. In fact, more children under five died from drowning in bathtubs than children under ten or even under fifteen from accidental gun shots (167 and 291 respectively).

Of course, no one would advocate getting rid of bathtubs. Bathtubs do create a possibility of drowning, but cleanliness is also important. A similar trade-off exists for guns—some accidents do happen, but guns also protect law-abiding people from death or injury.

When they involve a child, even accidental gun woundings can get national coverage. In April 2016, the Associated Press covered a case where a mother dropped her purse and a gun inside went off. The woman's two-year-old daughter suffered a "superficial" wound and was "expected to be fine."[4] In less than twenty-four hours, the story was picked up by over forty-four different news organizations, including Fox News.[5] It's hard to think of any other product that produced a minor injury attracting equal national attention.

National news programs have staged experiments where a single gun is placed in a toy-filled room.[6] Shocking pictures show five- and six-year-olds picking up and playing with the gun like it was a toy. The fear is understandable but will end up costing more lives than it will save. It gives a misleading impression of what poses the greatest dangers to our children. We may eliminate one danger by not owning guns or by keeping them under lock-and-key, but at the same time we expose ourselves and our children to other dangers. Guns are the most effective way for people to defend themselves against criminals, and making it so that people can no longer use guns for self-defense means that criminals will be more successful in harming people. There is also evidence that making crime easier will encourage criminals to commit more crime.

Accidental gun deaths among children are fortunately much rarer than most people believe. According to the CDC, thirty-eight children under age ten died from accidental gunshots in 2014. With some 130 million gun owners and about 40 million children under ten, it is hard to find any other commonly-owned, potentially lethal item that has as low a rate of accidental death.

These deaths rarely involve children shooting themselves or other children. In a study that I did on the years 1995–2001, I found that children under ten were involved in an average of only nine such shootings per year.[7] Overwhelmingly, the shooters are adult males with alcohol addictions, suspended or revoked driver's licenses, and a record of arrests for violent crimes.

Asking patients about guns not only strains doctor patient relationships, it exaggerates the dangers and risks lives. It makes more sense for doctors to ask if "daddy" has a violent criminal record than it does to ask if he owns a gun.

FEAR DOESN'T CHANGE THE STATISTICS

Fear about guns seems to be greatest among those who know the least about them. It takes some familiarity to know that young children can't simply fire a typical semi-automatic pistol. Few are likely to know that the slide needs to be pulled back to put a bullet in the chamber. Those who do are unlikely to have the strength to do so. And, of course, they may not be aware that the safety has to be switched off.

Maybe more media attention should be given to the dangers posed by everyday items. In 2014, motor vehicles killed 303 pedestrians under age ten.[8] Bicycle and space heater accidents take many times more children's lives than guns do. Suffocation claimed over 1,100 lives. The most recent yearly data available indicate that five-gallon plastic water buckets claimed the lives of more than thirty children under age five.

Again, the problem with gun-phobia is that without guns, victims are much more vulnerable to criminal attack. Guns are used defensively some 2 million times each year.[9] Even though the police are extremely important in reducing crime, they simply can't be there all the time. In fact, they virtually always arrive after the crime has been committed. Having a gun is by far the safest course of action when one is confronted by a criminal.

We rarely hear about the cases where young children use guns to save family members. And we don't hear at all about cases where children's lives were clearly lost because of locked and inaccessible guns.

I have done research examining juvenile accidental gun deaths for all U.S. states from 1977 to 1998. I couldn't find any positive effects from the gun-lock mandates that existed in sixteen states.[10] What did happen, however, was that criminals were emboldened to attack people in their homes. These states experienced 300 more murders and 4,000 more rapes after adopting gun lock mandates. Burglaries also rose dramatically. Overall, the evidence indicates that states with the largest increases in gun ownership had the largest drops in violent crime.

SHOULD MOTOR VEHICLE REGULATIONS GUIDE FIREARM REGULATIONS?

Which is more likely to kill you: a car or a gun? In January 2015, numerous publications such as *The Economist, Forbes, Washington Post, Slate, The Atlantic,* and *Vox* all reported that gun deaths were set to overtake road deaths before the year ended.[11] That probably didn't happen.

In 2014, the Center for American Progress predicted that the year's data would show firearm deaths equalling motor vehicle deaths among fifteen-to-twenty-four-year-olds.[12] Many were convinced that this was going to happen. Gun control advocates brag that this gives them a "statistic that really resonates with people."[13]

In fact, the gap between these types of deaths was slightly larger in 2014 than in 2013.[14]

The latest data we have are from 2014. A total of 35,631 Americans died from motor vehicle deaths, and 32,856 died from gun deaths (suicides, murders, and accidental fatalities). The gap has narrowed since 2000, when there were 43,563 motor vehicle deaths and 25,855 gun deaths. And the 2014 firearm deaths fall somewhat to 30,044 when we exclude justifiable homicides.

The drop in motor vehicle deaths is generally attributed to stringent safety regulations. The Coalition to End Gun Violence recently told the Associated Press: "Starting in the 1960s, the United States began to take a look at the carnage that we were seeing on our roads and made a serious effort to strictly regulate drivers, cars, and roads. We've done none of this for guns."

FIGURE 1

Figure 1: Center for American Progress' February 2014 Prediction that in 2014 Gun Deaths and Vehicle Deaths would equal each other

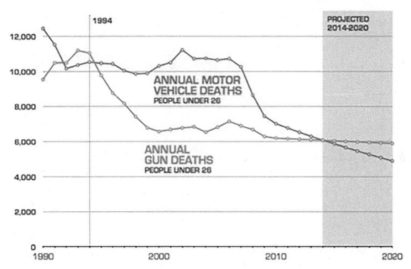

If increased safety regulations are the solution, why is it that accidental firearm death rates have fallen more quickly than accidental motor vehicle death rates? They fell 22 percent faster from 2000 to 2014: 33 percent versus 27 percent (Figure 3).

Since 2000, motor vehicle deaths only really changed between 2007 and 2009, when deaths fell by more than 20 percent. Why the sudden drop? It wasn't because of any safety regulations suddenly going into effect in late 2007. The explanation is much more prosaic: during the recession and anemic recovery, people drove a lot less.

There is a more basic problem with comparing motor vehicle deaths to firearm deaths. The causes of death are very different (Figure 4). In 2014, 99.4 percent of car deaths were accidental in nature. By contrast, only 1.8 percent of gun deaths were accidental. A staggering 65 percent of gun fatalities are suicides.

Although murders and accidental gun death rates have fallen, the firearm suicide rate has risen by 14 percent since 2000 (Figure 5). But the non-firearm suicide rate rose by 49 percent during the same period.

FIGURE 2

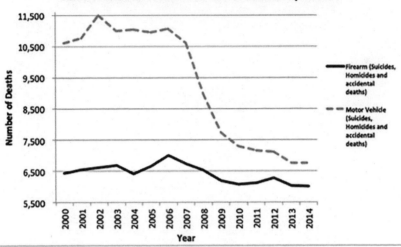

Figure 2: Actual Total Deaths from Firearms and Motor Vehicles between 2000 and 2014 for 15 to 24-year-olds

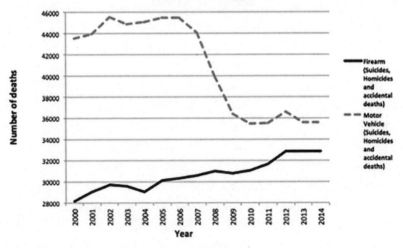

Total deaths from firearms and motor vehicles between 2000 and 2014 for all ages

The motor vehicle suicide rate went up 53 percent.[15] Something is causing a general rise in suicide.

Regulations and licensing rules haven't prevented motor vehicle suicides, and they aren't going to prevent firearm suicides. Beyond prohibiting people with psychiatric disorders from owning a gun or driving

FIGURE 3

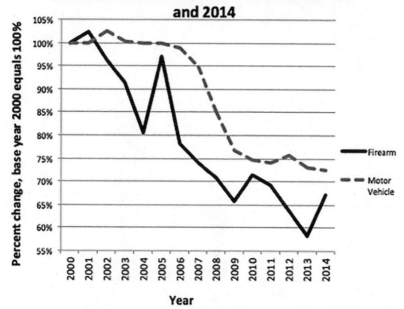

Figure 3: Percent change in accidental firearm and motor vehicle deaths rates between 2000 and 2014

a car, as is already done, there is essentially nothing that regulations can do to prevent suicides.[16]

A 2004 National Research Council report found that "Some gun control policies may reduce the number of gun suicides, but they have not yet been shown to reduce the overall risk of suicide in any population."[17]

Even if regulations could be credited with the sudden drop in motor vehicle deaths from 2007 to 2009, that doesn't imply that gun control regulations would have the same result.

The current gun control system is a mess. In the vast majority of cases in which a gun sale is stopped, law-abiding citizens are denied because their names happen to be similar to those of criminals. This is only one reason why academic studies consistently find that background checks have failed to reduce violent crime.

FIGURE 4

Figure 4: Firearm and Motor Vehicle Deaths by Cause

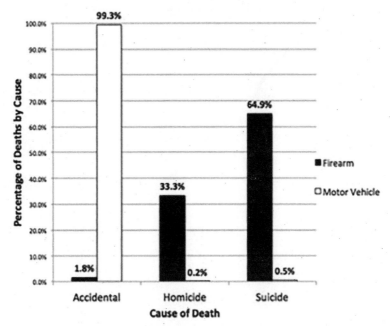

We have no easy answers. Take gun locks, for example. One might think that they are an obvious solution to accidental deaths involving children. But we are dealing with relatively small numbers here—in 2014, fifty children under fifteen died from accidental gun shots. In most of these cases, the child was not playing with the weapon, but was accidentally shot by an adult male.

And, of course, locks aren't going to stop adults from firing their own guns. Except, perhaps, when they actually need to protect themselves. When their homes get broken into, these adults are going to wish that their guns were unlocked and readily accessible. Indeed, peer-reviewed, academic studies find that mandating gun locks causes an increase in death rates.[18]

So will gun control advocates ever explain why accidental gun deaths have fallen more than accidental motor vehicle deaths? Or why non-firearm suicides rose twice as quickly as firearm suicides? We're unlikely

FIGURE 5

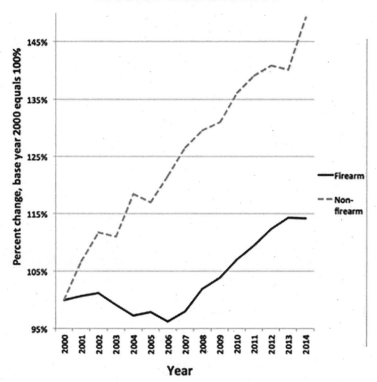

Figure 5: Percent change in firearm and non-firearm suicide rates between 2000 and 2014

to ever get an explanation, since these people have such trouble even correctly reporting numbers.

HAVE REGULATIONS REALLY REDUCED MOTOR VEHICLE FATALITIES?

According to the Violence Policy Center in January 2016, "Experts agree that the formation of the federal National Highway Traffic Safety Administration (NHTSA) in 1966, coupled with a sustained, decades-long effort to develop and implement a series of injury-prevention

FIGURE 6

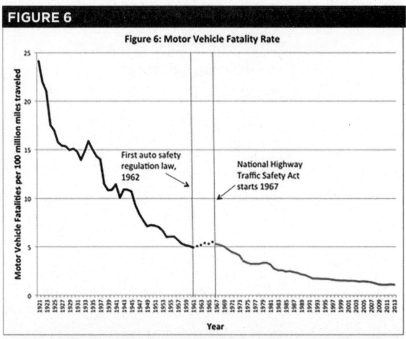

Figure 6: Motor Vehicle Fatality Rate

FIGURE 7

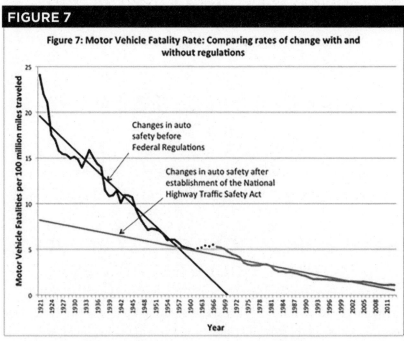

Figure 7: Motor Vehicle Fatality Rate: Comparing rates of change with and without regulations

initiatives, have saved countless lives. ... Between 1966 and 2000, the combined efforts of government and advocacy organizations reduced the rate of death per 100,000 population by 43%, which represents a 72% decrease in deaths per vehicle miles traveled."[19]

The post-1966 drop in deaths per vehicle mile is often cited as evidence that federal regulation has dramatically improved safety. As touched on earlier, it is sometimes assumed that the same sort of safety improvements could have been achieved with guns. Of course, over the last fifteen years, the drop in gun accidents has greatly exceeded the drop in motor vehicle accidents.

While it is true that motor vehicle safety improved in the wake of federal regulations, the rate of safety improvement was actually much faster prior to adoption of the first auto safety law in 1962 (Figure 6).[20] Figure 7 shows the average trend in fatalities before and after federal involvement. The rate of motor vehicle fatalities fell almost five times more quickly *before* the federal government got involved (see Table 1).

Table 1: Average yearly change in motor vehicle fatality rate per 100 million miles traveled before federal auto safety regulations and after the National Highway Traffic Safety Act		
	Change in rate per year	Absolute t-statistic	Significant level for a two-tailed t-test
Before federal regulations	-0.40	22.90	0.00%
After NHTSA	-0.083	19.45	0.00%

Virtually every year from 1921 to 2013 has a lower death rate than the year before. So there's nothing magical about the post-1966 drop.

CONCLUSION

If government regulations were really so effective, motor vehicle safety should have improved relative to firearm. Yet neither point turned out to be true.

There is no evidence that safety regulations reduced total suicides. There are simply too many ways for people to kill themselves. To the extent that the two products are comparable, it appears that motor vehicles might have more to learn from firearms than the reverse.

CHAPTER 12

BACKGROUND CHECK MYTHS

O ver and over, Democrats keep pointing to background checks on private transfers of guns as the solution to mass public shootings and crime. Such "universal" background checks have been the crux of their gun control proposals. But as we have already seen, background checks have not been successful in stopping criminals from getting guns.

Obama pushes for universal background checks after seemingly every mass public shooting. He has claimed, "The Republican Party is just uniformly opposed to all gun safety laws." Hillary Clinton said Republicans "refuse to do anything" about mass shootings.

Democrats could pass universal background checks if only they addressed three seemingly straightforward problems:

1. *Who pays for it?* Gun buyers and sellers are stuck with all the fees for universal background checks. In New York City and D.C., these fees are at least $125.[1] In Washington

state and Oregon, the costs of transferring a gun are about sixty dollars and fifty-five dollars, respectively.[2] But the background checks are supposed to benefit everyone, so why not pay for them out of general revenue? It isn't as if gang members are the ones paying the fees. These are law-abiding citizens who may really need a gun for protection. Some of them are poor people living in high-crime urban areas. Often, the most likely victims of violent crime can least afford these costs.

Paying for these background checks out of general government revenue would not only be fair, it would go a long way toward putting opponents' minds at ease. This should be an easy fix, if gun control advocates cared more about passing universal background checks than about just making it costly to own guns.

2. *Stop only prohibited people from buying guns.* The background check system is a mess. Virtually everyone who fails the check is someone who is legally eligible to buy a gun. Obama says that background checks have stopped 2.4 million dangerous or prohibited people from buying a gun.[3] He should have said that there were 2.4 million "initial denials."

It's like when someone is mistakenly stopped from flying because his name matches that of someone on the anti-terror "No Fly" list. This happened five times to the late Sen. Ted Kennedy.[4] By Obama's method of counting, five terrorists were stopped from flying.

About 96 percent of "initial denials" are dropped after the first two stages of review.[5] Many more are dropped during the three remaining stages.

Bill Clinton, George W. Bush, and President Obama have all been criticized for not prosecuting prohibited purchasers. In 2010, 76,152 denials resulted in only forty-nine federal prosecutions. State prosecutions were also few in number.[6] But there wasn't really a failure to prosecute. Many of these denials were not real cases. Having a similar name and birthdate to a felon isn't the same thing as actually being a felon.

For many of these 2.4 million people, a mistaken denial might be a mere inconvenience. But some people really do have an urgent need to protect themselves from stalkers or enemies. For those people, these delays can have very serious consequences.

These mistakes will particularly hurt people in certain racial groups for a simple reason: people are particularly likely to share similar names with others in their racial group. For instance, some 40 percent of Vietnamese people bear the name Nguyen.[7] Hispanics are more likely to have similar names to other Hispanics. The same is true of blacks. And because blacks have higher rates of felony convictions, law-abiding blacks are more likely to have their names confused with those of prohibited people.

The solution? Hold the government to the same standards that private companies are held to by the federal government. If private companies made even a tiny fraction of the government's mistakes, they would be sued out of existence. The current government system is clearly racist in its impact.

3. *Background checks as de facto registration.* It is not just other countries that use gun registries as a tool for mass confiscation. People in California, New York, and Chicago have all seen their registered guns confiscated.[8] Tellingly, Obama has hailed Great Britain and Australia as examples to follow. Both of these countries have engaged in mass confiscation.

Since 2004, the FBI has been required to destroy federal background check records within twenty-four hours of the check being approved. Proposed federal legislation, however, would require federally licensed dealers to keep these records indefinitely. Right now, the government is forbidden from consolidating that information into a central database. But the time may come when the government would decide to create such a database. With new data on private gun transfers, the government could potentially figure out the identities of everyone who legally owns a gun.

Gun control proponents assure us that they aren't setting up a registration program. Yet, in the same breath, they defend gun registration as a crime-fighting tool.

The idea is that police could find a gun at a crime scene and then be able to trace it to the registered owner. In fact, guns are very rarely left at crime scenes. Those that are left are virtually always unregistered. In the few cases where a registered gun has been left at the scene, it is because the criminal has been killed or seriously injured.

Police can't seem to point to a single instance in which gun registration has helped them solve a crime. During a recent deposition, the Washington, D.C. police department could not "recall any specific instance where registration records were used to determine who committed a crime." Police in Hawaii, Canada, and other places have made similar admissions. The best way of preventing such a government database would be to require that licensed dealers destroy background check records after a certain period of time.

WILL GUN CONTROL ADVOCATES AGREE TO THESE CHANGES?

I have made these suggestions for a decade, with no success. Gun control advocates feel particularly strongly about making gun owners pay the fees for firearms transfers. Colorado's 2013 bill on expanded background checks mandated both a fee to the state and another fee to the federally licensed gun dealer. Assembly Republicans proposed an amendment to waive the state fee for people below the poverty line, but Democrats voted it down.[9] A similar move was stopped by Democrats in Maryland.[10] Of course, when it comes to other taxes, one can count on Democrats to vote almost unanimously in favor of exemptions for the poor.

That universal background checks don't reduce mass public shootings or other kinds of violent crime isn't the question here. But if gun control advocates believe it, are they willing to make these fair, simple changes? If not, they're probably more interested in reducing gun ownership than stopping crime.

WHY THE "CHARLESTON GUN PURCHASE LOOPHOLE" WASN'T A LOOPHOLE

Clinton regularly claims that Dylann Roof was a convicted felon who wasn't supposed to be able to buy a gun.[11]

> We also have to close what is called the Charleston loophole. … The information that he wasn't eligible because he had a felony conviction didn't come through until after he went and used that gun and murdered nine people…. So we have work to do.[12]

In fact, Roof was *not* a convicted felon. He was arrested on misdemeanor drug possession, which carries a maximum prison time of six months. In addition, Roof was charged only with possession, not use. Even if you haven't yet been convicted of a crime, you are prohibited from buying guns if you are charged with a felony that could result in a prison term of at least two years or if you are a drug addict. *Neither case applied to Roof.*

The FBI released a statement trying to substantiate the claim that Roof was prohibited from buying a gun.[13] It explains that Roof could be prohibited from owning a gun on the basis of "a conviction for use or possession of a controlled substance within the past year; multiple arrests for such offenses within the past five years with the most recent arrest occurred within the past year; or persons found through a drug test to use a controlled substance unlawfully, provided that the test was administered within the past year."

But Roof had never been convicted of anything. Nor did he have previous arrests of any kind, let alone for drugs. Is the FBI seriously claiming that a first arrest for misdemeanor drug possession is all it takes to make someone ineligible to buy a gun?

Having been chief economist at the United States Sentencing Commission, I am quite familiar with these types of cases. I suspect that the FBI would unequivocally answer, *No*, if asked whether a person with a misdemeanor arrest for marijuana possession is prohibited from owning a gun. Its statement smacks of the FBI selectively changing its standards for political reasons.

It may not have made much difference even if he were banned from legally acquiring a gun. Roof's mother had taken the gun from him, and he stole it back.[14] Since his family apparently owned multiple guns, he could presumably have stolen one of those guns and used it to commit his heinous act.

WAS THE VIRGINIA TECH KILLER REALLY BANNED FROM BUYING A GUN?

Clinton again misstated what happened in the Virginia Tech case, as well:

> The mental health piece of this is especially troubling.... You've got to have information. The killer at Virginia Tech, you might remember, had been committed. But that information was not in the records....[15]

The Virginia Tech Review Panel report was very clear about killer Seung Hui Cho's history of mental health evaluation (emphasis added):

> The evaluator completed the evaluation form certifying his findings that Cho "is mentally ill; *that he does not present an imminent danger to (himself/others)*, or is not substantially unable to care for himself, as a result of mental illness; and that he does not require involuntary hospitalization." The independent evaluator did not attend the commitment hearing, however, both counsel for Cho and *the special justice signed off on the form certifying his findings.*
>
> Shortly before the commitment hearing, the attending psychiatrist at St. Albans evaluated Cho. When he was interviewed by the panel, the psychiatrist did not recall anything remarkable about Cho, other than that he was extremely quiet. The psychiatrist did not discern dangerousness in Cho, and, as noted, his assessment did not differ from that of the independent evaluator—that Cho was not a danger to himself or others. He suggested that Cho *be treated on an outpatient basis with counseling*. No medications were prescribed, and no primary diagnosis was made.[16]

Cho was *not* involuntary committed. The panel's report noted that he did *not* meet the legal standards for involuntary commitment: "The judge or special justice ordering commitment must find by clear and convincing evidence that the person presents (1) an imminent danger to himself or others or is substantially unable to care for himself, and (2) less restrictive alternatives to involuntary inpatient treatment have been investigated and are deemed unsuitable." One could argue that mistakes were made by both the independent evaluator and the psychiatrist. But Cho was *not* involuntarily committed, and the law did *not* prohibit him from buying a gun.

CHAPTER 13

STAND YOUR GROUND LAWS

More than thirty states have passed Stand Your Ground laws, which allow people to defend themselves without having first tried to retreat.[1]

Some states have had Stand Your Ground for several decades. The laws were signed by both Democratic and Republican governors and often passed the legislatures by overwhelming bipartisan majorities. In some states, such as California and Washington, Stand Your Ground provisions came about from state Supreme Court decisions.

Florida has had Stand Your Ground since 2005, when the law passed the state senate unanimously and by a vote of 94-to-20 in the state house.[2] In 2004, even Illinois State Senator Barack Obama cosponsored and voted for a bill that significantly broadened Illinois' 1961 Stand Your Ground law. The state already allowed its citizens to defend themselves without retreating. Obama's bill provided civil immunity to those who use deadly force in defense of themselves or their property.[3] The bill received overwhelming support, passing unanimously through the state senate and receiving just two "nay" votes in the state house.[4] People of all races and political beliefs feel the threat of violent crime. It is not surprising that these laws have received such bipartisan support.

There also exist Castle Doctrine laws which remove the duty to retreat within one's own home (and sometimes on one's property). Once you step off your property, Stand Your Ground laws apply.

Unfortunately, Stand Your Ground laws have recently become the subject of a racially-charged debate. President Obama and then-Attorney General Holder have weighed in, suggesting that Stand Your Ground laws do not apply equally to all races. And in 2013 on ABC News's *This Week*, Tavis Smiley declared: "It appears to me, and I think many other persons in this country, that you can in fact stand your ground unless you are a black man."[5]

In fact, blacks living in high-crime urban areas are the most likely victims of violent crime and the most likely beneficiaries of Stand Your Ground laws. Blacks are disproportionately affected by rules that make self-defense more difficult.

From 2005 through October 1, 2014, blacks made up 16.7 percent of Florida's population and 34 percent of the defendants who invoked Stand Your Ground.[6] Black defendants who invoke this statute are actually acquitted four percentage points more frequently than whites who use this very same defense.

Prior to Stand Your Ground, citizens had to retreat as far as possible and then warn the criminal that they were going to shoot. Under Stand Your Ground law, lethal force is justified if a reasonable person would believe that an attacker intends to inflict serious bodily harm or death. The response has to be proportionate to the threat.

Proponents of the federal "Trayvon Martin Act" want to prevent Stand Your Ground laws from being used by someone who was the initial aggressor.[7] But Florida and other state laws already make clear that under the Stand Your Ground provision, the law's protection is "not available to a person who...initially provokes the use of force against himself or herself, unless: (a)...he or she has exhausted every reasonable means to escape such danger other than the use of force which is likely to cause death or great bodily harm to the assailant...or (b) In good faith, the person withdraws from physical contact with the assailant and indicates clearly to the assailant that he or she desires to withdraw and terminate the use of force, but the assailant continues or resumes the use of force."[8] The bottom line is simple: under Stand Your Ground, you must retreat if you provoked the situation.

There are real problems with requiring someone to retreat. The concept of "appropriate retreat" is vague and potentially confusing to a defendant whose life may depend on taking immediate, decisive action. Overzealous prosecutors can try to define this concept and claim that the defendant could have retreated even farther. Even when people are acquitted, trials are very costly and destroy people's lives. Here are a few cases that helped motivate the push for Stand Your Ground laws in certain states.

- Black Oak, Arkansas (February 1999): A seventy-five-year-old man was knocked down and kicked repeatedly. After trying to get away and being knocked down for a second time, the seventy-five-year-old man pulled out his revolver and fatally shot his assailant once in the chest. The prosecutors successfully convicted the elderly man by arguing that he could have retreated further.[9]
- East Baltimore, Maryland (June 2001): Two businessmen were acquitted of gunning down a drug addict who had broken into their warehouse late at night.[10]
- Palmer, Alaska (October 2003): A preacher was acquitted of two counts of manslaughter, after shooting two burglars who broke into his chapel at about 5 AM.[11]
- West Palm Beach, Florida (October 2006): Norman Borden was walking his dogs at 2 AM when he was approached by three men. Borden displayed his firearm after the men threatened to hurt Borden's dogs. The men left, only to return with bats. This time, Borden fired his gun. Borden was acquitted as having acted in self-defense.[12]

- Kennesaw, Georgia (November 2006): Brian Epp, a white man, allegedly refused to leave the property of John McNeil (a black man). Epp charged at McNeil, who fired his gun, killing Epp. Prosecutors argued that McNeil could have done more to avoid Epp. McNeil was convicted but given an early release from prison. "State NAACP President Rev. William Barber called Tuesday's release 'a kind of partial repentance' by the Georgia criminal justice system."[13]

Much of the controversy over Stand Your Ground stems from the high profile case of George Zimmerman and the less well-known cases of Michael Dunn and Marissa Alexander. All three of these killings occurred in Florida, and have been pointed to extensively by gun control advocates. In the Zimmerman and Dunn cases, the mothers of the victims claim that Stand Your Ground laws allowed the killers to get away with murder.[14]

Despite all the controversy, Stand Your Ground was actually irrelevant to the Dunn and Zimmerman cases. Neither defense team used the Stand Your Ground law as a defense. After all, forensic and eyewitness evidence indicates that Zimmerman was on his back and being held down by Trayvon Martin. Zimmerman had no option to retreat.

In Dunn's case, a young Jordan Davis supposedly pointed a shotgun at him and announced: "I'm going to kill you." Again, retreat would have been out of the question.[15] But Davis was convicted of first degree murder and four other charges. The jury heard testimony that Dunn had fired ten shots at a car after he had argued with the teens in the car about their loud music. Just because someone invokes Stand Your Ground as a defense doesn't change the facts of the case.

Marissa Alexander said that she had fired a warning shot during a dispute with her husband. The prosecutor, however, argued that it wasn't a warning shot, and that by firing the gun Alexander had endangered her husband and two children.[16] Gun control advocates claimed that the case against Alexander, who is black, showed that Stand Your Ground laws discriminated against blacks. After Alexander's initial conviction, Florida changed its Stand Your Ground law to allow warning shots and that change lead to her eventual acquittal.[17]

No Stand Your Ground law has ever been repealed. For so many decades and in so many states, these laws have existed without controversy. Maybe that's because they save lives. Since 2005, eighteen black Florida men have defended themselves against attackers and then successfully used Stand Your Ground to defend themselves in court.[18]

STAND YOUR GROUND STANDS UP FOR MINORITIES

Stand Your Ground laws have saved black lives in dramatic cases around the country. Three years ago, Darrell Standberry of Detroit was confronted by an armed man who was trying to take his car. He told WJBK: "If it wasn't for [the] 'stand your ground' law, right now I would be in jail, and my life could've been taken at that point."[19]

Or take the case of a black Florida man in Duval County who was "beaten and bloody" after being attacked in a parking lot. The case, decided just a couple of weeks after the Zimmerman verdict, was aptly-summarized by headlines such as: "Man says 'stand your ground' law saved his life."[20]

Those who claim racism point to data compiled by the *Tampa Bay Times*. Up through October 1, 2014, the newspaper had collected 119 cases in which people charged with murder relied on Florida's Stand Your Ground law.[21] The *Times*' "shocking" finding? Defendants who killed a black person got off with no penalty in 67 percent of cases. This is greater than the 57 percent of defendants who killed a white person and got off.[22]

They never discussed the fact that those who kill Hispanics are even more likely to face no penalty (80 percent of the time). If these results really imply discrimination, why would Florida's Hispanics be discriminated against so much more frequently than blacks?

Black and white victims are usually killed by members of their own race. The *Tampa Bay Times* data show that in cases where Stand Your

Ground was invoked as a defense, 76 percent of blacks were killed by other blacks. Similarly, the vast majority of whites were killed by other whites. This, however, does not appear to be true of Hispanics.

Table 1: Race of killer and person killed in Florida's Stand Your Ground Cases			
	Race of person killed		
Race of person claiming to have acted in self-defense	Black	White	Hispanic
Black	76.3%	11.9%	22.2%
White	18.4%	80.6%	55.6%
Hispanic	5.3%	7.5%	22.2%

Since blacks are most often killing each other, there is a flip side to the high acquittal rate in Stand Your Ground cases involving black victims. It means a lower conviction rate for the black defendants in these cases. *In fact, blacks were more likely than whites to succeed with the Stand Your Ground defense.* The success rate was 64 percent for blacks and 60 percent for whites. Hispanic defendants had a 67 percent success rate, making them the mostly likely to be acquitted.

If blacks are supposedly being discriminated against because their killers so often are not facing any penalty, wouldn't it also follow that blacks are being discriminated *in favor* of when blacks who claim self-defense under the Stand Your Ground law are convicted at a lower rate than whites? If this is indeed a measure of discrimination, rather than merely reflecting something different about these particular cases, why are conviction rates so low for Hispanics who raise the Stand Your Ground defense? The figures used to support claims of racism are cherry-picked from the data.

Table 2: Probability of no conviction			
Race of person killed		Race of person claiming to have acted in self-defense	
Black	67%	Black	64%
White	57%	White	60%
Hispanic	80%	Hispanic	67%

The *Tampa Bay Times* data suggest why people who shoot blacks and use the Stand Your Ground defense are more likely to be acquitted. The data show that, compared to whites, blacks who were killed in these Stand Your Ground confrontations were twenty-six percentage points more likely to be armed with a gun. The blacks who were killed were also twenty-five percentage points more likely to be in the act of committing a robbery, home invasion, or burglary. And, finally, both a witness and physical evidence are thirteen percentage points less likely to be present when a black person is killed. All of these factors may explain why convictions are less common when blacks are killed.

The *Tampa Bay Times* collected a lot of other useful information on things besides race, gender, and conviction rates. For instance: whether the victim initiated the confrontation, whether the defendant was on his own property when the shooting occurred, and whether the defendant pursued the victim. There is also information on the circumstances of the case (a drug deal gone bad, home invasion, etc.). No other study has provided such detailed information about Stand Your Ground cases.[23]

However, the *Tampa Bay Times* never examined whether the data they collected might explain the different conviction rates of whites and blacks. So I ran two regressions that account for all of the different factors we've discussed (see Appendix 1). I did one regression on all of the cases and another regression that only examined cases where a single person was killed.

My regressions found no evidence of discrimination against blacks. Though there was no statistically significant difference in conviction rates for black and white defendents, both of my regressions suggested that racial bias actually worked in favor of blacks. It appears that killing a black rather than a white increases the defendant's odds of being convicted.

The regressions also indicate that, all other circumstances being equal, white defendants are more likely to be convicted than black defendants. The best predictors of conviction were the presence of an eyewitness and the defendent initiating the confrontation.

In my third edition of *More Guns, Less Crime*, I provided the first published, peer-reviewed, nationwide study on Stand Your Ground laws.

I found that these laws lowered murder rates by about 9 percent. Overall violent crime rates also declined.[24]

THE URBAN INSTITUTE REPORT AND WHAT IT DOESN'T TELL YOU

A recent Urban Institute study by John Roman claims to have found that, "Stand Your Ground laws appear to exacerbate those [racial] differences, as cases overall are significantly more likely to be justified in Stand Your Ground (SYG) states than in non-SYG states."[25] Roman acknowledges that his data is lacking sufficient detail to provide the "setting of the incident."[26] Indeed, Roman's estimates contain virtually none of the information available in the *Tampa Bay Times* data set. For example, he has no data on eyewitnesses and physical evidence. Roman also has no information on who initiated the confrontations, where the attacks occurred, or on the general circumstances of the incidents.[27]

Even using his limited information, Roman draws the wrong conclusions. To the extent to which the Urban Institute study proves anything, it proves the *opposite* of what Roman thinks that it does.

Roman's Table 3: Percentage of homicides ruled justified, attributes, 2005–2010 (Describes the likelihood a homicide is ruled justified when there is a single victim and single shooter, they are both male, both strangers, and a firearm is used. 2,631 cases)		
	Non-Stand Your Ground States	Stand Your Ground States
White on white	12.95	23.58**
White on black	41.14***	44.71***
Black on white	7.69**	11.10
Black on black	10.24***	9.94***
Total	2.15***	3.67

Source: 2005– 2010 FBI Supplementary Homicide Reports. * p<0.05, ** p<0.01, *** p<0.001

Roman thinks that homicides are more likely to be ruled justifiable if the victim is black.[28] He observes that white-on-black homicides are more likely to be ruled justifiable in SYG than in non-SYG states.[29]

However, this difference is not statistically significant. Furthermore, the difference between SYG and non-SYG states is much more pronounced when the homicide victim is white.[30] This can only support the notion that Stand Your Ground laws help blacks relative to whites.[31]

A second study has received some attention for claiming that Stand Your Ground laws lead to more homicides. "Estimates indicate that the laws increase homicides by a statistically significant 8%," conclude authors Mark Hoekstra and Cheng Cheng of Texas A&M University.[32] Hockstra and Cheng, however, never explain why they only look at Stand Your Ground laws passed in 2005 or later and crime data over the 2000 to 2010 period. Many states adopted Stand Your Ground laws long before 2005, and there is no excuse for omitting them from the analysis.[33] Many of these earlier states that were excluded experienced sharp drops in violent crime after adopting Stand Your Ground laws. Furthermore, why only look at crime data from 2000 to 2010? All of the data that they use is available going back to 1977.

Hoekstra and Cheng also do not account for the effects of any other gun control laws. Nor do they account for changes in numbers of concealed handgun permit holders. Instead, they seem to assume that Stand Your Ground laws are responsible for any and every change in violent crime.

My research, which does account for these various factors, finds that Stand Your Ground and Castle Doctrine laws reduce violent crime.[34]

CHANGES IN CRIME RATES

Since Stand Your Ground laws were being implemented by many states well before 2005, let's not limit ourselves to the 2000-2010 period as studied by these other authors, and look at how Stand Your Ground laws affected crime data from 1977 to 2012. We can include Washington State, which implemented its Stand Your Ground rules through a court decision in 1999.[35] And of course, we'll take into account the concealed carry laws in different states. The Stand Your Ground defense, after all, will have little impact in states that issue few permits. My past work indicates that the prevalence of concealed handgun permits depends strongly on the fees and training requirements that different states impose.

I examined Stand Your Ground laws in my book, *More Guns, Less Crime*. I accounted for a wide range of variables including arrest rates, percentage of adults in prison, median family income, poverty rate, and unemployment rate. I also factored in how the population breaks down according to age, race, and gender. After updating all of this data through 2012, I obtained the following figures.

Murder, rape, and aggravated assault rates all consistently fall after the adoption of Stand Your Ground laws. Robbery rates also initially fell, but by year ten end up roughly where they started. There is actually no sudden increase in robberies in year seven—the resurgence occurs because the sample no longer includes Florida, which adopted its law in 2005. Since we only have data going up to 2012, Florida has to be

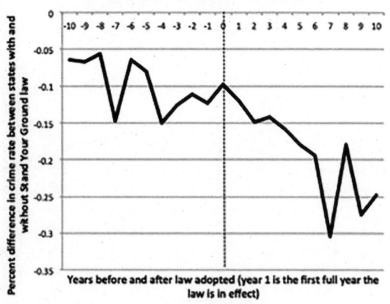

The Impact of Stand Your Ground Laws on the Murder rate (1977 to 2012)

Percent difference in crime rate between states with and without Stand Your Ground law

Years before and after law adopted (year 1 is the first full year the law is in effect)

The Impact of Stand Your Ground Laws on the Rape rate (1977 to 2012)

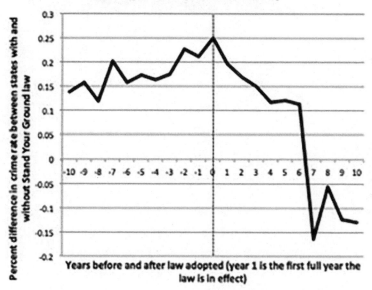

The Impact of Stand Your Ground Laws on the Robbery Rate (1977 to 2012)

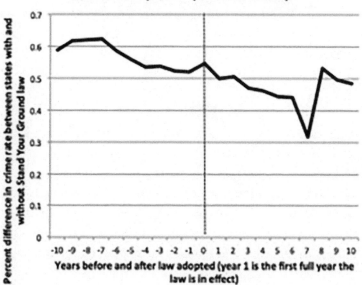

The Impact of Stand Your Ground Laws on the Aggravated Assault Rate (1977 to 2012)

removed from the sample when the graph gets to seven years after adoption of the law. The graph is dramatically affected, because Florida had been experiencing a relatively sharp drop in robbery rates.

CONCLUSION

It is a tragedy that blacks are much more likely to be victims of violent crime. But as police know all too well, they simply can't be there all the time to save people. Blacks have to defend themselves more often than any other racial group. Since they so frequently act in self-defense, it is no wonder that their homicides are more likely to be judged as "justifiable." Blacks have the most to gain from Stand Your Ground laws, and there is no evidence that the laws are applied in any way that discriminates against blacks. My research even suggests just the opposite.

But this conversation about discrimination should not be blown out of proportion. The most important thing is that Stand Your Ground saves lives.

CHAPTER 14

BACKGROUND CHECKS ON PRIVATE GUN TRANSFERS

P resident Obama keeps proposing gun control as the solution to mass public shootings. Time after time, he points to expanded background checks as key legislation.[1] After the San Bernardino shooting in December 2015, he said, "And there are some steps we could take, not to eliminate every one of these mass shootings, but to improve the odds that they don't happen as frequently: common-sense gun safety laws, stronger background checks."[2]

Hillary Clinton has also frequently pointed to background checks as the solution to mass shootings. After the shooting at a Planned Parenthood clinic in Colorado Springs, she called for "common-sense steps like comprehensive background checks, closing the loopholes that let guns fall into the wrong hands."[3]

People just assume that expanded background checks will stop these mass public shootings. Yet there has been no attempt to provide even the most basic statistical evidence. None of these shootings, nor others that the president has mentioned, would have been stopped if background checks on private transfers had been required.[4] The three most recent massacres occurred in states—California, Colorado, and Oregon—which already have such laws in place.[5] Mass public shootings have recently occurred in France, Belgium, Norway, Germany, and other European countries where these background checks also exist.

The theory behind background checks is simple: if you stop a potential killer from getting a weapon, you will stop him from committing a crime. But background checks also reduce gun ownership among law-abiding citizens who wish to defend themselves. And killers can try to obtain their guns from illegal sources, which isn't terribly difficult.[6]

Many academic studies have failed to produce evidence that background checks on private purchases actually make a difference in reducing violent crimes such as murder and robbery.[7] But no one has done a study on whether background checks help stop mass public shootings.

Looking at all mass public shootings from 2000 through 2015, this chapter asks: do states with background checks on private transfers experience fewer mass public shootings or casualties? Even if background checks don't stop the attacks from occurring, might they reduce casualties by preventing killers from obtaining the most destructive weapons?

STATE LAWS

Federal law requires a criminal and mental illness background check for every person who buys a gun through a federally licensed dealer. People with a felony conviction (or certain kinds of misdemeanors) are banned from legally purchasing a gun. Being involuntarily committed for mental illness also disqualifies someone from buying a firearm. Short of a pardon, these are life-time bans.

Eighteen states currently go beyond the federal regulations and require background checks on private transfers of guns (see Appendix 2 for a compilation of these laws). Originally, gun control advocates focused on what they called the "gun-show loophole," or the private transfer of guns at gun shows. This designation was misleading, because federally licensed dealers still had to conduct background checks even if the sales were made at gun shows. In most states, private individuals were allowed to transfer guns without a background check, whether at a gun show or at another place. Thus there was no "loophole," no special rule for gun shows.

The most recent surveys of state and federal prisoners, conducted all the way back in 1991 and 1997, indicate that only about 0.6 percent to 0.7 percent of guns obtained by criminals were from gun shows.[8]

Originally, states such as Colorado, New York, and Oregon focused specifically on gun shows. Since then, their laws have been broadened to encompass *all* private transfers. Many other states impose additional background check requirements on private transfers, whether they occur in or out of gun shows.

Eight states (California, Colorado, Connecticut, Delaware, New York, Oregon, Rhode Island, and Washington State) and the District of Columbia mandate "universal" background checks that apply to all gun transfers. Four other states (Hawaii, Illinois, Massachusetts, New Jersey,) are very similar and require people to obtain a license (for which a background check is required) before they can buy a gun. Six other states (Iowa, Maryland, Michigan, Nebraska, North Carolina, and Pennsylvania) require background checks on all private transfers of handguns.

Although there has been a movement toward more background checks, a couple of states have dropped their requirements for background checks on private transfers. Missouri and Tennessee did so in 2007 and 1998, respectively. On June 20, 2015, a commonwealth court in Puerto Rico struck down its licensing requirement for gun ownership as violating the Second Amendment.[9]

COMPARISONS ACROSS STATES

Using data from 2000 through 2015, we can compare mass public shooting rates in states with three different types of laws: no background checks on private transfers, background checks on at least some private transfers, and "universal" background checks on all private transfers. As we have done previously, mass public shootings are defined as non-gang attacks in which four or more people are killed in a public place.[10] During at least part of the time period from 2000–2015, nineteen states (plus Puerto Rico and D.C.) had background checks on the private transfer of guns for at least part of that period. States are only counted as having background checks on at least some private transfers during the years in which the regulations were in effect.

States with background checks had a 15 percent higher per capita rate of mass public shooting deaths and a 38 percent higher rate of injuries (Table 1 and Figure 1). Mass public shootings rose only very slightly—by just 0.44 percent. There was no clear, year-to-year pattern. In about half the years, states with background checks on private transfers had higher per capita rates of death and injury.

A comparison for so-called universal background checks is more difficult given the small number of states and the short time these laws have been in effect. Six of the eight states with these laws have only had them since 2013, thus limiting the period of time over which one can

FIGURE 1

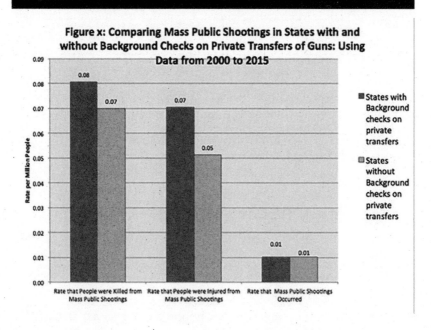

Figure x: Comparing Mass Public Shootings in States with and without Background Checks on Private Transfers of Guns: Using Data from 2000 to 2015

Table 1: Mass public shootings in states with and without background checks on private transfers								
Comparing the rate that people were killed from mass public shootings in the U.S. for states with and without background checks on private transfers (rate per million people)			Comparing the rate that people were injured from mass public shootings in the U.S. for states with and without background checks on private transfers (rate per million people)			Comparing the rate of mass public shootings in the U.S. for states with and without background checks on private transfers (rate per million people)		
	With background checks on at least some private transfers	Without background checks on private transfers	Was rate higher in states with private transfers checks?	With background checks on at least some private transfers	Without background checks on private transfers	Was rate higher in states with private transfers checks?	With background checks on at least some private transfers	Without background checks on private transfers	Was rate higher in states with private transfers checks?
2000	0.081	0.000	Yes	0.007	0.000	Yes	0.015	0.000	Yes
2001	0.029	0.027	Yes	0.029	0.000	Yes	0.007	0.007	Yes
2003	0.043	0.066	No	0.000	0.060	No	0.007	0.013	No
2004	0.035	0.065	No	0.014	0.033	No	0.007	0.013	No
2005	0.000	0.097	No	0.000	0.058	No	0.000	0.013	No
2006	0.084	0.000	Yes	0.035	0.000	Yes	0.014	0.000	Yes
2007	0.035	0.321	No	0.035	0.214	No	0.007	0.025	No
2008	0.000	0.060	No	0.000	0.018	No	0.000	0.012	No
2009	0.151	0.101	Yes	0.043	0.178	No	0.014	0.012	Yes
2010	0.057	0.024	Yes	0.014	0.018	No	0.007	0.006	Yes
2011	0.057	0.058	No	0.007	0.117	No	0.007	0.012	No
2012	0.319	0.098	Yes	0.532	0.040	Yes	0.021	0.017	Yes
2013	0.140	0.000	Yes	0.112	0.000	Yes	0.028	0.000	Yes
2014	0.027	0.048	No	0.013	0.006	Yes	0.007	0.012	No
2015	0.149	0.084	Yes	0.213	0.024	Yes	0.013	0.012	Yes
	Average	Average	Number of times "Yes"	Average	Average	Number of times "Yes"	Average	Average	Number of times "Yes"
	0.0805	0.0700	8	0.0704	0.0511	7	0.010308	0.010268	8
	Difference	14.9%		Difference	37.8%		Difference	0.44%	

Table 2: Mass public shootings in states with and without "universal" background checks on private transfers (Six of the eight states with these universal background checks didn't adopt them until the years 2013 to 2015. Shootings are only counted as occurring in a universal background check state if they occurred after the shooting took place.)

Comparing the rate that people were killed from mass public shootings in the U.S. for states with and without universal background checks (rate per million people)			Comparing the rate that people were injured from mass public shootings in the U.S. for states with and without universal background checks (rate per million people)			Comparing the rate of mass public shootings in the U.S. for states with and without universal background checks (rate per million people)		
With background checks on at least some private transfers	Without background checks on private transfers	Was rate higher in states with private transfers checks?	With background checks on at least some private transfers	Without background checks on private transfers	Was rate higher in states with private transfers checks?	With background checks on at least some private transfers	Without background checks on private transfers	Was rate higher in states with private transfers checks?
2013 0.2320	0.0231	Yes	0.2030	0.0115	Yes	0.0290	0.0058	Yes
2014 0.0523	0.0476	Yes	0.0261	0.0060	Yes	0.0131	0.0119	Yes
2015 0.2833	0.0841	Yes	0.4065	0.0240	Yes	0.0246	0.0120	Yes
Average	Average	Number of times "Yes"	Average	Average	Number of times "Yes"	Average	Average	Number of times "Yes"
0.1892	0.0516	3	0.2119	0.0138	3	0.0222	0.0099	3
Difference	267%		Difference	1431%	Difference	124%		

make a reasonable comparison. Naturally, shootings are only counted as occurring in a universal background check state if they occurred *after* the law was in place. The narrowest time gap came before the Umpqua Community College shooting in Oregon. The law went into effect on August 9, 2015, and the attack occurred at the beginning of October. In this case, however, the shooter legally obtained all of his guns through a federally licensed firearms dealer. The law wouldn't have made a difference even if it had been enacted years earlier.[11]

FIGURE 2

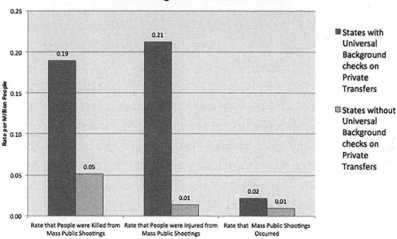

Figure x: Comparing Mass Public Shootings in States with and without Universal Background Checks on Private Transfers of Guns: Using Data from 2000 to 2015

But since 2013, states with "universal" background checks have experienced 124 percent more mass public shootings and dramatically higher rates of death and injury. Per capita, there were 267 percent more deaths and 1,431 percent more injuries (Table 2). In addition, in each year, all three rates were higher in states with universal background checks. Yet, even eight states is a small sample, and with so few years of data, it is hard to put a lot of weight on these results. What is clear is that the initial data on universal background checks definitely does not confirm the claims of supporters.

DO BACKGROUND CHECKS ON PRIVATE TRANSFERS STOP MASS PUBLIC SHOOTINGS?

Looking across places at only one point in time can be extremely misleading. Mass public shootings may vary between states for many reasons that have nothing to do with background checks. States with expanded background checks may have had higher rates of mass public shootings even before they adopted the law. Consequently, the best way to handle this is to look at how mass public shooting rates changed in the states that adopted these expanded background checks. We would then compare these states with those that didn't change their laws.

To analyze this, I have put together what is called a *panel* data set. We follow each state, by year, from 2000 to 2015. We can thus test whether the rate of mass public shootings or casualties changed before and after the adoption of more restrictive background checks.[12]

One other factor needs to be taken into account. After the San Bernardino attack, Alison Anderman, with the Law Center to Prevent Gun Violence, noted: "California is leading the way [with stricter gun control laws], but California is surrounded by a country that has much weaker laws, and we know that a lot of the guns used in crime in California are trafficked in from other states. What we do need is a comprehensive Federal system that puts tough strict regulations in place that make it hard for people who mean to do harm to get guns."[13] There are only two cases where all the guns used in an attack were obtained outside the state that the attack occurred in.

- Aaron Alexis, Washington, D.C., Navy Yard, 2013. Alexis legally purchased a shotgun in Virginia, where he lived. He then carried out the shooting at his workplace in D.C.
- Jennifer San Marco, Goleta, California, 2006. San Marco purchased a gun in New Mexico, where she lived. She then drove to her old place of employment in California where she committed the crime.

The reason there are so few attacks that use out-of-state guns is that in both cases these individuals could have passed background checks in either the state where they lived or the place where they committed their crimes.[14] In any case, gun control advocates believe that this ability to buy a gun in a different state without an expanded background check is important, so we will account for it.

Table 3 shows four sets of estimates. None confirm the claim that additional background checks are beneficial. Columns (1) and (2) look at the entire time period from 2000 to 2015 and separately examine the impacts of universal background checks and background checks specifically on some private transfers. They control for differences across states and years, as well as whether all the guns used in the crime were purchased in another state and state population.

The results in column (1) show that additional background checks on private transfers actually have a statistically significant association with higher rates of death (80 percent higher) and injury (101 percent) from mass public shootings.

The estimates in column (2) show that universal background checks are also associated with more mass public shootings and more deaths and injuries. The effect, however, is not statistically significant. The suggested impact is also smaller—implying a 26 percent higher rate of fatalities and a 27 percent higher rate of injuries.

Columns (3) and (4) account for the variables that were controlled for in the first two columns. In addition, it accounts for state murder rate, what percent of the population is black, what percent is Hispanic, poverty rate, median income, percent of population in prison, divorce rate, and unemployment rate. Since the additional variables are not yet available for 2015, these regressions are limited to the years 2000 to 2014. None of the results are statistically significant.[15]

Finally, there is the question of how much time it takes for background check laws to achieve their full effect. In instances where the law had been in effect for only a short time before a shooting, gun control advocates would probably jump to the conclusion that the killer had armed himself before the law was enacted. Some killers do in fact plan their attacks years in advance (e.g., Adam Lanza, who attacked the Sandy Hook Elementary School), so the benefits from these laws could be delayed.[16]

Table 3: Impact of background checks on mass public shootings after accounting for average differences across states and years and other factors (the estimates are shown below as follows: the regression coefficient for background check laws; the percent change in murders, injuries, or events from these laws is shown in brackets; absolute t-statistics are shown in parentheses; and the level of statistical significance below that)

	Explanatory variables			
	Data for years from 2000 through 2015		Data for years from 2000 through 2014	
	Fixed state and year effects as well as whether all the guns used in crime were purchased in another state and state population		Same variables used in columns (1) and (2) as well as murder rate, percent of population black, percent Hispanic, poverty rate, median income, percent of population in prison, divorce rate, and the unemployment rate	
Endogenous variable	Background checks on at least some private transfers	Universal background checks	Background checks on at least some private transfers	Universal background checks
	(1)	(2)	(3)	(4)
Log of number killed in mass public shootings per million people	.620 [80%]	.228 [26%]	.2676 [31%]	.027 [3%]
	(2.06)	(0.73)	(0.79)	(0.07)
	0.04	0.467	0.427	0.947
Log of number wounded in mass public shootings per million people	.725 [101%]	.239 [27%]	.3656 [44%]	-.031 [-3%]
	(2.79)	(0.89)	(1.28)	(0.09)
	0.01	0.376	0.201	0.928
Log of total casualties in mass public shootings per million people	.709 [96%]	.242 [27%]	.3066 [36%]	.002 [0%]
	(2.13)	(0.70)	(0.83)	(0.00)
	0.03	0.484	0.409	0.996
Log of number of mass public shootings per million people	. 235 [24%]	.168 [18%]	.005 [1%]	.059 [6%]
	(1.30)	(0.90)	(0.03)	(0.25)
	0.19	0.370	0.979	0.806

Estimates in bold are statistically significant at least at the ten percent level for a two-tailed t-test.

(The estimates are shown below as follows: the regression coefficient for background check laws; the percent change in murders, injuries, or events from these laws is shown in brackets; absolute t-statistics are shown in parentheses; and the level of statistical significance below that)

	Explanatory variables	
	Data for years from 2000 through 2015	
	Fixed state and year effects as well as whether all the guns used in crime were purchased in another state and state population	
Endogenous variable	Background checks on at least some private transfers	Number of years that background checks on private transfers have been in effect
Log of number killed in mass public shootings per million people	.600 [82%]	.0077 [1%]
	(1.82)	(0.15)
	0.069	0.880
Log of number wounded in mass public shootings per million people	.676 [97%]	.019 [2%]
	(2.39)	(0.44)
	0.017	0.664
Log of total casualties in mass public shootings per million people	.655 [93%]	.021 [2%]
	(1.80)	(0.37)
	0.072	0.713
Log of number of mass public shootings per million people	.2045 [23%]	.0116 [1%]
	(1.04)	(0.38)
	0.299	0.700

Estimates in bold are statistically significant at least at the 10 percent level for a two-tailed t-test.

Table 4 indicates that the number of years for which private transfer background checks have been in place has no statistically significant, additional impact on the frequency of mass shootings or the number of people harmed in those attacks. If anything, each additional year that they are in effect is associated with an extremely small percent increase in the number of people killed in mass public shootings.

Accounting for the penalty for not conducting a background check or for providing false information doesn't alter any of the results

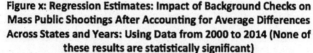

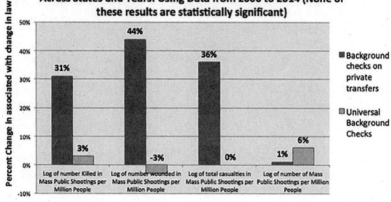

Figure x: Regression Estimates: Impact of Background Checks on Mass Public Shootings After Accounting for Average Differences Across States and Years: Using Data from 2000 to 2014 (None of these results are statistically significant)

presented in Tables 3 and 4, and these factors (whether included separately or together) are not statistically significant.

OTHER SUPPOSED BENEFITS FROM EXPANDED BACKGROUND CHECKS

While the gun violence debate often focuses on mass shootings of strangers, hundreds of Americans are fatally shot every year by spouses or partners…. Between 2008 and 2012, states that required background checks on private sales had 46% fewer gun homicides of women by partners, adjusted for population, than states with no such requirement.[17]
—Editorial, New York Times, January 16, 2016

Bloomberg's Everytown is responsible for the above claim by *the New York Times*. Everytown has also claimed that expanded background

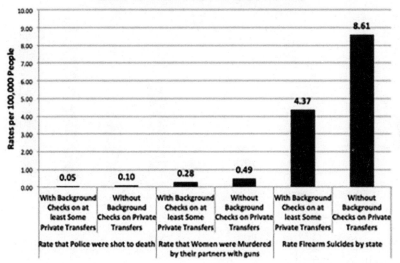

FIGURE 4

Expanded Background Checks and the Crime Categories Examined by Bloomberg's Everytown: Comparing State with and without Expanded Background Checks 2000 to 2014 (except for women where the data is for 2000 to 2013)

checks on private gun transfers reduced firearm suicides and police gun deaths by similarly extreme margins of between 46 and 48 percent.[18] Figure 4 shows the results for those same categories over the years from 2000 to 2014, and the pattern is very similar to what they showed over 2008 to 2012.

But the problem isn't only with looking across places at one point in time. There is also the issue of what types of crimes to compare. It is no surprise that a Bloomberg organization would selectively pick whatever categories appeared to support their conclusions. Look at murder, robbery, or aggravated assault, and we find that states with expanded background checks experienced higher rates from 2000 to 2014 (see Figure 5). If Bloomberg's group really believes that this is the proper way to analyze data, are they going to accept the fact that murders are 49 percent higher and robberies are 75 percent higher in states with expanded background checks?

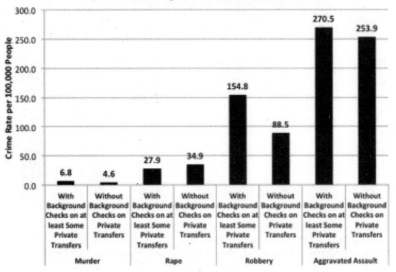

FIGURE 5

What if you used the Bloomberg Approach to look at other Crime Rates Across States?: Looking at Violent Crime for their years from 2000 to 2014

Of course, this fact doesn't mean that expanded background checks cause higher violent crime rates any more than looking across states proves that these laws lowered police shooting deaths or the other claimed benefits. In my book *More Guns, Less Crime*, I found no change in violent crime rates after states passed these background checks on private transfers.[19] There was a small 2 percent increase in murder rates, but the effect wasn't statistically significant.

Table 5 looks at changes in the suicide rate and in the murder rate against women and police. We looked again at states before and after they changed their laws and compared these states with those that didn't change their laws. But twenty-two of the twenty-four estimates show *no change* in crimes or suicides as a result of these new background checks; half of these statistically insignificant results imply that background checks make things worse and half imply that they get better. I obtained only two statistically significant results. One showed that states with expanded background checks on transfers had a large increase in police

gun deaths. The other showed a relatively miniscule drop in total suicides. But even these results are no longer statistically significant when
other factors are taken into account.

The bottom line is that these background checks on private transfers
don't help. Economists, criminologists, and public health researchers
have yet to find that the Brady background checks did *anything* to reduce
violent crime. Additional checks aren't the solution. We've been about
as successful in stopping criminals from getting guns as we have been in
preventing people from obtaining illegal drugs.

Table 5: Impact of background checks on police and female murders after accounting for average differences across states and years and other factors (the estimates are shown below as follows: the regression coefficient for background check laws; the percent change in murders, injuries, or events from these laws is shown in brackets; absolute t-statistics are shown in parentheses; and the level of statistical significance below that)

	Explanatory variables			
	Data for years from 2000 through 2014 for police and suicides, 2000 to 2013 for women's murder rate			
	Fixed state and year effects as well as whether all the guns used in crime were purchased in another state and state population		Same variables used in columns (1) and (2) as well as murder rate, percent of population black, percent Hispanic, poverty rate, median income, percent of population in prison, divorce rate, and the unemployment rate. In the case of female murder rate regression, the overall murder rate is replaced with the male murder rate. Data for 2000-2013.	
Endogenous variable	Background checks on at least some private transfers	Universal background checks	Background checks on at least some private transfers	Universal background checks
	(1)	(2)	(3)	(4)
Log of number police murdered by guns per 100,000 police	.0118 [1.2%]	.696 [101%]	.6015 [82%]	-.211 [24%]
	(0.03)	(1.22)	(1.28)	(0.22)

	0.01	0.223	0.202	0.825
Log of number police murdered per 100,000 police	.0024 [0.2%]	.558 [75%]	.818 [127%]	.4054 [50%]
	(0.02)	(0.91)	(1.71)	(1.13)
	0.974	0.363	0.089	0.261
Log of women shot to death by partner, rate per 100,000 women	.2651 [30.4%]	-.2073 [23%]	-.039 [4%]	-.989 [169%]
	(0.81)	(0.36)	(0.11)	(1.42)
	0.418	0.715	0.909	0.155
Log of women's murder rate per 100,000 women	.00235 [0.2%]	.2108 [23%]	-.1388 [15%]	.1099 [12%]
	(0.02)	(1.01)	(1.15)	(0.47)
	0.984	0.311	0.250	0.648
Log of firearm suicide rate per 100,000 people	-.0500 [5.1%]	.0026 [0.3%]	-.0688 [7%]	-.132 [14%]
	(1.52)	(0.06)	(0.59)	(1.28)
	0.130	0.949	0.555	0.202
Log of total suicide rate per 100,000 people	-.0065 [0.7%]	-.0036 [0.4%]	-.0685 [7%]	-.0577 [5.9%]
	(0.29)	(0.14)	(1.86)	(1.17)
	0.772	0.892	0.064	0.243

Estimates in bold are statistically significant at least at the 10 percent level for a two-tailed t-test.

CONCLUSION

Despite the continual calls for expanded background checks after mass public shootings, there is *no* evidence that background checks on private transfers of guns would have prevented any of the attacks. Nor is there any statistical evidence that indicates that these mass public shootings are rarer in states with background checks on private transfers.

What we do find is that fatalities and injuries from mass public shootings *increased* in states *after* they imposed background checks on private transfers. States with background checks on private transfers tended to have relatively low rates of murders and injuries from mass public shootings before the passage of background checks on private transfers, and these rates became relatively high *afterwards*. Clearly, there is no evidence that these laws lower mass public shootings.

There are real costs of expanding background checks to private transfers. In particular, the fees on private transfers reduce gun ownership, particularly among law-abiding poor blacks who live in high crime urban areas and who benefit the most from protecting themselves; they will be the ones most likely priced out of owning guns for protection.

Without some benefits in terms of either reduced crime or mass public shootings, it is hard to see how these rules pass any type of cost-benefit test.

CONCLUSION

People just say well, we should have firearms in kindergarten and we should have machine guns in bars. You think I'm exaggerating—I mean, you look at some of these laws that come up.[1]
—President Obama, March 6, 2015

There are neighborhoods where it's easier for you to buy a handgun and clips than it is for you to buy a fresh vegetable.[2]
—President Obama, March 6, 2015

The idea, for example, that we couldn't even get a background check bill in to make sure that if you are going to buy a weapon you have to go through a fairly rigorous process so that we know who you are so that you can't just walk up to a store and buy a semi-automatic weapon makes no sense.[3]
—President Obama, June 11, 2014

L ike many gun control advocates, President Obama doesn't seem to mind making a few completely outlandish claims. For him, the ends appear to justify the means. Sure, there are people who want to eliminate all gun-free zones, but no one is asking to be able to carry machine guns into bars. As to vegetables, there are no forms to fill out to buy a vegetable. There are no background checks to complete. And despite Obama's claims, every store in the United States that sells guns has to have background checks.

When it comes to television advertising, Michael Bloomberg outspends the NRA and all other self-defense groups by 6.3 to one. The money produces political attack ads that accuse supporters of right-to-carry on college campuses of "allowing criminals to carry hidden, loaded guns in our schools."[4]

Many gun control academics use language that is hardly scholarly, attacking academics they disagree with as being paid off by the "execrable NRA." They claim that "gun sellers call the shots at the NRA."[5] They accuse others of having "blood on [their] hands" or being a "blight on democracy." Apparently, finding evidence of defensive gun uses brings "harm to the democratic process."[6]

There are other less obvious claims that are just as outrageous. No, the United States isn't unique in terms of mass public shootings or homicides. No, gun bans don't make people safer. Background checks on private transfers haven't stopped mass public shootings or any other type of crime in the U.S. or other countries. Background checks are racist. And there are real problems with background checks that harm the most vulnerable. Gun control advocates have it backwards when they claim that gun makers have something to learn about how to reduce accidents from looking at government regulation of cars.

I have continually seen how intense and personal this debate can get. While I was at the University of Chicago, I wrote several opinion pieces that criticized Chicago Mayor Richard Daley's positions on guns. I also published my book *More Guns, Less Crime* in May 1998. In December 1998, Mayor Daley called University of Chicago President Hugo Sonnenschein. Daley reportedly told Sonnenschein that my continued presence at the university would cause "irreparable harm" to the school's relationship with the city of Chicago. I was then faced with two different termination options: immediately resign from the university or stay until July and promise not to talk to the press any more while I was there.

What had I done? On December 10, 1998, Daley had organized a conference with four other mayors to discuss suing the gun makers. Because of my book *More Guns, Less Crime*, which argued that Daley's gun laws did more harm than good, reporters from the local CBS and Fox stations who were already at the conference asked me to meet them to talk about the lawsuits. I had originally planned to arrive after the mayors had finished their post-conference presentations. But the mayors were running behind schedule when I arrived, so CBS reporter Mike Flannery suggested that I attend the presentations. That way, I could better answer any questions that he might have.

The presentations were followed by a question-and-answer period with press, some students, and others in the audience. When the audience started yelling questions, I raised my hand in an attempt to get called on. At that point a woman walked over to me and asked me if I was John Lott from the University of Chicago. I said that I was, and she informed me that I was not allowed to ask any questions. No explanation was given. Some audience members took notice. Joe Mathews, a reporter with *The Baltimore Sun*, gave me his card and said he'd be happy to talk to me about what happened.

After the mayors' presentation, Mike Flannery interviewed me outside. After the interview, I tried to re-enter the building to use a pay phone. I just wanted to get in touch with the reporter from the local Fox station. However, a man stood at the door and told me I was not allowed to enter. He said that I had "lied" to get in to begin with. He claimed that I had entered the building by pretending to be a member of the press. He also told me that I was not a real professor and that I was abusing the University of Chicago's name in my public criticism of Mayor Daley's gun policies.

That was the spin that the Daley people put on what happened. After the phone call from Daley, the University of Chicago presented me with my two termination options. I wrote back to Dean Fischel—whom I believed I had been on good terms with—that I was "stunned and shocked at being requested to resign." I told him that I had gone to the conference simply to answer reporters' questions about my research. I asked him whether, if I took the second option, I could still talk about my book and other research.

Fischel responded, "I cannot give you a specific answer to your questions." He noted, "With respect [to] damage to your reputation, many think you have only yourself to blame by winding up in a public confrontation at the mayor's press conference." He added in a later email: "If you cannot make yourself for all practical purposes invisible (at least in terms of any mention of the university), you should resign."

I took the second option and completely stopped talking to the media for over three months. This pause concluded the fairly busy media schedule I had been keeping after the release of *More Guns, Less Crime.* Only towards the very end of my contract did I again start accepting requests to write op-ed pieces and do interviews about my book. In retrospect, I probably should have immediately gone to the press and told them what happened. At the time, I was concerned that doing so could make life difficult for people such as Fischel. I also knew that academia frowns on people who stir up controversy.

Years later, in June 2007, *Chicago Magazine* described the events this way: "A man in the audience, a fierce defender of the right to carry a gun, tried to interrupt the mayor with pointed questions. That was John R. Lott.... [S]tories made the rounds that he had heckled the mayor until police took him from the room. Lott denies this account vigorously."[7] All I had done was raise my hand. Others in the audience were yelling questions. I shared all of this with James Merrier, the author of the *Chicago Magazine* piece. After the piece ran, he told me: "I did talk with Mike Flannery and his memory of the incident largely squared with yours. Largely for that reason, I did not go into more detail about who was there and why. Had I done so, I doubt it would have survived the editing process."

Unfortunately, *Chicago Magazine* was more interested in repeating the sensational, false charges against me. Alas, not even the University of Chicago had been willing to check whether my version of events was true. The university never contacted the reporters that I have mentioned here. It was simply more convenient to accept Mayor Daley's version of events. Indeed, the University of Chicago Press even refused to allow me to discuss these events in the third edition of *More Guns, Less Crime.*

I ran into similar, though less dramatic events after moving to Yale Law School, where I spent two years as a Senior Research Scholar. Hawaii's two Democratic U.S. Senators once contacted the law school to complain about testimony that I gave before the Hawaii state legislature. They blamed me for somehow single-handedly scuttling the new gun registration laws that were being considered. The associate dean of the law school called me up about the complaints and grilled me about my testimony.

I am certain that neither of these incidents would have occurred if I had been on the other side the gun debate. Over the years, many academics have told me that they would have studied gun control if not for fear of damage to their careers. They didn't want to run the risk of coming out on the wrong side of the debate. From my experience, that is understandable. Eventually, I was forced out of academia. There is only an abundance of funding for those researchers who *support* gun control.

There *is* a war on guns. Just like with any war there are real casualties. Police are probably the single most important factor in reducing crime, but police themselves understand that they almost always show up at the crime scene *after* the crime has been committed. When the police can't be there, guns are by far the most effective way for people to protect themselves from criminals. And the most vulnerable people are the ones who benefit the most from being able to protect themselves: women and the elderly, people who are relatively weaker physically, as well as poor blacks who live in high crime urban areas—the most likely victims of violent crime.

When gun control advocates can't simply ban guns outright, they impose high fees and taxes on guns. When the Northern Mariana

Islands, a U.S. territory, had their handgun ban struck down as uncon-
stitutional by a federal judge in March 2016, they passed a $1,000 excise
tax on guns—a tax they hoped would serve as a model for the rest of the
U.S.[8]

   I hope that this book provides the ammunition people need for some
of the major battles ahead. We must fight to keep people safe.

APPENDIX 1

Table 1.1a: For question six in the survey of economists and criminologists, we asked to "please cite one academic study that best supports your answer as to how allowing people to carry a permitted concealed handgun will affect the murder rate." Studies with at least two citations are listed here. Ten of those surveyed could not reference a single "best" study to support their answer.

Table 1.1a: For economists: "Please cite one academic study that best supports your answer as to how allowing people to carry a permitted concealed handgun will affect the murder rate."	
Studies that got at least two cites	
John Lott and David Mustard, Journal of Legal Studies, 1997	5
John Lott, More Guns, Less Crime, University of Chicago Press	3
F. Plassmann & T.N. Tideman, "Does the Right to Carry Concealed Handguns Deter Countable Crimes-Only a Count Analysis Can Say," Journal of Law & Economics, 2001	2

Carl Moody and Teb Marvell, Southern Economic Journal, 2005	2
Eric Helland and Alex Tabarrok, Advances in Economic Analysis & Policy, 2004	2
Other answers	
Papers that got only one cite	11
Researchers who said that they could not point to a "best study"	10

Table 1.1b: For criminologists: "Please cite one academic study that best supports your answer as to how allowing people to carry a permitted concealed handgun will affect the murder rate."

Studies that got at least two cites	
John Lott and David Mustard, Journal of Legal Studies, 1997	4
John Lott, More Guns, Less Crime, University of Chicago Press	4
Carl Moody and Teb Marvell, "The Debate on Shall-Issue Laws," Econ Journal Watch, 5(3) September 2008	2
Nagin (unspecified)	2
Other answers	
Papers that got only one cite	9
Researchers who said that they could not point to a "best study"	18

Table 1.2a: Do economists and criminologists have clear views on the issue of guns? (Researchers from entire world with undecideds)

Question	Is the difference between "yes" and "no" answers for economists statistically significant? (Probability of significance shown in parentheses)	Is the difference between "yes" and "no" answers for criminologists statistically significant? (Probability of significance shown in parentheses)
In the United States, are guns used in self-defense more often than they are used in the commission of crime?	Yes (0.0%)	No (71.1%)

Are gun-free zones, areas where civilians are banned from having guns, more likely to attract criminals than they are to deter them?	Yes (0.0%)	No (85.6%)
Would you say that, in the United States, having a gun in the home causes an increase in the risk of suicide?	Yes (0.0%)	No (86.8%)
Would you say that concealed handgun permit holders are much more law-abiding than the typical American?	Yes (0.0%)	Yes (2.1%)
	Is the difference between "Decrease" and "Increase" answers for economists statistically significant? (Probability of significance shown in parentheses)	Is the difference between "Decrease" and "Increase" answers for criminologists statistically significant? (Probability of significance shown in parentheses)
How does allowing people to carry a permitted concealed handgun affect the murder rate?	Yes (0.0%)	Yes (7.0%)
These estimates assume that the distributions for economists and criminologists have unequal variances.		

Table 1.2b: Do economists and criminologists give statistically significantly different answers to survey questions on guns? (Researchers from entire world with undecides)	
Question	Is the difference between the percentage of economists and criminologists who answer "yes" statistically significant for a two-tailed t-test? (Probability of significance shown in parentheses)
In the United States, are guns used in self-defense more often than they are used in the commission of crime?	Yes (6.6%)
Are gun-free zones, areas where civilians are banned from having guns, more likely to attract criminals than they are to deter them?	Yes (0.15%)
Would you say that, in the United States, having a gun in the home causes an increase in the risk of suicide?	Yes (3.5%)

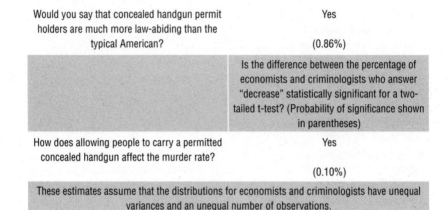

Would you say that concealed handgun permit holders are much more law-abiding than the typical American?	Yes
	(0.86%)
	Is the difference between the percentage of economists and criminologists who answer "decrease" statistically significant for a two-tailed t-test? (Probability of significance shown in parentheses)
How does allowing people to carry a permitted concealed handgun affect the murder rate?	Yes
	(0.10%)
These estimates assume that the distributions for economists and criminologists have unequal variances and an unequal number of observations.	

EVERYTOWN'S ERRORS IN IDENTIFYING MASS SHOOTINGS AND GUN-FREE ZONES

As noted in Chapter 2, Everytown's report on mass shootings contains many errors. In addition, it muddies the discussion on mass public shootings by including shootings in private homes along with ones in public places, and the vast majority of the cases they include are in private homes. But there is a distinction between what motivates mass public shooters who are committing their crimes to get media attention and those who engage in attacks in private residences.

There are three mass public shootings since at least 1950 that have not been part of some other crime where at least four people have been killed in an area where civilians are generally allowed to have guns. These are the International House of Pancakes restaurant in Carson City, Nevada on September 6, 2011; the Gabrielle Giffords shooting in Tucson, Arizona on January 8, 2011; and the Kalamazoo shooting on February 20, 2016, where four people died in one attack at a Cracker Barrel restaurant and two others in another one (while the Cracker Barrel restaurant didn't ban guns, Uber does ban its drivers from carrying guns and the killer was on the job when he did the shootings, and the shooting was done while he was in his car).

Here are some general points about how to classify mass public shootings that have occurred in gun-free zones.

1. A lot of work is involved in obtaining information on whether the attacks occurred in gun-free zones. This includes calling the businesses or other facilities involved. But many times those organizations are uncooperative, and in those cases much time is spent contacting individuals in the area of the attack and asking them if they can provide pictures or other information on the facilities. Indeed, the media virtually always refuses to mention whether the attack occurred in a gun-free zone. Unfortunately, Everytown for Gun Safety/Mayors Against Illegal Guns did not do this work, and they have also inaccurately stated, ignored, or simply missed facts that are readily available in news stories.

2. What motivates mass public shootings where the killer is trying to kill or injure as many people as possible to get publicity is quite different from what motivates robbers or gang fights (see Lott and Landes). The issue of gun-free zones is particularly important for mass public shootings.

3. The word "public" is also key to these cases. Shootings that occur in people's homes will often involve killers who know if guns are owned in the home. And if there is a gun in the home, the killer will know who has access to it.

4. There is also the distinction between right-to-carry and may-issue laws. If virtually no one, especially no civilian, is allowed to get a concealed handgun permit as occurs in most may-issue jurisdictions, the area is essentially a gun-free zone.

EXAMPLES: BLOOMBERG'S EVERYTOWN ORGANIZATION INCORRECTLY REPORTS AS MASS PUBLIC SHOOTINGS AND/OR SHOOTINGS IN GUN-FREE ZONES

The Bloomberg discussions are indented and put in block quotes. After the quotes there is an explanation for why they shouldn't be counted as mass public shootings. The Bloomberg report doesn't number these events, but we will assign numbers just to make them easier to reference.

> 1) **Terrell, TX, 10/28/13**: The shooter shot and killed his mother, his aunt, two acquaintances, and a store clerk in a spree of attacks before he was captured by police. He killed the first four victims in their respective homes and the final one—the clerk—at Ali's Market on W. Moore Avenue, apparently in an attempt to rob the store. Shooter Name: Charles Everett Brownlow Jr. Gun details: Unknown. Ammo details: Unknown. Gun acquired: Unknown. Prohibiting criteria: The shooter had a criminal record that prohibited him from possessing firearms. He was convicted of burglarizing a vehicle in 1996, a Class A misdemeanor, and convicted of felony burglary in 1997. In 2008, he was served a three-year sentence for unlawful possession of a firearm and in 2011 he was convicted of misdemeanor assault against a family member. Not a gun-free zone: The manager of the Ali's Market reported that customers are allowed to carry firearms in the store.

FACTS: There was not a mass public shooting at Ali's Market. Only one person was killed at that store. Permitted concealed handguns can deter many attacks from occurring and can limit the harm that does occur. But permit holders aren't expected to limit the harm for those attacks that do occur to zero. Permitted concealed handguns deter mass shootings because they can limit the harm and take away the incentive that these killers obtain from their warped desire to get media attention.

2) **Washington, DC, 9/16/13**: The alleged shooter, who was a civilian contractor and former non-combat military, killed twelve and wounded three more in an attack on Building 197 at the Navy Yard. Shooter Name: Aaron Alexis, 34. Gun details: The shooter arrived with a shotgun and also obtained a handgun from a security guard that he killed. Ammo details: Unknown. Gun acquired: Two days before the incident the shooter passed a National Instant Criminal Background Check System (NICS) at the licensed gun dealer Sharpshooters in Lorton, VA, and purchased the shotgun. Prohibiting criteria: The shooter had been arrested at least three times including: in September 2010 in Fort Worth, Texas for shooting a firearm into a neighbor's apartment; in August 2008 in Dekalb County, Georgia for disorderly conduct; and in 2004 in Seattle, Washington for shooting out the tires of another man's vehicle. But court records do not indicate he was convicted in any of these cases, and this record did not prohibit him from buying guns. He had also received treatment for mental health conditions at two VA hospitals beginning in August, 2013 following an incident where he called Newport Rhode Island Police to report hearing voices. But these incidents did not rise to the level of prohibiting from buying guns. And during his military service he was reportedly cited on at least eight occasions for misconduct ranging from traffic tickets and showing up late for work to insubordination, extended absences from work, and disorderly conduct. On account of this the Navy sought to offer him a

"general discharge" but he was ultimately honorably discharged through the early-enlisted transition program in January 2011. Not a gun-free zone: There were armed guards at the Washington Navy Yard, and the shooter was familiar with the premises, so he did not select it as a target on the presumption he would not faced armed resistance. In fact, the shooter reportedly used a gun that he took from a guard after killing him.

FACTS: Whether one is looking at the attacks at the Washington Navy Yard or Fort Hood, letting military police carry guns is much different than letting other soldiers protect themselves. While military police tend to be at the entrances to military bases, they largely patrol the rest of the base in the same way that police patrol a city. One no more expects military police to instantly arrive at the scene of a mass public shooting than one expects police to arrive at one. In Alexis's attack, since he worked at the Navy Yard, he knew what entrance to go to that would have only one guard and that is where he went. For related discussions, read my April 2014 Fox News articles.

3) **Crab Orchard, TN, 9/11/13:** The shooters killed a woman and three teenagers, apparently during an attempted robbery during a marijuana exchange. The victims' bodies were discovered in a car parked along the side of the road in the Renegade Mountain resort community near Crossville. Shooter Name: Jacob Allen Bennett, 26 and Brittany Lina Yvonn Moser, 25. Gun details: Handgun. Ammo details: Unknown. Gun acquired: Unknown. Prohibiting criteria: Bennett was prohibited from possessing firearms. In 2010 he received a 6-year prison sentence for charges of theft, forgery, and possession of a handgun during a felony, but was paroled on March 4, 2013. The Cumberland County sheriff's office estimated they had previously arrested Bennett five

times. Not a gun-free zone: We could find no evidence that permit holders were prohibited from carrying guns in this area. In Tennessee, concealed weapons would be prohibited only if the county or municipality declared itself a gun-free zone.

FACTS: This shooting was part of another crime, a robbery of illegal marijuana (see point two in the introduction). It was not a mass public shooting where the point of the crime was to kill as many people as possible so as to obtain media coverage.

4) **Herkimer, NY, 4/13/13:** The shooter killed two people and critically wounded one at John's Barber Shop and then killed two more people at Gaffey's Fast Lube, a car care facility. He was killed by responding officers. Shooter Name: Kurt Myers, 64. Gun details: According to the police superintendent, Myers used a shotgun. Additional guns and ammunition were found by emergency crews after Myers set fire to the apartment. Ammo details: Unknown. Gun acquired: Unknown. Prohibiting criteria: There is no reason to believe Myers was prohibited him from possessing a gun. He was arrested in 1973 for drunk driving. Not a gun-free zone: Gaffey's Fast Lube does not have a specific policy prohibiting guns and allows permit holders to carry concealed weapons on the premises. John's Barbershop did not reopen following the shooting but the owner of a neighboring business did not recall the barbershop having any explicit firearm policy or ban, which would have been required to prohibit customers from carrying guns on the premises.

FACTS: New York is a May-Issue state, not a right-to-carry state. We don't yet have the number of civilian concealed carry permits, but they seem to be extremely rare. The possession of a handgun in New

York State requires a NYS Pistol Permit. In 2012 there were only 154 permits issued to own a pistol in Herkimer county. Over the previous five years, there were 667 permits issued, though not all of those permits to own a handgun would have been active at the beginning of 2013. When talking to the pistol permit office, Lott was told that there were zero restricted licenses that allowed people to carry for business purposes (concealed carry licenses that allow a business owner to carry in the course of doing business) and zero restricted for self defense purposes (e.g., a woman who is being actively stalked).

Report from February 2013: At this point, the Everytown for Gun Safety report mainly repeats cases previously discussed by Bloomberg's Mayors Against Illegal Guns on MASS SHOOTING INCIDENTS, JANUARY 2009–JANUARY 2013. An earlier report on the problems with their claims about the attacks not being in gun-free zones was never corrected. Here is the analysis of these previous cases.

> 5) **Geneva County, AL, 3/10/09**: The shooter killed ten, including four members of his family, before killing himself. Shooter Name: Michael Kenneth McLendon, 28. Gun details: Bushmaster AR-15, SKS Rifle, Shotgun, and .38 Pistol. Ammo details: Police recovered additional ammunition from his vehicle after the shooting. Gun acquired: Unknown. Prohibiting criteria: The shooter had no criminal record and there is no indication he was prohibited from owning a gun. Not a gun-free zone: It was lawful to carry a firearm in the public intersection and gas station where two of the individuals were shot.

FACTS: Nine people were killed by McLendon. In the first shooting in a house on Pullum Street, five people were killed. There was also a second shooting in another home that left two people dead. Neither were public places. It is true that two individuals were killed in separate public places as McLendon was driving along, but that is not a multiple victim public shooting in which at least four are killed in a public place.

However, MAIG's report implies that all these shootings occurred in public places.

> 6) **Lakewood, WA, 11/29/09**: The shooter killed four police officers in a Tacoma Coffee shop, eluding police for two days before being killed as he fled. Shooter Name: Maurice Clemmons, 37. Gun details: When he was killed, he was in possession of the handgun of one of the officers he had killed. Ammo details: Unknown. Gun acquired: Unknown. Prohibiting criteria: The shooter was prohibited from purchasing a firearm, having been charged with at least 13 felonies across two states. He had posted bail for raping a child just six days before the attack. Not a gun-free zone: The police officers were armed at the time of the shooting.

FACTS: Lott and Landes didn't define gun-free zones in terms of whether police were allowed to carry guns, but whether private citizens are able to readily obtain concealed handguns for their protection. What is important is that the coffee shop was posted to prevent concealed carry permit holders from carrying. Presumably MAIG understood this point and that is the reason why they focused on police officers being able to carry in this venue. Obviously, however, on-duty police can carry any place. The problem for uniformed police is that they provide an easily identifiable target and it is easy to take them out. Possibly if the attacker had to worry about permit holders who he could not identify, it would have dissuaded him from attacking. While Lott had checked when this event originally occurred, he reconfirmed this information with Dave Workman who lived nearby via email on January 8, 2013.

> 7) **Carthage, NC, 3/29/09**: The shooter opened fire at a nursing home where his estranged wife worked, killing eight and injuring three before he was shot and arrested

by a police officer. Shooter Name: Robert Stewart, 45. Gun details: .357 Magnum handgun and Winchester 1300 shotgun. Ammo details: Unknown. Gun acquired: The guns were acquired legally from a local sporting good store. Prohibiting criteria: There is no indication the Stewart was prohibited from owning a gun. Not a gun-free zone: We could find no indication that the property-owner forbid carrying of firearms on their property.

FACTS: This facility informed Lott in April 2009 that it did not allow guns in the facility for either the people living there or the staff. He called up to ask what its policies had been before the attack.

Here are places listed by Bloomberg's group that may have allowed people with permits to carry in places, but that made it extremely difficult or impossible for civilians to get a concealed handgun permit.

8) **Boston, MA, 09/28/10**: The shooter killed four and wounded one during a drug-related robbery. Shooter Name: Edward Washington, 33, and Dwayne Moore, 35, were both charged in the killings. Washington was acquitted. In Moore's first trial, the jury deadlocked 11-1 in favor of his guilt, but he was later convicted in a retrial. Gun details: 40-caliber Iberia handgun and 9mm Cobray semiautomatic. The Cobray has not been recovered, but the weapon was identified based on recovered bullets and shell casings. Ammo details: 14 rounds fired. Gun acquired: Unknown. Prohibiting criteria: Unknown. Not a gun free zone: A person with a Massachusetts Class A license could lawfully carry a firearm in this area.

9) **Buffalo, NY, 8/14/10**: The shooter opened fire on a group of people outside a bar, killing four and wounding four others. Shooter Name: Riccardo McCray, 24. Gun details: Unknown. Ammo details: Unknown. Gun

acquired: Unknown. Prohibiting criteria: McCray had been arrested earlier that year on felony drug charges and the previous year for having a loaded rifle in his car. If he was found guilty of either crime, he would have been prohibited from possessing firearms. Not a gun-free zone: We could find no indication that it was unlawful to carry a firearm in the area.

10) **Northridge, CA, 12/2/12**: The shooter arrived at an unlicensed boarding house on Devonshire street, reportedly in search of his girlfriend, and after a dispute shot and killed four people out- side. Shooter Name: Ka Pasasouk, 31. Gun details: semiautomatic handgun. Ammo details: Unknown. Gun acquired: Unknown. Prohibiting criteria: The shooter was prohibited from possessing guns, having been convicted for car theft and felony robbery. While on probation in September 2012, he was arrested again for possession of methamphetamine. According to the district attorney, a prosecutor then released him on probation over the objection of probation officials, who believed he posed a threat to the safety of the community. Not a gun-free zone: Permit holders were not prohibited from carrying guns in this area.

11) **East Oakland, CA, 3/21/09**: The shooter used a semi-automatic handgun to kill two police officers after they stopped his car and then fled on foot to an apartment where he killed two SWAT officers with an assault weapon and injured a third before being killed by police. Shooter Name: Lovelle Mixon Gun details: 9mm semiautomatic handgun and SKS assault-style rifle Ammo details: Police said the assault weapon had a high-capacity magazine. Gun acquired: The shooter took part in a home invasion robbery in Modesto, CA, on February 21 2009 in which a rifle was reported stolen. Police did not comment on whether the stolen rifle was the one used in the

shooting. Prohibiting criteria: The shooter had a lengthy criminal history, including a conviction for armed battery, which would have prohibited him from possessing a gun, and he was on parole for assault with a deadly weapon at the time of the shootings. Not a gun-free zone: Two of the victims were shot on a public roadway—the 7400 block of Macarthur Boulevard in East Oakland—where no state law would have prohibited a citizen with the appropriate permit to carry a gun. All of the police officers killed in the incident were armed.

12) **Medford, NY, 6/9/11:** The shooter killed four people at a pharmacy, Haven Drugs, and stole thou- sands of hydrocodone pills before fleeing in a vehicle. During the trial he acknowledged that he and his wife were addicted to prescription medication. Shooter Name: David Laffer. Gun details: A .45 caliber handgun was used in the shoot- ing. Several other legally registered guns were also recov- ered from the shooter's home. Ammo details: Unknown. Gun acquired: Unknown. Prohibiting criteria: The gun was legally registered to the shooter, and there is no evi- dence he was prohibited from possessing a gun. But five months before the shooting, Suffolk County Detective Kenneth Ripp investigated an identity theft claim made by the shooter's mother, who said the shooter had stolen her debit card. After questioning the shooter and his mother, Ripp advised the Suffolk County Pistol License Bureau that the shooter was dangerous and that his guns should be confiscated. Despite Ripp's report, the guns were not removed. Not a gun-free zone: We could find no evidence that Haven Drugs posted a sign or had a policy prohibiting the carrying of firearms. Current employees declined to comment.

13) **Brockport, NY, 2/14/09:** The shooter killed a nurse in the Lakeside Memorial Hospital parking lot and a

motorist who intervened, and wounded the motorist's girlfriend. The shooter had been fired from the hospital after the nurse filed a sexual harassment complaint against him. He then drove 50 miles and killed another nurse — who had filed a similar complaint against the shooter— and her husband in their home. Shooter Name: Frank Garcia, 34. Gun details: .40 caliber Glock handgun Ammo details: Unknown. Gun acquired: Unknown. Prohibiting criteria: There is no evidence that the shooter was prohibited from owning a gun. However, he had applied for concealed carry permits and been denied three times. In his 1995 application, he omit- ted information about his criminal record—including arrests for criminal possession of a weapon, assault, and harassment. In 2001 and 2006 he made further omissions, and was evaluated as lacking moral character. But in 2007, a judge reversed the denial and granted Garcia a concealed weapon permit. Not a gun-free zone: We found no indication that permit holders were prohibited from carrying guns in this area at the time of the incident.

FACTS: All these cities either forbid or make it incredibly difficult for law-abiding citizens to carry concealed handguns for protection. In Boston, it is so bad that even off-duty and retired police are regularly denied unrestricted license to carry permits. Northridge, California is part of Los Angeles County, which refuses to issue permits to regular citizens. In September 2011, there were 240 permits in all of Los Angeles County when the population was about 7.6 million adults. That equals a permit rate of 0.0032 percent. In addition, the attack was at a residential dwelling, not a public place.

By contrast, we estimate that there are 10.82 million permits in right-to-carry states with an adult population of 161 million—that is a permit rate of about 6.7 percent (209 times the rate of permits issued in Los Angeles). (This doesn't include the six states that allow carrying concealed handguns without a permit, and these states presumably have higher rates of carrying.) In these states, the general population is simply not able to carry a gun for protection.

Similarly, East Oakland, California is part of Alameda County. In 2010, Alameda County had granted concealed handgun permits to seventy-five people out of 1,182,534—a permit rate of 0.006 percent.

Just as with Herkimer, New York; Medford in Suffolk County, New York, and Brockport in Monroe County, New York were similarly very restrictive in issuing May-Issue permits. In Suffolk County, the police and sheriff's departments each handle permits in half of the permits for the county. For the sheriff's office, Robert E. Draffin (the Suffolk County Sheriff's Freedom of information officer) informed us that there were 569 sportsman permits (limited to carrying to or from a shooting range or to go hunting) and seventy-nine business permits (where a business owner is allowed to carry only in the course of doing business). For the police department, Inspector Derrocco noted that the department "virtually never gives out permits for anything other than sportsmen to carry to and from the range and for premises and dwellings." Given that there are about 1.2 million adults in Suffolk County, even assuming that the police department issued permits at the same rate as the sheriff's office, this implies a permit rate of about 0.1 percent and virtually none of these permits would have allowed a concealed handgun to be carried in the pharmacy where the attack occurred.

> 14) **Oak Creek, WI, 8/5/12:** The shooter killed six people at a Sikh temple and injured three others, including a responding police officer, before killing himself. Shooter Name: Wade Michael, 40. Gun details: 9mm semiautomatic handgun. Ammo details: Page reportedly bought three 19-round magazines when he purchased the gun. Gun acquired: Page acquired the gun at a local gun shop a week before the shooting. Prohibiting criteria: Page was involved with the white supremacist movement but he does not appear to have been prohibited from purchasing

a gun. Federal officials investigated Page's ties to supremacist groups more than once prior to the shooting, but did not collect enough evidence to open an investigation.

FACTS: From FoxNews.com: "No guns [were] allowed in the temple," Kulbir Singh, an attendee of the Sikh Temple of Wisconsin, told FoxNews.com. "Everyone knows that it's not allowed, anywhere in the temple."

15) **Norcross, GA, 2/22/12:** The shooter returned to a Korean spa from which he'd been kicked out after an altercation, where he shot and killed two of his sisters and their husbands before committing suicide. Shooter Name: Jeong Soo Paek, 59. Gun details: .45 caliber handgun. Ammo details: Unknown. Gun acquired: Police reported that he acquired the gun legally. Prohibiting criteria: Paek does not appear to have been prohibited, although he had allegedly served two months in jail for assaulting his sister six years earlier. Not a gun-free zone: We could find no indication that the property owner forbade possession of a firearm on their property.

FACTS: Lott spoke with someone at the spa after the attack and was told that the killer knew "nobody there had a gun." The person at the spa indicated that they were sure that neither the sisters nor their husbands had guns at the spa and that the killer who was the brother of the women knew that was the case. While the official policy at the spa isn't clear because the conversation was very short, the important thing was that the killer knew that there were no guns for people to defend themselves there. This was a small family owned establishment so it is most likely that this was the official policy of the family. Note that they have the wrong date on this event. (UPDATE: Mayors Against Illegal Guns originally claimed that this event occurred on February 22, but the event actually occurred on February 20, 2012. After Lott wrote his analysis, they corrected the data but did not update their discussion of gun-free zones.) Note also that the business has since closed.

> 16) **Hialeah, FL, 6/6/10:** The shooter killed four women, including his wife—who had just separated from him. He injured three others before shooting and killing himself. The shooting occurred in Yoyito-Cafe Restaurant, where the shooter's wife was employed as a waitress, and in the parking lot immediately outside. Shooter Name: Gerardo Regalado, 38. Gun details: .45 caliber handgun. Ammo details: Unknown. Gun acquired: The shooter had a concealed weapons permit. Prohibiting criteria: There is no evidence that the shooter was prohibited from owning a gun. However, relatives said the shooter had abused and terrorized women in the past, and had been imprisoned in Cuba for a particularly violent incident, but he did not have a criminal record in the United States. Not a gun-free zone: We could find no indication that guns were prohibited in this area. Guns are prohibited in Florida restaurants only in areas primarily devoted to the serving of alcohol.

FACTS: Strangely, while Bloomberg's group mentions the restaurants that get 50 percent of their revenue from alcohol, it didn't actually go and check whether that was the case for this restaurant, which apparently was at the time a very popular venue for parties serving alcohol. If Bloomberg's group had checked, it would have found that the restaurant was a gun-free zone.

> 17) **Washington, DC, 3/30/10:** Three gunmen killed four and wounded five in retaliation for another murder. Shooter Name: Nathaniel D. Simms, 26; Orlando Carter,

20, and unnamed 14-year-old juvenile. Gun details: An AK-47 assault rifle and 9mm and .45-caliber handguns. Ammo details: Unknown. Gun acquired: Unknown. Prohibiting criteria: The adults were reported to have lengthy criminal histories, which prohibited them from purchasing guns, and the 14-year-old was too young to purchase or own a gun.

FACTS: This is one case where Bloomberg's Everytown doesn't include this as a place that allows guns (obviously D.C. completely bans the carrying of concealed handguns); we include it here simply as an example of one of the many cases where it is including what are pretty obviously drive-by gang shootings. Even the D.C. police chief, Cathy Lanier, indicated that it was a "gang retaliation." The AK-47 was used to spray bullets into a group in another gang's territory in retaliation for another murder. We are focused on cases identified by Everytown as occurring in gun-free zones, but gang shootings are obviously quite different from the types of mass public shootings that garner national attention.

18) **Mount Airy, NC, 11/1/09:** The shooter killed four people outside a television store before eventually surrendering to the police. Shooter Name: Marcos Chavez Gonzalez, 29. Gun details: Assault rifle. Ammo details: Unknown. Gun acquired: Unknown. Not a gun-free zone: It was lawful to carry a firearm in the area of the shooting.

FACTS: Indications are that the attack was part of gang related crime. As explained above, that would exclude it from the mass public shootings done specifically to harm people as distinct from other types of violent crime.

TABLE 1.3: THE FBI'S CASES WHERE ZERO OR ONE PERSON HAS BEEN KILLED

Year	Month	Day	City	State	Attacker Name	Killed
2001	3	22	El Cajon	California	Jason Anthony Hoffman	0
2003	7	17	Charleston	West Virginia	Richard Dean Bright	0
2004	2	9	East Greenbush	New York	Jon William Romano	0
2005	2	13	Kingston	New York	Robert Charles Bonelli Jr.	0
2005	11	20	Tacoma	Washington	Dominick Sergil Maldonado	0
2006	3	25	Reno	Nevada	James Scott Newman	0
2006	10	9	Joplin	Missouri	Thomas White	0
2007	3	5	Signal Hill	California	Alonso Jose Mendez	0
2007	10	10	Cleveland	Ohio	Asa Halley Coon	0
2009	4	26	Hampton	Virginia	Odane Greg Maye	0
2009	5	18	Cut Off	Louisiana	Justin Doucet	0
2010	2	3	Macomb	Illinois	Jonathan Joseph Labbe	0
2010	2	10	Knoxville	Tennessee	Mark Stephen Foster	0
2010	2	23	Littleton	Colorado	Bruco Strongeagle Eastwood	0
2010	3	4	Arlington	Virginia	John Patrick Bedell	0
2010	5	7	Bloomfield	New Jersey	Rasheed Cherry	0
2010	5	27	New York Mills	New York	Abraham Dickan	0

Year	Month	Day	City	State	Attacker Name	Killed
2010	9	22	Crete	Nebraska	Akouch Kashoual	0
2010	10	8	Carlsbad	California	Brendan O'Rourke	0
2010	10	29	Reno	Nevada	John Dennis Gillane	0
2010	12	14	Panama City	Florida	Clay Allen Duke	0
2011	8	27	Queens	New York	Tyrone Miller	0
2011	9	13	Girard	Kansas	Jesse Ray Palmer	0
2012	2	8	Middletown	New York	Timothy Patrick Mulqueen	0
2012	7	17	Tuscaloosa	Alabama	Nathan Van Wilkins	0
2012	8	27	Baltimore	Maryland	Robert Wayne Gladden Jr.	0
2012	12	15	Birmingham	Alabama	Jason Heath Letts	0
2013	1	10	Taft	California	Bryan Oliver	0
2013	4	12	Christiansburg	Virginia	Neil Allen MacInnis	0
2013	6	21	Greenville	North Carolina	Lakin Anthony Faust	0
2013	10	26	Albuquerque	New Mexico	Christopher Thomas Chase	0
2001	4	23	San Jose	California	Cathline Repunte	1
2001	12	6	Goshen	Indiana	Robert L. Wissman	1
2003	4	24	Red Lion	Pennsylvania	James Sheets	1
2003	5	9	Cleveland	Ohio	Biswanath A. Halder	1
2003	8	19	Andover	Ohio	Richard Wayne Shadle	1
2005	1	26	Toledo	Ohio	Myles Wesley Meyers	1

Year	Month	Day	City	State	Attacker Name	Killed
2005	11	8	Jacksboro	Tennessee	Kenneth S. Bartley	1
2005	11	22	North Augusta	South Carolina	Unknown	1
2006	6	25	Denver	Colorado	Michael Julius Ford	1
2006	7	28	Seattle	Washington	Naveed Afzal Haq	1
2006	8	30	Hillsborough	North Carolina	Alvaro Castillo	1
2006	9	29	Cazenovia	Wisconsin	Eric Jordan Hainstock	1
2007	8	30	Bronx	New York	Paulino Valenzuela	1
2007	10	8	Simi Valley	California	Robert Becerra	1
2008	3	3	West Palm Beach	Florida	Alburn Edward Blake	1
2009	4	7	Temecula	California	John Suchan Chong	1
2009	6	1	North Little Rock	Arkansas	Carlos Leon Bledsoe	1
2009	6	10	Washington D.C.	Washington D.C.	James Wenneker von Brunn	1
2009	7	1	Simi Valley	California	Jaime Paredes	1
2009	7	25	Houston	Texas	Unknown	1
2009	11	6	Orlando	Florida	Jason Samuel Rodriguez	1
2009	11	7	Vail	Colorado	Richard Allan Moreau	1
2009	11	10	Tualatin	Oregon	Robert Beiser	1
2010	1	4	Las Vegas	Nevada	Johnny Lee Wicks Jr.	1
2010	3	9	Columbus	Ohio	Nathaniel Alvin Brown	1
2010	3	30	Tarpon Springs	Florida	Arunya Rouch	1
2010	4	19	Knoxville	Tennessee	Abdo Ibssa	1

Year	Month	Day	City	State	Attacker Name	Killed
2010	9	20	El Paso	Texas	Steven Jay Kropf	1
2010	10	4	Gainesville	Florida	Clifford Louis Miller Jr.	1
2010	10	13	Washington	D.C.	Unknown	1
2011	1	5	Omaha	Nebraska	Richard L. Butler Jr.	1
2012	3	8	Pittsburgh	Pennsylvania	John Schick	1
2013	10	21	Sparks	Nevada	Jose Reyes	1
2013	11	1	Los Angeles	California	Paul Anthony Ciancia	1
2013	12	13	Centennial	Colorado	Karl Halverson Pierson	1
2013	12	17	Reno	Nevada	Alan Oliver Frazier	1

APPENDIX 2

ENACTMENT DATES OF LAWS REQUIRING BACKGROUND CHECKS IN PRIVATE TRANSFER OF HANDGUNS OR RIFLES. NOTED WHEN HANDGUNS ONLY. (STATES IN BOLD REQUIRE BACKGROUND CHECKS ON ALL PRIVATE TRANSFERS OF GUNS AT POINT OF SALE.)

State	Date law went into effect*	Type of crime for not conducting check	Type of crime for providing false information
California	1/1/91	Misdemeanor	Misdemeanor
Colorado	3/31/01		
	Expanded background checks at gun shows	Class 1 misdemeanor	Class 1 misdemeanor

State	Date law went into effect*	Type of crime for not conducting check	Type of crime for providing false information
Colorado	7/1/2013		
	Expanded background checks on all guns	Class 1 misdemeanor	Class 1 misdemeanor
Connecticut	10/1/94		
	Handgun certificate of eligibility	Class D felony	Fined not more than $500 and/or imprisoned for not more than three years
Connecticut	April 1, 2014		
	Long-gun eligibility certificate requiring state and federal background checks	Class D felony	Class D felony For which two years of the sentence imposed may not be suspended or reduced by the court, and $5,000 of the fine imposed may not be remitted or reduced by the court unless the court states on the record its reasons for remitting or reducing such fine
Delaware	July 1, 2013		
	Expanded background check on all guns	Class A misdemeanor for first offense, Class G felony there after	Class G felony
District of Columbia	Pre-1977		
	license necessary to own a gun and that requires background check	First violation is a $100 civil fine, Second violation is a $500 civil fine and five-year prohibition on owning a gun	Fine of not more than $2,500 and not more than one year in prison

State	Date law went into effect*	Type of crime for not conducting check	Type of crime for providing false information
Hawaii	Pre-1977		
	permit required to purchase any gun, and background check required for permit	Misdemeanor	Class C felony
Illinois	Pre-1977		
	permit required to purchase any gun, and background check required for permit	Class A misdemeanor	Perjury
Iowa	7/1/91		
	Handguns	Simple misdemeanor	Class D felony
Maryland	10/1/96		
	Handguns	Misdemeanor	Misdemeanor
Massachusetts	Pre-1977		
	permit required to purchase any gun, and background check required for permit	Felony	$500–1000 and/or six months to two years imprisonment
Michigan	Pre-1977		
	handguns	Felony	Felony
Missouri	9/28/81 Started		
	handguns	Class A misdemeanor	Class A misdemeanor
Missouri	9/28/2007 Ended		
	handguns		
Nebraska	9/6/91		
	Handguns	Class 1 misdemeanor	Class 4 felony
New Jersey	Pre-1977		
	Permit required to purchase any gun, and background check required for permit	Crime of the fourth degree	Crime of the third degree

State	Date law went into effect*	Type of crime for not conducting check	Type of crime for providing false information
New York	Pre-1977		
	expanded background checks at gun shows	Class A misdemeanor	Class A misdemeanor
New York	March 15, 2013		
	Expanded background checks on all guns	Class A misdemeanor	Class A misdemeanor
North Carolina	12/1/95		
	Handguns	Class 2 misdemeanor	Class H felony
Oregon	12/7/00		
	Expanded background checks at gun shows	Class A misdemeanor	Class A misdemeanor
Oregon	8/9/2015		
	Expanded background checks on all guns	First violation Class A misdemeanor, subsequent violations Class B felony	Class A misdemeanor
Pennsylvania	10/11/95		
	Handguns	Misdemeanor of the second degree	Felony of the third degree
Puerto Rico	Pre-1977 license necessary to own a gun and that required background check		
Puerto Rico	June 20, 2015 Ended licensing requirement		
Rhode Island	Pre-1977		
	All private transfers	Not more than $1000 and/or imprisonment of up to five years	Imprisonment of up to five years

State	Date law went into effect*	Type of crime for not conducting check	Type of crime for providing false information
Tennessee	Until 11/11/98 on handguns	Class A misdemeanor	Class A misdemeanor
Washington	12/4/2014		
	All private transfers	For first violation a Gross misdemeanor (imprisonment of up to 364 days, fine up to $5,000); for additional violations class C felony	Gross misdemeanor

NOTES

INTRODUCTION

1.   Alana Goodman and Stephen Gutowski, "Leaked Audio: Clinton Says Supreme Court Is 'Wrong' on Second Amendment," Washington Free Beacon, October 1, 2015, http://freebeacon.com/politics/leaked-audio-clinton-says-supreme-court-is-wrong-on-second-amendment/.

2.   *District of Columbia v. Heller,* 554 U. S. (2008), https://www.law.cornell.edu/supct/pdf/07-290P.ZO.

3.   *McDonald v. City of Chicago,* 561 U. S. (2010), https://www.law.cornell.edu/supct/pdf/08-1521P.ZO.

4.   Justice Breyer, dissent, *Otis McDonald, et al v. City of Chicago,* et *al.* Supreme Court decision, June 28, 2010, https://www.law.cornell.edu/supct/pdf/08-1521P.ZD, 1-2.

5.   Alana Goodman and Stephen Gutowski, "Leaked Audio: Clinton Says Supreme Court is 'Wrong' on Second Amendment," The Washington Free Beacon, October 1, 2015, http://freebeacon.com/politics/leaked-audio-clinton-says-supreme-court-is-wrong-on-second-amendment/.

6. "Hillary Clinton Lauding Australia and UK Gun Control Laws," Crime Prevention Center, October 16, 2015, http://crimeresearch. org/2015/10/hillary-clinton-lauding-australia-and-uk-gun-control-laws/.

7. John R. Lott Jr., "Reaction to D.C. Gun Ban Decision," Fox News, July 1, 2008, http://www.foxnews.com/story/2008/07/01/john-lott-reaction-to-dc-gun-ban-decision.html.

8. "Obama supports DC Handgun Ban," YouTube video, posted by ObamaDCGunBan, June 26, 2008, https://www.youtube.com/ watch?v=-wu9jE1MnAE.

9. Ben Smith, "Obama on small-town Pa.: Clinging to religion, guns, xenophobia," Politico, April 11, 2008, http://www.politico.com/ blogs/ben-smith/2008/04/obama-on-small-town-pa-clinging-to-religion-guns-xenophobia-007737.

10. Among Garland's other decisions was a 2005 vote against rehearing *Seegars v. Gonzales*, a case that had protected D.C.'s strict gun prohibitions. See *Seegars v. Gonzales*, 396 F. 3d 1248–Court of Appeals, Dist. of Columbia Circuit 2005, https://scholar.google. com/scholar_case?case=18408735856908207861&hl=en&as_ sdt=6&as_vis=1&oi=scholar. In an earlier case, Garland voted to ignore federal law prohibiting the government's retention of gun background check information. See *National Rifle Association* of *America v. Janet Reno*, Court of Appeals, Dist. of Columbia Circuit 2000, https://www.gpo.gov/fdsys/pkg/USCOURTS-caDC-99-05270/pdf/USCOURTS-caDC-99-05270-0.pdf. The prohibition was in place to prevent a back-door gun registry.

11. Alan Zarembo, "Obama pushes to extend background checks to Social Security," *Los Angeles Times*, July 18, 2015, http://www. latimes.com/nation/politics/la-na-gun-law-20150718-story. html#page=1.

12. Senator Chuck Grassley, "Veterans, Dependents Account for Disproportionate Share of 'Mental Defective' Category on Gun Ban List," April 15, 2015, http://www.grassley.senate.gov/news/news-releases/veterans-dependents-account-disproportionate-share-%E2%80%98mental-defective%E2%80%99-category.

13. Lawrence Southwick Jr., "Self-Defense with Guns: The Consequences," Journal of Criminal Justice, vol. 8 (2000), tables 5 and 6; see also Gary Kleck, Point Blank: Guns and Violence in America (Hawthorne: Aldine de Gruyter Publishers, 1991).

14. Mike Lillis, "Democrat's bill targets 'junk' handguns," *The Hill*, March 4, 2013, http://thehill.com/homenews/house/286029-dem-bill-targets-junk-handguns-.

15. Staff, "From Veep to Lobbyist: Biden Pressures CO Democratic Lawmakers to Pass Gun Control," Colorado Peak Politics, February 15, 2013, http://coloradopeakpolitics.com/2013/02/15/from-veep-to-lobbyist-biden-pressures-co-democratic-lawmakers-to-pass-gun-control/.

16. Based on numerous discussions with Colorado State Representative Lori Saine.

17. Four hours of training is required in Maryland to own a handgun. The least expensive class is $125, though many others are $150 or more. The fee for the three-year permit is fifty dollars and the renewal cost is twenty dollars. The cost of fingerprinting is thirty dollars. For information on the Handgun Qualification License in Maryland, see http://mdsp.maryland.gov/Organization/Pages/CriminalInvestigationBureau/LicensingDivision/Firearms/HandgunQualificationLicense.aspx.

18. Three-and-a-half years after the Heller decision, you still only had about 1,500 in D.C. with a legal handgun. See Emily Miller, "D.C.'s only gun source," *Washington Times*, October 11, 2011, http://www.washingtontimes.com/blog/guns/2011/oct/11/miller-dcs-only-gun-source/.

19. Andrea Noble, "No changes—yet—to D.C. gun sales law after federal ruling in Texas," *Washington Times*, February 12, 2015, http://www.washingtontimes.com/news/2015/feb/12/dc-gun-sales-law-remain-the-same-after-federal-rul/?page=all.

20. Robert A. Levy, "The real story in D.C.'s gun data," *Washington Post*, February 11, 2011, http://voices.washingtonpost.com/local-opinions/2011/02/the_real_story_in_dcs_gun_data.html.

21. Emily Miller, "Inside D.C.'s gun registry," *Washington Times*, October 6, 2011, http://www.washingtontimes.com/blog/

guns/2011/oct/6/miller-inside-dcs-gun-registry/; and Emily Miller, "Steps to gun ownership in D.C.," *Washington Times*, October 14, 2011, http://www.washingtontimes.com/blog/guns/2011/oct/14/miller-steps-gun-ownership-dc/.

22.   Paul Duggan, "Since D.C.'s handgun ban ended, well-heeled residents have become well armed," *Washington Post*, February 8, 2011, http://www.washingtonpost.com/wp-dyn/content/story/2011/02/07/ST2011020706491.html?sid=ST2011020706491.

23.   William Lee, "Getting a Chicago gun permit," *Chicago Tribune*, December 12, 2000, http://articles.chicagotribune.com/2010-12-12/news/ct-met-chicago-gun-registry-steps-20101212_1_applicants-gun-owners-chicago-gun. In 2013, Illinois passed a state preemption of firearm laws for "the regulation, licensing, possession, and registration of handguns and ammunition for a handgun, and the transportation of any firearm and ammunition." See Public Act 098-0063, http://ilga.gov/legislation/publicacts/98/098-0063.htm.

24.   Chicago ordinance No. 006-75 is quite clear that people are forbidden "to possess or carry any pistol, revolver, firearm, dagger, stiletto, billie club, knife, stun gun, taser, mace, bludgeon, explosive device or other weapon on property owned, operated or maintained by the CTA." See http://www.transitchicago.com/assets/1/ordinances/Ordinance_006-75.pdf.

25.   The data discussed here was originally obtained from a FOIA request submitted by the *Washington Times*. See Kelly Riddell, "Data divulges racial disparity in Chicago's issuance of gun permits," *Washington Times*, September 29, 2014, http://www.washingtontimes.com/news/2014/sep/29/chicago-concealed-carry-gun-permit-law-disarms-poo/.

26.   The permit fee in Illinois is $150 and it costs around $350 to get a class that satisfies the sixteen-hour training requirement.

27.   For eleven states, there is no permit required to carry inside their state.

28.   A video of Hillary Clinton's testimony before the Senate Finance Committee on September 30, 1993: "Newly Released Footage Shows Hillary's 25% Gun Tax Endorsement," Americans for Tax

Reform, April 14, 2016, http://www.atr.org/newly-released-footage-shows-hillary-s-25-gun-tax-endorsement.

29. Crime Prevention Research Center, "Concealed Carry Permit Holders Across the United States," July 16, 2015, http://ssrn.com/abstract=2629704.

30. For information on permit fees for the two states, see http://www.txdps.state.tx.us/RSD/CHL/documents/LTCFeeSchedule.pdf and http://www.in.gov/isp/2829.htm.

31. Aaron Goldstein, "Obama blasts Voter ID laws in Selma Speech," The American Spectator, March 7, 2015, http://spectator.org/blog/61981/obama-blasts-voter-id-laws-selma-speech.

32. Jeff Jacoby, "Crime soared with Mass. gun law," *Boston Globe*, February 17, 2013, https://www.bostonglobe.com/opinion/2013/02/17/the-nation-toughest-gun-control-law-made-massachusetts-less-safe/3845k7xHzkwTrBWy4KpkEM/story.html.

33. CNN Townhall, "Guns in America town hall with Obama transcript (full text)," CNN, January 7, 2016, http://www.cnn.com/2016/01/07/politics/transcript-obama-town-hall-guns-in-america/.

34. Noble, "No changes—yet—to D.C. gun sales law after federal ruling in Texas."

35. "Hillary Clinton Townhall Talks Guns," YouTube video, posted by Live Satellite News, October 7, 2015, https://www.youtube.com/watch?v=HOc50YcRZmM.

36. Fox News, "Sanders turns up attacks on Clinton at feisty debate, Dem front-runner fights back," Fox News, March 7, 2016, http://www.foxnews.com/politics/2016/03/07/sanders-turns-up-attacks-on-clinton-at-feisty-debate-dem-front-runner-fights-back.html.

37. Chris Murphy, "Sanders 'is standing in clear opposition to the families of Sandy Hook'," Grabien, April 7, 2016, https://grabien.com/story.php?id=52813&utm_source=cliplist20160407&utm_medium=email&utm_campaign=cliplist&utm_content=story52813.

38. CNN, "Full results: CNN/ORC poll on guns in America," CNN Politics, January 7, 2016, http://www.cnn.com/2016/01/07/politics/obama-guns-executive-action-poll-results/.

CHAPTER 1

1. See Pew Research Center, http://www.pewresearch.org/data-trend/
    domestic-issues/gun-control/; and Roper Center, http://images.
    huffingtonpost.com/2015-08-31-1441034960-3827073-
    favorstrictergunlaws.gif.

2. See Gallup, http://www.gallup.com/poll/1645/guns.aspx; http://
    www.gallup.com/poll/186236/americans-desire-stricter-gun-laws-
    sharply.aspx; and PollingReport.com, http://www.pollingreport.
    com/guns.htm.

3. Frank Newport, "Majority Say More Concealed Weapons Would
    Make U.S. Safer," Gallup, October 20, 2015, http://www.gallup.
    com/poll/186263/majority-say-concealed-weapons-safer.aspx?utm_
    source=alert&utm_medium=email&utm_content=heading&utm_
    campaign=syndication.

4. Jeffrey M. Jones, "Public Wary About Broad Concealed Firearm
    Privileges," Gallup, June 14, 2005, http://www.gallup.com/
    poll/16822/public-wary-about-broad-concealed-firearm-privileges.
    aspx.

5. John Merline, "Obama Fails To Sway Public On Gun Control:
    Poll," *Investor's Business Daily*, January 8, 2016, http://www.
    investors.com/politics/policy/obama-fails-to-convince-public-on-
    gun-control-poll-finds/.

6. Rasmussen Reports, "Americans Prefer Living in Neighborhoods
    With Guns," June 12, 2015, http://www.rasmussenreports.com/
    public_content/politics/current_events/gun_control/americans_
    prefer_living_in_neighborhoods_with_guns.

7. Steve Visser, "Rockdale sheriff calls store patron 'hero' for firing on
    gunman," *Atlanta Journal Constitution*, June 1, 2015, http://www.
    ajc.com/news/news/crime-law/rockdale-sheriff-calls-store-patron-
    hero-for-firin/nmSbG/; and Alice Queen, "Customer who returned
    fire at Rockdale County murder suspect called 'hero'," *Rockdale
    Citizen*, May 31, 2015, http://www.rockdalecitizen.com/news/
    customer-who-returned-fire-at-rockdale-county-murder-suspect-
    called/article_4ee4f1bf-8f25-5969-8360-0b9eb21e6c98.html.

8. Chad Mills, "CWPs likely stopped deaths of children, firefighters,"
    Fox Carolina, May 6, 2015, http://www.foxcarolina.com/

story/28998992/firefighter-cwps-likely-stopped-a-massacre-of-children-firefighters.

9. David Chang, "Gunman Shot, Killed Inside West Philly Barbershop," NBC Channel 10 Philadelphia, March 22, 2015, http://www.nbcphiladelphia.com/news/local/Man-Shot-in-the-Chest-Inside-West-Philly-Barbershop-297176271.html.

10. John R. Lott, Jr., "Armed Doctor Saved Lives," *Philadelphia Inquirer*, July 29, 2014, http://johnrlott.tripod.com/op-eds/PhillyInqArmedDoctor072914.html.

11. Daily Mail Reporter, "Veteran shoots gunman after he opened fire on him and his friends in the street," Daily Mail (UK), July 7, 2014, http://www.dailymail.co.uk/news/article-2683197/Gunman-22-shot-veteran-opening-fire-friends.html; and Geoff Ziezulewicz, "Authorities: Military service member with concealed carry permit shoots attacker," *Chicago Tribune*, July 7, 2014, http://www.chicagotribune.com/news/local/breaking/chi-military-member-concealed-carry-shoots-attacker-20140706-story.html.

12. Lara Greenberg, "Guilty Plea Entered In Plymouth Shooting Death," ABC Channel 16 WNEP, October 13, 2013, http://wnep.com/2013/10/15/guilty-plea-entered-in-plymouth-shooting-death/; and Bob Kalinowski, "Man who ended Plymouth shooting rampage wants gun back," Citizensvoice.com, March 6, 2014, http://citizensvoice.com/news/man-who-ended-plymouth-shooting-rampage-wants-gun-back-1.1645788.

13. "Man charged in supermarket stabbing," ABC Channel 4 News, April 30, 2012, http://www.good4utah.com/news/local-wasatch-front-/man-charged-in-supermarket-stabbing. Some of the original stories are no longer available. See Crime Prevention Research Center, "Compiling Cases Where Concealed Handgun Permit Holders Have Stopped Mass Public Shootings," April 21, 2015, http://crimeresearch.org/2015/04/uber-driver-in-chicago-stops-mass-public-shooting/.

14. Jenny Arnold, "Sheriff: Man kicks in church side door, points shotgun," GoUpState.com, March 25, 2012, http://www.goupstate.com/article/20120325/articles/120329781.

15. Chuck Ross, "Man With Gun Saves Toddler From Lunatic With 2 Guns," Daily Caller, July 27, 2015, http://dailycaller. com/2015/07/27/man-with-gun-saves-toddler-from-lunatic-with-2-guns/; and Maxine Bernstein, "Mystic club shooting: Bouncer wondered 'Is this real?' when bullets started flying," The Oregonian, February 01, 2014, http://www.oregonlive.com/ portland/index.ssf/2014/01/post_414.html.

CHAPTER 2

1. Emanuella Grinberg, "Gun violence not a mental health issue, experts say, pointing to 'anger,' suicides," CNN, January 25, 2016, http://www.cnn.com/2016/01/25/health/gun-violence-mental-health-issue/.

2. John R. Lott Jr., *More Guns, Less Crime* 3rd ed. (Chicago: University of Chicago Press, 2010).

3. Charles F. Wellford, John V. Pepper, and Carol V. Petrie, *Firearms and Violence: A Critical Review* (Washington, DC: The National Academies Press, 2005), 183, http://www.nap.edu/read/10881/ chapter/9#182.

4. David M. Cutler, Edward Glaeser, and Karen Norberg, "Explaining the Rise in Youth Suicide," in *Risky Behavior Among Youths*, ed. Jonathan Gruber (Chicago: University of Chicago Press, 2001).

5. Hiroko Tabuchi and Rachel Abrams, "Obama's Gun Initiative Seen as Having Limited Effect on Unlicensed Dealers," *New York Times*, January 7, 2016, http://www.nytimes.com/2016/01/08/business/ obamas-gun-initiative-seen-as-having-limited-effect-on-unlicensed-dealers.html.

6. The list of economists was obtained using JSTOR (www.jstor.org), selecting their Economics subset (632 sources), and doing a full-text search for "gun control" for all years, limited to peer-reviewed books and articles (not book reviews, miscellaneous). We obtained 234 hits. We then obtained copies of all the articles to determine if the articles contained empirical work on the issues of guns and crime or accidents or suicides. Empirical studies that only dealt with voting behavior by politicians or the electorate or were surveys themselves were excluded.

For criminologists, the samples were drawn from two databases of academics who had published at least one empirical study on firearms and violence in peer-reviewed criminology articles between January 2000 and December 2013 (the databases are PROQUEST and EBSCO Host). Again, we only included criminologists who had published empirical studies in peer-reviewed criminology journals (excluding forensics or injury publications). The original sample was of emails was eighty-one criminologists, but one of the participants wrote back and said that they did not consider themselves to have any expertise for the questions in the survey.

We know the identity of the individuals who took the survey and how they answered the survey, but individuals were promised anonymity from having their survey answers publicly revealed.

7. On average, the survey took economists about three minutes to complete. Respondents had the option of answering, "yes," "no," or "I don't know." If a researcher answered, "I don't know," the question was repeated a second time. This time, the answers were limited to "yes" or "no." Both sets of results are reported. (Unfortunately, the "I don't know" option was by error still included for a few respondents.) The survey was conducted using Surveygizmo.com.

8. Gary Becker, "Crime and Punishment: An Economic Approach," *Journal of Political Economy* 76 (1968): 169–217.

9. Julia Lurie, "When the Gun Lobby Tries to Justify Firearms Everywhere, It Turns to This Guy," *Mother Jones*, July 28, 2015 (for a general discussion of the other errors in the article see http://crimepreventionresearchcenter.org/2015/08/a-response-to-mother-jones-mistake-filled-effort-to-discredit-john-lott/).

10. At the time James Q. Wilson made a statement on concealed handguns, he was possibly "the most influential criminal justice scholar of the 20th century." Brian Frost, "James Q. Wilson," Oxford Bibliographies, September 30, 2013, http://www.oxfordbibliographies.com/view/document/obo-9780195396607/obo-9780195396607-0156.xml; and Charles F. Wellford, John V. Pepper, and Carol V. Petrie, eds., *Firearms and Violence: A Critical*

Review (Washington, D.C.: The National Academy Press, 2005), http://www.nap.edu/openbook.php?record_id=10881page=271.

11. Christopher F. Cardiff and Daniel B. Klein, "Faculty Partisan Affiliations in All Disciplines: A Voter-Registration Study," *Critical Review* 17 (2005).

12. Peltzman provides one of the classic examples of the unintended effects of regulation in his analysis of auto safety regulations. Gilles and Lund as well as Lott and Whitley provide a couple examples of the unintended consequences of gun regulations. See Stephen G. Gilles and Nelson Lund, "Insurance as Gun Control?" *Regulation* (Fall 2013): 38-43; and John R. Lott, Jr. and John Whitley, "Safe Storage Gun Laws: Accidental Deaths, Suicides, and Crime," *Journal of Law and Economics* 44, no. 2 (October 2001): 659-689.

13. Our survey is unique in that it only asks questions of those who have actually published empirical work on gun issues, not just those who mention the words "firearm" or "gun." See Harvard Injury Control Research Center, http://www.hsph.harvard.edu/hicrc/ firearm-researcher-surveys/. This survey by Professor David Hemenway at Harvard cherry-picked authors. Surprisingly, he found the vast majority agreed that we need more gun control. So let's look at the details. He polled authors who had published in the fields of "public health, public policy, sociology, or criminology." Most notably, half of the authors picked were within Hemenway's own field of public health and another third were sociologists/criminologists, followed by public policy and a few economists. The poll dramatically over-weighted those in public health. It didn't matter whether the publications even contained any empirical work or related to the survey questions.
Economists have done a lot of work on crime. Unlike the vast majority of work in public health, economists' work is usually much more rigorous with more detailed, statistical evidence dealing with issues of causality. Economists are also much more open to the notion of deterrence than the vast majority of authors surveyed by Hemenway. I myself was chief economist at the United States Sentencing Commission. But Hemenway steers away from economics journals. In addition, looking at publications from only

2011 through 2013 also picks up a recent surge in public health studies and skews the sample towards those types of authors. Authors were asked if they agreed with the statement: "In the United States, guns are used in self-defense far more often than they are used in crime." Hemenway reports that 73 percent disagreed. However, many respondents may have believed that a net benefit from gun ownership still exists—just not enough to say that guns are used defensively "far more often."

14. Ibid.
15. Carlisle E. Moody and Thomas B. Marvell, "The Debate on Shall Issue Laws, Continued," *Econ Journal Watch* 6(2) (May 2009): 203-217; and John R. Lott, Jr., "What a balancing test will show for right-to-carry laws," *University of Maryland Law Review* 71 (2012): 1205-1218. See also various editions of Lott's *More Guns, Less Crime* (Chicago: University of Chicago Press, 1998).
16. There was one other part to the survey that is not reported in the text that asked academics the research that they relied on for their conclusions (Appendix 1.1a-b).
17. Perry Chiaramonte, "Media misfire? Columbia J-school, Bloomberg unite to teach gun coverage," Fox News, March 31, 2015, http://www.foxnews.com/us/2015/03/31/media-misfire-vaunted-journalism-school-pairs-with-bloomberg-to-teach-gun.html.
18. Amy Goodman, "Pima County Sheriff Clarence Dupnik: 'People Who Are Mentally Unstable Are Susceptible to the Rhetoric Going on in this Country,'" DemocracyNow!, January 10, 2011, http://www.democracynow.org/2011/1/10/pima_county_sheriff_clarence_dupnik_people.
19. Megan Canterbury, "Tucson police chief meets with Obama," Tucson News Now, February 4, 2013, http://www.waff.com/story/20757773/tucson-police-chief-meets-with-obama).
20. About 15,000 members participated in this survey. "Gun Policy Law Enforcement: Survey Results," PoliceOne.com, survey conducted between March 4 and March 13, 2013, http://ddq74coujkv1i.cloudfront.net/p1_gunsurveysummary_2013.pdf.
21. When the National Association of Chiefs of Police surveyed chiefs of police and sheriffs in the U.S. in 2014 they asked five firearms

related questions. Typical of those questions was: "Would national
recognition of state-issued concealed weapons permits facilitate the
violent crime fighting efforts of the professional law enforcement
community?" where 63.2 percent answered "yes" and 32.3 percent
answered "no."

When *Police Magazine* asked police officers "Would tighter
restrictions on handgun ownership increase or enhance public safety
in your jurisdiction?" only 11.8 percent said "yes" and 88.2 percent
said "no." A follow up question asked, "if you answered 'no' to gun
control, please select the closest answer that describes why not."
The three most frequent answers were: "law would only be obeyed
by law-abiding citizens" (76.5 percent), "criminals would know
public was unarmed" (12.7 percent), and "ready availability of guns
anyway" (9.2 percent).

Typical of surveys of local police associations was one given of
police officers in the Lehigh and Northampton Counties,
Pennsylvania. Asked if "outlawing civilian gun ownership will result
in less crime," 11.4 percent said "agree" and 88.6 percent said
"disagree." See National Association of Chiefs of Police,"26th
Annual National Survey Results," 2014, http://www.nacoponline.
org/sr14.pdf; page copied from *Police Magazine* (2012),http://1.
bp.blogspot.com/-yXmOongpnOg/UBbdSQePl7I/
AAAAAAAADD8/Ki6JfMptgeA/s1600/Police percent2BMagazine
percent2BMarch percent2B2007.bmp; and survey of police officers
in Lehigh and Northampton Counties Pennsylvania, October 1997,
conducted from June 20, 1997 to September 10, 1997 (survey
response rate: 56 percent), http://www.sightm1911.com/lib/rkba/
police_survey.htm.

22. Jay Crane, "Obama comes home, talks gun violence," Chicago
    Maroon, February 19, 2013, http://chicagomaroon.
    com/2013/02/19/obama-comes-home-talks-gun-violence/.

23. Lois Beckett, "Fact-Checking Feinstein on the Assault Weapons
    Ban," ProPublica, September 24, 2014, https://www.propublica.org/
    article/fact-checking-feinstein-on-the-assault-weapons-ban.

24. Sasha Abramsky, "Wresting Gun Policy From the Hands of the
    Radical Fringe: A Q&A With Garen Wintemute," The Nation,

December 16, 2012, http://www.thenation.com/article/wresting-gun-policy-hands-radical-fringe-qa-garen-wintemute/.

25. For information on Jill Messing publications see https://webapp4.asu.edu/directory/person/1271146.

26. For a copy of Rosenthal's CV, see https://www.chapman.edu/our-faculty/files/curriculum-vita/Rosenthal-Lawrence-CV.pdf.

27. See for example, Tim Evans, "Indiana mom launches online crusade for gun control," *USA Today*, December 18, 2012, http://www.usatoday.com/story/news/nation/2012/12/18/mom-launches-gun-control-crusade/1776929/. For information on Marc Cooper, see John Stoehr, "We need gun laws that address the whole problem, not part," Al Jazeera, December 19, 2012 http://www.aljazeera.com/indepth/opinion/2012/12/2012121973233283925.html.

28. See Federal Bureau of Investigation,"Crime in the United States: 2014," Expanded Homicide Data, Table 8 https://www.fbi.gov/about-us/cjis/ucr/crime-in-the-u.s/2014/crime-in-the-u.s.-2014/tables/expanded-homicide-data/expanded_homicide_data_table_8_murder_victims_by_weapon_2010-2014.xls.

29. For a copy of the Dart Center's post on "Covering Guns" see http://crimeresearch.org/wp-content/uploads/2015/03/Dart-Center-Announcement-Bloomberg.png.

30. Michelle Ye Hee Lee, "Has there been one school shooting per week since Sandy Hook?" *Washington Post*, June 29, 2015, https://www.washingtonpost.com/news/fact-checker/wp/2015/06/29/has-there-been-one-school-shooting-per-week-since-sandy-hook/.

31. Bloomberg's updated numbers between January 1, 2013 and March 10, 2016, show 170 shootings in just over 166 weeks.

32. For videos from the show and Alcorn's response, see http://crimeresearch.org/2015/04/cprc-on-c-spans-washington-journal-on-peoples-changing-views-on-guns-bloombergs-research-director-explains-why-he-wont-debate/.

33. For a video of the segment I was on for the Stossel show, see https://www.youtube.com/watch?v=Ak9Lhd1riD0.

CHAPTER 3

1.   Clare Foran, "The Missing Data on Gun Violence," *The Atlantic*,
      January 21, 2016, http://www.theatlantic.com/politics/
      archive/2016/01/gun-control-laws-research/424956/.
2.   There are literally hundreds of such stories in the media. In April
      2013, ABC News 20/20 ran a segment titled: "CDC Ban on Gun
      Research Caused Lasting Damage." Sydney Lupkin, "CDC Ban on
      Gun Research Caused Lasting Damage," ABC News, April 9, 2013,
      http://abcnews.go.com/Health/cdc-ban-gun-research-caused-
      lasting-damage/story?id=18909347.
      In December 2013, NBC News warned: "While that money may be
      allocated in 2014…so far, that lack of funding has failed to entice
      researchers to answer the president's call [for more research]." Bill
      Briggs, "Obama's unlocking of federal funding ban on gun research
      yields little upshot in first year," NBC News, December 13, 2013,
      http://www.nbcnews.com/health/health-news/obamas-unlocking-
      federal-funding-ban-gun-research-yields-little-upshot-f2D11733547.
3.   Brad Plumber, "Gun research is allowed again. So what will we find
      out?" *Washington Post*, January 17, 2013, http://www.
      washingtonpost.com/blogs/wonkblog/wp/2013/01/17/gun-research-
      is-allowed-again-so-what-will-we-find-out/; and Joe Davidson,
      "Federal scientists can again research gun violence," *Washington
      Post*, January 17, 2013, http://www.washingtonpost.com/national/
      federal-scientists-can-again-research-gun-
      violence/2013/01/17/19d959fc-60e5-11e2-b05a-605528f6b712_
      story.html.
4.   Peter Henderson, "Scientists urge end to limits on gun safety
      research," Reuters, January 10, 2013, http://www.reuters.com/
      article/2013/01/10/us-usa-guns-scientists-
      idUSBRE90915F20130110.
5.   Lauren Pearle, "Unanswered Questions Gun Violence Researchers
      Would Tackle If They Had The Money," ABC News, January 31,
      2014, http://abcnews.go.com/US/unanswered-questions-gun-
      violence-researchers-tackle-money/story?id=22322439.
      The list of additional related quotes is quite long. On January 21,
      2014, Healthline News had this headline: "With Ban Lifted, New

Research Shows How Firearm Access Increases Homicides, Suicides," http://www.healthline.com/health-news/policy-gun-violence-research-ban-lifted-after-newtown-shooting-012114.

6. Michael Luo, "N.R.A. Stymies Firearms Research, Scientists Say," *New York Times,* January 25, 2011, http://www.nytimes.com/2011/01/26/us/26guns.html?ref=us&_r=0; and Michael Luo, "In Firearms Research, Cause Is Often the Missing Element," *New York Times,* January 25, 2011, http://www.nytimes.com/2011/01/26/us/26gunsresearch.html.

7. *Access Denied: How the Gun Lobby is Depriving Police, Policy Makers, and the Public of the Data We Need to Prevent Gun Violence,* Mayors Against Illegal Guns, January 2013, 2,15, http://libcloud.s3.amazonaws.com/9/c1/6/1017/3/access_denied.pdf.

8. Ibid., 15. The claim by Rosenberg that they "terrorized people" is available from this CBS News report: Mark Strassmann, "NRA, Congress stymied CDC gun research budget," CBS Evening News with Scott Pelley, January 17, 2013, http://www.cbsnews.com/news/nra-congress-stymied-cdc-gun-research-budget/. For Rosenberg's affiliation see http://www.taskforce.org/our-team/our-staff/mark-rosenberg-president-and-ceo.

9. Eliot Marshall, "Obama lifts ban on funding gun violence research," Science, January 16, 2013, http://news.sciencemag.org/2013/01/obama-lifts-ban-funding-gun-violence-research.

10. The quote is POLITICO's description of Ms. Sorenson's beliefs. Brett Norman, "Mayors: Do gun research right," POLITICO, January 9, 2013, http://www.politico.com/story/2013/01/mayors-group-blasts-restrictions-on-gun-research-85928_Page2.html.

11. Letter to Vice President Joseph P. Biden by 102 academics, January 10, 2013, https://crimelab.uchicago.edu/sites/crimelab.uchicago.edu/files/uploads/Biden%20Commission%20letter_20130110_final.pdf.

12. Letter to Senators Thad Cochran and Barbara Mikulski and Congressmen Harold Rogers and Nita Lowey, April 6, 2016, http://www.aafp.org/dam/AAFP/documents/advocacy/prevention/safety/LT-CON-GunResearch-040616.pdf.

13. National Institute of Justice, "Awards Related to: Research on Firearms and Violence," October 2013, http://nij.gov/funding/awards/pages/awards-list.aspx?solicitationid=3455.

14. National Institute of Health, "NIH calls for research projects examining violence," September 27, 2013, http://www.nih.gov/news/health/sep2013/nih-27.htm.

15. Briggs, "Obama's unlocking of federal funding ban on gun research yields little upshot in first year."

16. Steven Sumner et al., "Elevated Rates of Urban Firearm Violence and Opportunities for Prevention—Wilmington, Delaware," Division of Violence Prevention, National Center for Injury Prevention and Control, and Centers for Disease Control and Prevention, November 3, 2015, http://dhss.delaware.gov/dhss/dms/files/cdcgunviolencereport10315.pdf.

17. Anne Hoffman, "CDC releases final report on Wilmington's high rates of gun violence," Delaware Public Media, November 3, 2015, http://delawarepublic.org/post/cdc-releases-final-report-wilmington-s-high-rates-gun-violence#stream/0.

18. Reporting on fundraising; as of November 2013 they had raised 16 million dollars. See New Venture Fund, "The Fund for a Safer Future—2013 Action Fund," http://www.newventurefund.org/wp-content/uploads/FSF-2013ActionFund.pdf; Mitch Nauffts, "5 Questions for Ellen Alberding, President, Joyce Foundation," Philanthropy News Digest, January 10, 2013, http://www.philanthropynewsdigest.org/5-questions-for/ellen-alberding-joyce-foundation; and Open Society Foundations, "New Venture Fund,"http://www.opensocietyfoundations.org/about/programs/us-programs/grantees/new-venture-fund.

19. New Venture Fund, "The Fund for a Safer Future— 2013 Action Fund."

20. "Obama: $30 million for gun research," UPI, April 10, 2013, http://www.upi.com/Health_News/2013/04/11/Obama-30-million-for-gun-research/UPI-34631365653165/.

21. Briggs, "Obama's unlocking of federal funding ban on gun research yields little upshot in first year." .

22. Reid J. Epstein, "White House gun plan: An end run around the NRA," POLITICO, January 11, 2013, http://www.politico.com/

story/2013/01/wh-gun-plan-out-organize-the-nra-86049.html; and
Rick Cohen, "Will Deep-Pocket Foundations Join the Call for Gun
Control?" *Nonprofit Quarterly*, January 10, 2013, http://
nonprofitquarterly.org/policysocial-context/21621-will-deep-
pocket-foundations-join-the-call-for-gun-control.html.

23. Patrick McGreevy, "Lawmakers propose California center on gun
violence research," *Los Angeles Times*, March 17, 2016, http://
www.latimes.com/politics/la-pol-sac-california-gun-violence-center-
20160317-story.html.

24. Mayors Against Illegal Guns, *Access Denied*, 2.

25. Brad Plumber, "Gun research is allowed again. So what will we find
out?" *Washington Post*, January 17, 2013, http://www.
washingtonpost.com/blogs/wonkblog/wp/2013/01/17/gun-research-
is-allowed-again-so-what-will-we-find-out/); Liz Goodwin, "Can
Obama end the long fight over gun violence research?" Yahoo
News, January 17, 2013, http://news.yahoo.com/blogs/lookout/
obama-end-long-fight-over-gun-violence-research-201708897.html;
and Peter Henderson, "Scientists urge end to limits of gun safety
research," Reuters, January 10, 2013, http://www.reuters.com/
article/2013/01/10/us-usa-guns-scientists-
idUSBRE90915F20130110.

26. The 1997 appropriations bill covered the period from October 1,
1996 to September 30, 1997. The bill stated: "None of the funds
made available for injury prevention and control at the Centers for
Disease Control and Prevention may be used to advocate or promote
gun control."
The 2003 appropriations bill covered spending from October 1,
2002 to September 30, 2003, and it amended the 1997 bill to
include the words "in whole or in part." The funding debate rarely
mentions this change, and there are no obvious changes in research
output that occurred after this date. One of the very rare exceptions
that mentions this is provided by Lupkin, "CDC Ban on Gun
Research Caused Lasting Damage."
Finally, the 2012 appropriations bill, which expanded the
restrictions to all Health and Human Services agencies, was delayed
by disagreements between the Republican-controlled House and

Democrat Senate until December 23, 2011, so virtually none of the appropriations bill covered 2011.

27. I really want to thank Bret Jessee, a senior fellow with the Crime Prevention Research Center who is also a research director in the biomedical industry, for putting together all the data for us in this section on medical journal publications.

28. Whether one looks at the impact of the research immediately after the Dickey Amendment or whether you allow for a lag doesn't seem to make any real difference.

Table 1B: Funding Sources for Firearms Research: assuming no lag in impact on research (1992 to 2013)

	Share of research funded	Share of research federally funded
Pre-1997	7.8%	2.5%
1997 and later	16.7%	3.4%
Average over entire period	14.7%	3.2%

29. Ana Radelat, "ROI Miss: Gun-Control Groups Outspent Opponents 7 to 1 on TV," Advertising Age, December 12, 2013, http://adage.com/article/news/battle-gun-regulation-lobbying-beats-advertising/245640/.

30. John R. Lott Jr., "NFL hypocrisy—Bloomberg anti-gun ads ok but ad about 'protection' is banned?" Fox News, December 4, 2013, http://www.foxnews.com/opinion/2013/12/04/nfl-hypocrisy-bloomberg-anti-gun-ads-ok-but-ad-about-protection-is-banned.html.

31. "Putting Football Rivalries Aside, Mayors Unite Against Illegal Guns," YouTube video, posted by "maigcoalition," February 2, 2012, https://youtu.be/BO94AdhCg0k.

32. Zach Schonbrun and Michael Barbaro, "N.B.A. Lends Its Name and Its Stars to Campaign Against Gun Violence," *New York Times*, December 23, 2015, http://www.nytimes.com/2015/12/24/sports/basketball/nba-gun-violence-campaign-michael-bloomberg.html?_r=0.

33. Padmananda Rama, "Gun-Control Battle Spills Over To Super Bowl Ads," NPR, February 3, 2013, http://www.npr.org/sections/

thetwo-way/2013/02/03/170987600/gun-control-battle-spills-over-to-super-bowl-ads; Associated Press, "Gun-control group airs Super Bowl ad," Politico, February 2, 2013, http://www.politico.com/story/2013/02/super-bowl-2013-bloomberg-mayors-group-gun-control-ad-087095; Amy Davidson, "The Gun Bowl: Bloomberg's Super Bowl Ad," *The New Yorker*, February 3, 2013, http://www.newyorker.com/news/amy-davidson/the-gun-bowl-bloombergs-super-bowl-ad; Brett LoGiurato, "Mike Bloomberg's Gun Control Group Will Air This Devastating Super Bowl Ad Slamming A Big NRA Flip-Flop," Business Insider, February 3, 2013, http://www.businessinsider.com/bloomberg-gun-control-super-bowl-ad-nra-wayne-lapierre-children-2013-2; and Taylor Bigler, "Bloomberg-funded gun control ad airs during Super Bowl," The Daily Caller, February 4, 2013, http://dailycaller.com/2013/02/04/bloomberg-funded-gun-control-ad-airs-during-super-bowl-video/.

34. For the amazingly inaccurate Bloomberg gun control ad, see "Bloomberg ad on gun free zones in Nevada," YouTube video, posted by John Lott, March 3, 2015, https://www.youtube.com/watch?v=AxzY4mqABhE.

35. George Pabst, "Bloomberg's PAC makes $150,000 ad buy against Clarke," *Milwaukee Wisconsin Journal Sentinel*, August 8, 2014, http://www.jsonline.com/news/statepolitics/bloombergs-pac-makes-150000-ad-buy-against-clarke-b99327098z1-270469951.html.

36. For Sheriff David Clarke's appearance on Fox Friends on August 16, 2016, see $150,000 Plan To Oust PRO-GUN Sheriff BACKFIRES: Bloomberg BLOW$ It !", YouTube video, posted by "61ys," August 16, 2014, https://www.youtube.com/watch?v=3AP3-GDxAzc.

37. Rachelle Baillon, "'The voters of this county have said they like my style:' Sheriff Clarke, on his primary victory," Fox 6 Now, August 13, 2014, http://fox6now.com/2014/08/13/the-voters-of-this-county-have-said-they-like-my-style-sheriff-clarke-on-his-primary-victory/.

38. Laura Vozzella, "Bloomberg's gun-control group bankrolls $1.5 million ad buy in second Va. race," *Washington Post*, October 22, 2015, https://www.washingtonpost.com/local/virginia-politics/bloomberg-gun-control-group-pours-15-million-into-va-senate-

race/2015/10/22/8e1ee96a-78d6-11e5-b9c1-f03c48c96ac2_story.
html.

39. Russ Choma, "Gun Groups Locked and Loaded for Nov. 4," OpenSecrets.org, October 6, 2014, http://www.opensecrets.org/ news/2014/10/gun-groups-locked-and-loaded-for-nov-4/.

40. John M. Leventhal, Julie R. Gaither, and Robert Sege, "Hospitalizations Due to Firearm Injuries in Children and Adolescents," *Pediatrics* 133, no. 2 (February 2014), http:// pediatrics.aappublications.org/content/pediatrics/early/2014/01/22/ peds.2013-1809.full.pdf; and Michelle Healy, "Study: 20 young people a day hospitalized for gun injuries," *USA Today*, January 27, 2014, http://www.usatoday.com/story/news/nation/2014/01/27/ guns-children-hospitalizations/4796999/.

41. John R. Lott Jr., "ABC News reports on guns mislead Americans," Fox News, February 7, 2014, http://www.foxnews.com/ opinion/2014/02/07/abc-news-reports-on-guns-mislead-americans. html. For the video for the ABC "World News Tonight" segment, see Diane Sawyer, "Young Guns," ABC News, January 31, 2014, http://abcnews.go.com/video/embed?id=2225837.

42. "Guns in America town hall with Obama transcript (full text)," CNN, January 7, 2016, http://www.cnn.com/2016/01/07/politics/ transcript-obama-town-hall-guns-in-america/.

43. Arthur L. Kellermann et al., "Gun Ownership as a Risk Factor for Homicide in the Home," *The New England Journal of Medicine* (October 1993).

44. Ibid., 1084–91.

45. The interesting letter that provoked this response from Kellermann et al. was written by students in a graduate statistics class at St. Louis University. See the New England Journal of Medicine (Feb. 3, 1994): 366, 368. The estimated rate at which defensive gun uses result in the death of the criminal is derived by comparing the estimated number of defensive gun uses with the number of justifiable homicides. The justifiable-homicide number is obviously an underestimate, and it implies that the actual rate of criminal deaths from defensive gun uses is somewhat higher than reported in

the text, but it could be several times higher and not affect the overall statement.

46. The cases for 2013 are as follows:

1) Colorado Springs, Colorado, December 24, 2013: UK Daily News reports: "The Colorado man who police say shot and killed his 14-year-old stepdaughter after allegedly mistaking her for a burglar has been identified as a highly decorated Army officer." Alexandra Klausner and Snejana Farberov, "Distraught Bronze Star-winning stepdad who shot girl dead 'as she tried to sneak into the house' could face no charges under 'Make My Day' law," UK Daily News, December 24, 2013, http://www.dailymail.co.uk/news/article-2528912/Pictured-Girl-14-shot-dead-stepfather-mistaken-burglar-trying-sneak-house.html.

2) Chickamauga, Georgia, November 27, 2013: New York Daily News describes the tragedy this way: "The shooter, Joe Hendrix, is not facing charges for fatally shooting 72-year-old Ronald Westbrook, who tried to get into his northwest Georgia home early Wednesday. Authorities say Westbrook was lost and disoriented." Philip Caulfield, "Wandering man with Alzheimer's disease mistaken for a burglar, shot and killed," *New York Daily News*, November 29, 2013, http://www.nydailynews.com/news/national/wandering-man-alzheimer-mistaken-burglar-shot-killed-article-1.1532714.

3) Winter Haven, Florida, November 27, 2013: Bay News 9 (St. Petersburg, Florida) has this: "A 26-year-old Winter Haven woman is dead and her 52-year-old mother has been charged with shooting her in an apparent case of mistaken identity, police said." Erin Maloney, "Police: Polk mom mistakes daughter for boyfriend, shoots and kills her," Bay News 9, November 28, 2013, http://www.baynews9.com/content/news/baynews9/news/article.html/content/news/articles/bn9/2013/11/26/wither_haven_mother_.html.

4) Dearborn, Michigan, November 7, 2013: The UK Independent reports: "Renisha McBride was shot on 2 November while reportedly seeking help after a car accident at 2.30am.... [The homeowner] mistook Ms. McBride for an intruder." Heather Saul and Tomas Livanda, "Renisha McBride death: Man who shot

teenager claims his gun discharged by accident," UK Independent, November 8, 2013, http://www.independent.co.uk/news/world/ americas/renisha-mcbride-death-man-who-shot-teenager-claims-his-gun-discharged-by-accident-8928919.html.

5) Longmont, Colorado, September 8, 2013: CNN describes the tragedy this way: "Galley and Pranil heard a noise and went to check it out, the brother told CNN affiliate KUSA on Sunday. 'We thought maybe there was an intruder in the house and maybe some people knew we moved, and they were coming to check if we got everything so we started clearing the house,' Pranil told KUSA. But the intruder turned out to be Premila, who jumped out of a closet as a harmless joke, according to her family. 'The door opened and she kind of, like, screamed and then Nerrek pulled the trigger,' her 12-year-old cousin told KUSA." Emma Lacey-Bordeaux, "Colorado teen shot and killed in prank gone wrong," CNN, September 9, 2013, http://www.cnn.com/2013/09/08/justice/colorado-teen-accidental-shooting/index.html.

6) Orlando, Florida, March 23, 2013: New York Daily News notes: "A 12-year-old mistaken for a home invader in Florida was shot and killed by his older brother in a heartbreaking tragedy." Sasha Goldstein, "Orlando boy shoots, kills younger brother, 12, after mistaking him for a home invader," New York Daily News, March 23, 2013, http://www.nydailynews.com/news/national/boy-shoots-brother-12-thinking-intruder-article-1.1297242.

7) Sterling, Virginia, March 18, 2013: ABC News writes: "[A very drunk] Caleb Gordley climbed in through the window of the house he thought was his.... But it wasn't Caleb Gordley's house. It was the home two doors down from his own...Startled, Wilder grabbed the 40-caliber pistol equipped with a laser and flashlight that he kept next to his bed, thinking a thief was breaking into his home at 2:30 a.m." Despite multiple warnings to stop and leave the house, Gordley continued to go up the stairs to where Wilder's girlfriend was staying. After a warning shot, Wilder fatally shot Gordley. Gwen Gowen and Alexa Valiente, "Parents Cry Murder After Drunk Teen Killed in Home Invasion," ABC News, January 10, 2014, http://abcnews.go.com/US/parents-cry-murder-drunk-teen-

killed-home-invasion/story?id=21474534.

8) Yakima County, Washington, March 10, 2013: The Associated Press describes the case where a man mistook his wife for an intruder early in the morning actually shooting her once. "Yakima man shoots pregnant wife, mistaking her for an intruder," Associated Press, March 10, 2013, http://www.oregonlive.com/ pacific-northwest-news/index.ssf/2013/03/yakima_man_shoots_ pregnant_wif.html.

Cases for 2012:

1) Wendell man tells 911 dispatcher he shot teen who entered his home See http://www.wral.com/wendell-man-tells-911-dispatcher-he-shot-teen-who-entered-his-home/11919599/.

2) Mike Odom, "Three South Alabama teens charged with murder in Summer Moody case," GulfCoastNewsToday.com, November 30, 2012, http://www.gulfcoastnewstoday.com/area_news/ article_0587b800-3b05-11e2-abdb-001a4bcf887a.html.

3) "Man, 84, admits killing nephew after mistaking him for burglar," The Guardian, November 1, 2012, http://www. theguardian.com/uk/2012/nov/01/man-admits-killing-nephew-burglar.

4) Sam Baranowski, "Shooter mistakenly kills man while trying to scare burglars," Fox 21 News, October 17, 2012, http://www. fox21news.com/news/story.aspx?id=814252#.Uw6qNvldUWI.

5) "NorCal man shoots and kills his girlfriend after mistaking her for an intruder," CBS San Francisco, October 15, 2012, http:// sanfrancisco.cbslocal.com/2012/10/15/norcal-man-shoots-kills-girlfriend-after-mistaking-her-for-intruder/.

6) Father shoots and kills son after mistaking him for burglar. Rosemary Sobol and Jeremy Gorner, "Cops: Retired detective fatally shoots son after mistaking him for intruder," October 9, 2012, http://articles.chicagotribune.com/2012-10-09/news/chi-cops-retired-detective-fatally-shoots-son-after-mistaking-him-for-intruder-20121009_1_michael-griffin-james-griffin-stephen-griffin.

7) "Conn. man kills masked burglar, then discovers it's his 15-year-old son," USA Today, September 28, 2012, http://usatoday30. usatoday.com/news/nation/story/2012/09/28/conn-man-kills-

masked-teen-then-discovers-its-his-son/57850736/1.

8) "Charles Williams Shot, Killed By Wife Mistaking Him For Intruder: New Orleans Police" http://www.huffingtonpost. com/2012/09/11/charles-williams-shot-killed-wife-mistakes-him-for-intruder_n_1873644.html.

9) "Off-duty cop shoots, kills son after mistaking him for intruder," Fox News, July 22, 2012, http://www.foxnews.com/us/2012/07/22/ off-duty-cop-shoots-kills-son-after-mistaking-him-for-intruder/.

10) Youlande, Du Preez, "Dad mistakes daughter for burglar," IOL, May 19, 2012, http://www.iol.co.za/news/crime-courts/dad-mistakes-daughter-for-burglar-1.1300063#.Uw6khvldUWI.

11) NBC News Staff and WDSU 6, "Cops: Woman shoots, kills boyfriend thinking he's an intruder," NBC News, September 11, 2012, http://www.abc12.com/story/16589203/police-woman-shoots-kills-boyfriend-thinking-hes-an-intruder.

Cases for 2011:

1) Stewart Maclean, "Father 'shot dead teenage daughter he thought was a burglar,'" The Telegraph, November 4, 2011, http://www. telegraph.co.uk/news/worldnews/africaandindianocean/ southafrica/8870186/Father-shot-dead-teenage-daughter-he-thought-was-a-burglar.html.

2) Gary Taylor, "Son won't face charges after accidentally shooting father to death," Orlando Sentinel, June 8, 2011, http://articles. orlandosentinel.com/2011-06-08/news/os-son-shoots-father-killed-accident-20110608_1_shooting-father-criminal-charges-camper.

3) WALA, "Alabama college student mistaken for burglar shot to death" Private Officer News, January 13, 2011, http://privateofficer. org/alabama-college-student-mistaken-for-burglar-shot-to-death-www-privateofficer-com/.

4) Fox Carolina Staff, "Jackson Co. Uncle Accidentally Shoots, Kills Niece," Fox Carolina, February 18, 2011, http://www.foxcarolina. com/story/14757924/deputies-jackson-co-uncle-accidentally-shoots-kills-niece-2-18-2011

5) "Teenage boy thought his cousin was a burglar, gets his gun, and shoots her dead," January 12, 2011, http://www.

montgomeryadvertiser.com/article/20110112/NEWS02/101120336/
Police-Cousin-was-mistaken-for-burglar-shot-dead.

CHAPTER 4

1. Emily Miller, "Dick Heller challenges D.C.'s gun registration
    scheme, files for quick ruling in Heller II," *Washington Times*,
    December 11, 2013, http://www.washingtontimes.com/news/2013/
    dec/11/dick-heller-challenges-dcs-gun-registration-files-/print/.
2. Hawaii State Senate Joint Committee Hearing, Committee on the
    Judiciary and Committee on Transportation and Intergovernmental
    Affairs, Tuesday, (February 15, 2000).
3. Andrew Blake, "Maryland guts gun-control 'ballistic fingerprints'
    program after zero hits in 15 years," *Washington Times*, November
    9, 2015, http://www.washingtontimes.com/news/2015/nov/9/
    maryland-guts-gun-control-ballistic-fingerprints-p/.
4. Fredric Dicker, "Cuomo whacks Pataki gun law," *New York Post*,
    April 2, 2012, http://nypost.com/2012/04/02/cuomo-whacks-
    pataki-gun-law/.
5. Erin Cox, "Maryland scraps gun "fingerprint" database after 15
    failed years," *The Baltimore Sun*, November 7, 2015, http://www.
    baltimoresun.com/news/maryland/bs-md-bullet-casings-20151107-
    story.html.
6. John J. Tobin, Jr., *MD-IBIS Progress Report #2: Integrated
    Ballistics Identification System*, Maryland State Police Forensic
    Sciences Division, September 2004, http://www.ocshooters.com/
    Reports/cobis/ibis.pdf.
7. Fredric Dicker, "Cuomo whacks Pataki gun law," *New York Post*,
    April 2, 2012, http://nypost.com/2012/04/02/cuomo-whacks-
    pataki-gun-law/.
8. David Snyder, "Report Faults Md. Ballistics Database," *Washington
    Post*, January 18, 2005, http://www.washingtonpost.com/wp-dyn/
    articles/A16475-2005Jan17.html?tid=a_inl.
9. "Ballistic Fingerprints," Encyclopedia.com, 2004, http://
    crimeresearch.org/wp-content/uploads/2015/11/Webster-
    predictions-about-ballistic-fingerprinting.png.

10. Brian J. Heard, *Handbook of Firearms and Ballistics: Examining and Interpreting Forensic Evidence*, 2nd ed. (Hoboken: John Wiley Sons, 2008).

11. "Connecticut Handgun Licensing Law Associated With 40% Drop in Gun Homicides," John Hopkins Bloomberg School of Public Health, June 2015, http://www.jhsph.edu/news/news-releases/2015/connecticut-handgun-licensing-law-associated-with-40-percent-drop-in-gun-homicides.html.

12. The authors say that they limit the data to 2005 because one paper that they cite examined only ten years after a law that they were investigating (p. 4: "We conclude the post-law period in 2005 to limit extrapolation in our predictions of the counterfactual to 10 years, as has been done previously"). But just because a study on cigarette smoking looks at the twelve years after the law was in effect (not ten as claimed—Proposition 99 went into effect on January 1, 1989 and their sample went until 2000), doesn't explain why a study on crime would do the same thing. Indeed, the reason given by the authors that the Bloomberg School of Public Health researchers cite isn't applicable to the current paper (p. 16: "It ends in 2000 because at about this time anti-tobacco measures were implemented across many states, invalidating them as potential control units"). There was no similar adoption across the states of handgun licensing laws. Yet, if the Bloomberg School of Public Health researchers had gone for this twelfth year as the study that they cite does, it would have dramatically altered their results.

13. Here are the two states that the Bloomberg School of Public Health researchers claim are the best matches to create their synthetic Connecticut. Just because there were some states that could be combined using historical data to match the changes in Connecticut's doesn't mean that you expect them to continue to predict future changes. As a comparison, suppose that you found five stocks that when combined closely matched the changes in Apple stock over the last year, would you want to bet that those stocks would closely match changes in Apple's stock over the next year? Just because you had a historical relationship that matched the changes over the last year, it wouldn't tell you very much about what

would happen next year. The same thing applies to states; just because Nevada or California firearm homicides happened to move with Connecticut's over the years from 1984 to 1995, why would you expect political, police, economic, demographic, and other changes to cause their crime rates to change the same way from 1996 to 2005?

14. "Connecticut's 1995 gun permit law prompts federal bill offered by state's delegation," Fox Business, June 11, 2015, http://www. foxbusiness.com/markets/2015/06/11/connecticut-15-gun-permit-law-prompts-federal-bill-offered-by-state-delegation.html; Jeff Guo, "Gun killings fell by 40 percent after Connecticut passed this law," *Washington Post*, June 12, 2015, https://www.washingtonpost. com/blogs/govbeat/wp/2015/06/12/gun-killings-fell-by-40-percent-after-connecticut-passed-this-law/; Michelle Gorman, "Handgun Law in Connecticut Helped Decrease Gun Homicides," *Newsweek*, June 11, 2015, http://www.newsweek.com/handgun-law-connecticut-helped-decrease-gun-homicides-342363; Robert Preidt, "Tough Handgun Law Linked to Lower Gun-Related Murder Rate in Connecticut," US News World Report, June 11, 2016, http:// health.usnews.com/health-news/articles/2015/06/11/tough-handgun-law-linked-to-lower-gun-related-murder-rate-in-connecticut; "And then there's guns," *Philadelphia Inquirer*, June 11, 2015, http://www.philly.com/philly/blogs/attytood/And-then-theres-guns.html; Neal Colgrass, "Gun Law Saved 296 Lives in One State," Newser, June 13, 2015, http://www.newser.com/ story/208253/permit-law-sharply-cut-gun-violence-in-one-state. html; John Fritze, "Van Hollen crafts gun licensing bill," *Baltimore Sun*, June 11, 2015, http://www.baltimoresun.com/news/maryland/ politics/blog/bs-md-van-hollen-gun-20150611-story.html; John Timmer, "Connecticut gun controls estimated to have cut fatal shootings by 40%," Arstechnica, June 13, 2015, http://arstechnica. com/science/2015/06/connecticut-gun-controls-estimated-to-have-cut-fatal-shootings-by-40/; and Samantha Lachman, "Connecticut Gun Control Law Sharply Reduced Gun-Related Violence, Report Says," HuffPost Politics, June 15, 2015, http://www.huffingtonpost. com/2015/06/12/connecticut-gun-control-_n_7570852.html.

15. Bindu Kalesan et al., "Firearm legislation and firearm mortality in the USA: a cross-sectional, state-level study," *Lancet* 387, no. 10030 (March 2016), http://www.thelancet.com/journals/lancet/article/PIIS0140-6736(15)01026-0/abstract.

16. Ike Swetlitz, "Could these 3 laws reduce gun deaths by 90 percent?," PBS Newshour, March 11, 2016, http://www.pbs.org/newshour/rundown/could-these-3-laws-reduce-gun-deaths-by-90-percent/; Melissa Healy, "Aiming to drive down gun deaths? Put these three laws on the books, researchers say," *Los Angeles Times*, March 10, 2016, http://www.latimes.com/science/sciencenow/la-sci-sn-gun-deaths-three-laws-20160310-story.html; Carina Storrs, "Study: 3 federal laws could reduce gun deaths by more than 90%," CNN, March 10, 2016, http://www.cnn.com/2016/03/10/health/gun-laws-background-checks-reduce-deaths/; and Reuters,"Background checks for gun buyers could save lives, U.S. study finds," Business Insider, March 10, 2016, http://www.businessinsider.com/r-background-checks-for-gun-buyers-could-save-lives-us-study-finds-2016-3.

17. Bindu Kalesan and John Lott, "Lancet study: universal background checks effective in lowering gun-related deaths," KPCC 89.3 FM, March 14, 2016, http://www.scpr.org/programs/airtalk/2016/03/14/47175/lancet-study-universal-background-checks-effective/.

18. For the link to the U.S. Centers for Disease Control website, see http://webappa.cdc.gov/sasweb/ncipc/dataRestriction_inj.html.

19. Jens Ludwig and Philip J. Cook, "Homicide and suicide rates associated with implementation of the Brady Handgun Violence Prevention Act," *Journal of the American Medical Association* 284 (2000): 585-591.

20. John R. Lott Jr., "Impact of the Brady Act on Homicide and Suicide Rates," *Journal of the American Medical Association* 284, no. 21 (December 2000): 2718.

CHAPTER 5

1. "Officials: Gun-toting veteran saves life of Bastrop deputy," *Austin Statesman*, January 28, 2016, http://www.statesman.com/news/news/local/officials-gun-toting-veteran-saves-life-of-bastrop/nqD7c/.

2. Stephanie Farr, "Police: Gun owner saved cop from attack by kids," *Philadelphia Inquirer*, February 11, 2016, http://articles.philly.com/2016-02-11/news/70513387_1_chitwood-teens-gangsters.

3. David I. Swedler et al., "Firearm Prevalence and Homicides of Law Enforcement Officers in the United States," *American Journal of Public Health* (August 2015), http://crimeresearch.org/wp-content/uploads/2015/08/274428440-Firearm-Prevalence-Study.pdf.

4. Maggie Fox, "More Police Are Killed in States With More Guns, Study Finds," NBC News, August 14, 2015, http://www.nbcnews.com/health/health-news/more-guns-more-dead-cops-study-finds-n409356; Joanna Walter, "High gun ownership linked to high rate of police officer deaths, study shows," The Guardian, August 14, 2015, http://www.msn.com/en-us/news/us/high-gun-ownership-linked-to-high-rate-of-police-officer-deaths-study/ar-BBlKMmv?ocid=spartandhp; and Frank Main, "NRA blasts study linking more guns to more cop murders," *Chicago Sun-Times*, August 13, 2015, http://chicago.suntimes.com/news/nra-blasts-study-linking-more-guns-to-more-cop-murders/.

5. David Mustard, "The Impact of Gun Laws on Police Deaths," *Journal of Law and Economics* (October 2001): 635–657.

6. Here is a simple version of their regression explaining the number of police officers feloniously killed over the years from 1996 to 2013, but without accounting for the time effects that we just discussed. Before going through the results, the media coverage of this study is incorrect in claiming that more guns are associated with more police killings. What the journal article actually measures is not the gun ownership, but the percentage of suicides committed with guns. This regression looks at the total number of police feloniously murdered with their measure of "gun ownership" and the number of police officers. In this regression, it appears that a one percentage point increase in the percent of suicides committed with guns increase, there is a significant 1.8 percent increase in the total

number of police killed. Poisson regression with coefficients (shown as incident rate ratios) and the absolute z-statistics are shown in parentheses: Total Police Killed = 1.018 (1.98) percentage of suicides committed with guns + 1.00003 (2.46) Total Number of LEO + Dummy variable for each state + intercept

Number of Observations = 916 Chi-Square = 1018.55

Just accounting for the changes in crime rates over time, completely reverses the claims made in the American Journal of Public Health. It now appears that with a one percentage point increase in the percent of suicides committed with guns, there is a significant 2.25 percent decrease in the total number of police killed.

Total Police Killed = 0.9776 (1.59) percentage of suicides committed with guns + 1.00003 (2.22) Total Number of LEO + Dummy variable for each state + Dummy variable for each year + intercept

Number of Observations = 916 Chi-Square = 1139.02

Including the other variables that they have used in their estimates along with the year fixed effects produce an even more statistically significant drop in police felonious killings. In that case, a one percentage point increase in the percent of suicides committed with guns, there is a significant 3.7 percent decrease in the total number of police killed.

Total Police Killed = 0.9638 (2.65) percentage of suicides committed with guns + 1.00004 (2.65) Total Number of LEO + 1.87 (1.04) Alcohol Consumption + 1.000009 (0.50) Median Income + 0.0000000045 (2.69) Percent of the population that is black + 0.02226 (0.72) Percent of the population that is Hispanic + 0.9994 (0.09) Poverty Rate + 1.002 (2.29) Violent Crime Rate + .9994 (3.55) Property Crime Rate + 0.9732 (0.48) Urbanization +0.000068 (1.05) Percent of Population that is 15 to 29 years of age + Dummy variable for each state + Dummy variable for each year + intercept

Number of Observations = 864 Chi-Square = 1139.02

7.   David Olson and Michael Maltz, "Right–to-Carry Concealed Weapon Laws and Homicide in Large US Counties: The Effect of Weapon Types, Victim Characteristics, and Victim-Offender

Relationships," *Journal of Law Economics* (October 2001): 747–770.

8. Alan Dershowitz, "Gun Control in America," Piers Morgan Tonight, CNN, December 18, 2012, http://transcripts.cnn.com/TRANSCRIPTS/1212/18/pmt.01.html.

9. Alan Dershowitz, "Mayor Bloomberg Speaks on Guns; The Right to Bear Arms; Acts of Heroism," *Piers Morgan Tonight*, CNN, July 23, 2012, http://transcripts.cnn.com/TRANSCRIPTS/1207/23/pmt.01.html. There are many similar statements over time. "The NRA buys scholars. They buy statistics. It's just wrong." See Alan Dershowitz, "Guns in America," *Piers Morgan Tonight*, January 7, 2013, http://transcripts.cnn.com/TRANSCRIPTS/1301/07/pmt.01.html.

10. Intelligence2 Debates, "Guns reduce crime," October 28, 2008, http://intelligencesquaredus.org/debates/past-debates/item/598-guns-reduce-crime.

11. James Q. Wilson, email to author, November 25, 2008.

12. It is an old line of attack, and it shows how desperate gun control advocates can become in trying to destroy their opponents. Then Congressman, now Senator, Charles Schumer (D-NY) wrote the following on September 4, 1996 in the *Wall Street Journal*: "I'd like to point out one other 'association.' The Associated Press reports that Prof. Lott's fellowship at the University of Chicago is funded by the Olin Foundation, which is 'associated with the Olin Corporation,' one of the nation's largest gun manufacturers. Maybe that's a coincidence, too. But it's also a fact." Others were even more direct. In a letter that the Violence Policy Center mass-mailed to newspapers around the country, M. Kristen Rand, the Center's federal policy director, wrote:
"Lott's work was, in essence, funded by the firearms industry—the primary beneficiary of increased handgun sales. Lott is the John M. Olin fellow at the University of Chicago law school, a position founded by the Olin Foundation. The foundation was established by John Olin of the Olin Corp., manufacturer of Winchester ammunition and maker of the infamous 'Black Talon' bullet." (See, as one of many examples, "Gun Industry Paid," *Omaha World*

Herald, March 10, 1997, 8.)

Congressman Schumer's letter elicited a powerful response from William Simon, the Olin Foundation's president and former U.S. Secretary of the Treasury, in the *Wall Street Journal* for September 6, 1996:

An Insult to Our Foundation

As president of the John M. Olin Foundation, I take great umbrage at Rep. Charles Schumer's scurrilous charge (Letters to the Editor, Sept. 4) that our foundation underwrites bogus research to advance the interests of companies that manufacture guns and ammunition. He asserts (falsely) that the John M. Olin Foundation is "associated" with the Olin Corp. and (falsely again) that the Olin Corp. is one of the nation's largest gun manufacturers. Mr. Schumer then suggests on the basis of these premises that Prof. John Lott's article on gun-control legislation (editorial page, Aug. 28) must have been fabricated because his research fellowship at the University of Chicago was funded by the John M. Olin Foundation.

This is an outrageous slander against our foundation, the Olin Corp., and the scholarly integrity of Prof. Lott. Mr. Schumer would have known that his charges were false if he had taken a little time to check his facts before rushing into print. Others have taken the trouble to do so. For example, Stephen Chapman of the Chicago Tribune looked into the charges surrounding Mr. Lott's study, and published an informative story in the Aug. 15 issue of that paper, which concluded that, in conducting his research, Prof. Lott was not influenced either by the John M. Olin Foundation or by the Olin Corp. Anyone wishing to comment on this controversy ought first to consult Mr. Chapman's article and, more importantly, should follow his example of sifting the facts before reaching a conclusion. For readers of the Journal, here are the key facts.

The John M. Olin Foundation, of which I have been president for nearly 20 years, is an independent foundation whose purpose is to support individuals and institutions working to strengthen the free enterprise system. We support academic programs at the finest institutions in the nation, including the University of Chicago, Harvard, Yale, Stanford, Columbia, the University of Virginia, and many others. We do not tell scholars what to write or what to say.

The foundation was created by the personal fortune of the late John M. Olin, and is not associated with the Olin Corp. The Olin Corp. has never sought to influence our deliberations. Our trustees have never taken into account the corporate interests of the Olin Corp. or any other company when reviewing grant proposals. We are as independent of the Olin Corp. as the Ford Foundation is of the Ford Motor Co.

The John M. Olin Foundation has supported for many years a program in law and economics at the University of Chicago Law School. This program is administered and directed by a committee of faculty members in the law school. This committee, after reviewing many applications in a very competitive process, awarded a research fellowship to Mr. Lott. We at the foundation had no knowledge of who applied for these fellowships, nor did we ever suggest that Mr. Lott should be awarded one of them. We did not commission his study, nor, indeed, did we even know of it until last month, when Mr. Lott presented his findings at a conference sponsored by a Washington think tank.

As a general rule, criticism of research studies should be based on factual grounds rather than on careless and irresponsible charges about the motives of the researcher. Mr. Lott's study should be evaluated on its own merits without imputing motives to him that do not exist. I urge Mr. Schumer to check his facts more carefully in the future.

Finally, it was incorrectly reported in the *Journal* (Sept. 5) that the John M. Olin Foundation is 'headed by members of the family that founded the Olin Corp.' This is untrue. The trustees and officers of the foundation have been selected by virtue of their devotion to John Olin's principles, not by virtue of family connections. Of our seven board members, only one is a member of the Olin family. None of our officers is a member of the Olin family—neither myself as president, nor our secretary-treasurer, nor our executive director.

13. Alan Dershowitz, "Mayor Bloomberg Speaks on Guns; The Right to Bear Arms; Acts of Heroism," *Piers Morgan Tonight*, CNN, July 23, 2012, http://transcripts.cnn.com/TRANSCRIPTS/1207/23/pmt.01.html.

14.   Christopher Goins, "Gun Control Won't Make Mass Shootings
      Less Likely to Happen, Academic Says," CNSNews.com, September
      4, 2012, http://cnsnews.com/news/article/gun-control-won-t-make-
      mass-shootings-less-likely-happen-academic-says.

15.   This statement is taken from the Crime Prevention Research Center
      website at http://crimeresearch.org/about-us/.

16.   Frank Smyth, "The Times Has Finally (Quietly) Outed an NRA-
      Funded 'Independent' Scholar," The Progressive, April 23, 2014,
      http://www.progressive.org/news/2014/04/187663/times-has-
      finally-quietly-outed-nra-funded-"independent"-scholar; Eli Stokols,
      "NRA money behind lawsuit challenging new Colo. gun control
      laws," Fox 31 Denver, May 29, 2013, http://kdvr.com/2013/05/29/
      nra-money-behind-lawsuit-challenging-new-colo-gun-control-laws/.

17.   See Smyth, "The Times Has Finally (Quietly) Outed an NRA-
      Funded 'Independent' Scholar"; and Frank Smyth, "Senate witness
      on weapons ban funded by gun lobby," MSNBC, February 27,
      2013, http://www.msnbc.com/msnbc/senate-witness-weapons-ban-
      funded-gun-l.
      An op-ed that Kopel recently had at the *New York Times* had to be
      updated to acknowledge that he "has received grant money from the
      National Rifle Association's Civil Rights Defense Fund" (see David
      Kopel, "Bloomberg's Gun Control That Goes Too Far for the
      Average Citizen," *New York Times*, April 18, 2014, http://www.
      nytimes.com/roomfordebate/2014/04/17/can-bloomberg-take-on-
      the-nra/bloombergs-gun-control-that-goes-too-far-for-the-average-
      citizen.
      Kopel also caused some consternation at the *Wall Street Journal*.
      The newspaper had just criticized Jonathan Gruber for not
      acknowledging the money that he was getting from the Obama
      administration. Yet, Kopel put the *Wall Street Journal* in a difficult
      position as he had also not acknowledged his funding source in
      op-eds that he had published in their newspaper. See "Health
      Experts and Double Standards," *Wall Street Journal*, January 14,
      2010, http://www.wsj.com/articles/SB10001424052748704586504574654362679868966.

18. I was told by many people in the Bush Administration that Hart was rewarded for being a Democrat who had supported Bush during the 2000 election. See U.S. Department of Justice, National Institute of Justice Annual Report, 2001, https://www.ncjrs.gov/pdffiles1/nij/195076.pdf.

19. Devon B. Adams and Lara E. Reynolds, Bureau of Justice Statistics 2002: At a Glance, U.S. Department of Justice, August 2002, http://www.bjs.gov/content/pub/pdf/bjsg02.pdf.

20. Ed Meese, who had been the U.S. Attorney General during the Reagan administration, told me about Greenfeld's background.

21. Eric Lichtblau, "Profiling Report Leads to a Clash and a Demotion," *New York Times*, August 24, 2005, http://www.nytimes.com/2005/08/24/us/front%20page/profiling-report-leads-to-a-clash-and-a-demotion.html?_r=0.

CHAPTER 6

1. Taylor Pittman, "A How-To Guide On Dealing With A 'Gunsplainer'," Huffington Post, February 12, 2016, http://www.huffingtonpost.com/entry/a-how-to-guide-on-dealing-with-a-gunsplainer_us_56bdef3ae4b0c3c55050d743.

2. Hollye Dexter was interviewed on KABC's McIntyre in the Morning on January 8, 2016. http://crimeresearch.org/2016/01/cprc-on-los-angeles-big-talk-radio-station-kabc-to-discuss-obamas-new-gun-regulations/.

3. Emily Swanson, "U.S. gun ownership drops to lowest level, poll finds," Associated Press, March 10, 2015, http://www.mercurynews.com/nation-world/ci_27682228/u-s-gun-ownership-drops-lowest-level-poll.

4. Ibid.

5. Michael Dimock, Carroll Doherty, and Leah Christian, "Why Own a Gun? Protection Is Now Top Reason," Pew Research Center, March 12, 2013, http://www.people-press.org/files/legacy-pdf/03-12-13%20Gun%20Ownership%20Release.pdf.

6. John R. Lott Jr., *The Bias Against Guns: Why Almost Everything You've Heard About Guns is Wrong* (Washington, D.C.: Regnery Publishing, 2003).

7. John R. Lott, Jr., "ABC News reports on guns mislead Americans," Fox News, February 7, 2014, http://www.foxnews.com/opinion/2014/02/07/abc-news-reports-on-guns-mislead-americans.html.

8. Lydia Saad, "Self-Reported Gun Ownership in U.S. Is Highest Since 1993," Gallup, October 26, 2011, http://www.gallup.com/poll/150353/Self-Reported-Gun-Ownership-Highest-1993.aspx.

9. "CNN/ORC poll on guns in America," CNN/ORC International, January 7, 20016, http://www.cnn.com/2016/01/07/politics/obama-guns-executive-action-poll-results/.

10. Ibid.

11. The PollingReport.com checked on April 1, 2016. http://www.pollingreport.com/guns.htm.

12. Lauren Pearle, email messages and telephone calls to author, December 2013–January 2014.

13. For the different segments of Sawyer's reporting, see Diane Sawyer, "Young Guns," ABC News, January 31, 2014, http://abcnews.go.com/US/video/young-guns-diane-sawyer-special-21694484, http://abcnews.go.com/GMA/video/inside-young-guns-diane-sawyer-special-22312421; and http://abcnews.go.com/WNT/video/young-guns-hide-guns-children-22306882, and https://www.youtube.com/watch?v=iU77ZlSDtpQ.

14. Crime Prevention Research Center, "New Study: Over 12.8 million concealed handgun permits, last year saw by far the largest increase ever in the number of permits," July 16, 2015, (Updated March 1, 2016), http://crimeresearch.org/2015/07/new-study-over-12-8-concealed-handgun-permits-last-year-saw-by-far-the-largest-increase-ever-in-the-number-of-permits/.

15. For the FBI NICS by year, see https://www.fbi.gov/about-us/cjis/nics/reports/nics_firearm_checks_-_month_year.pdf.

16. "Zogby/O'leary Report Polls Reveals Americans' Domestic And International Concerns," PR Newswire, February 25, 2015, http://www.prnewswire.com/news-releases/zogbyoleary-report-polls-reveals-americans-domestic-and-international-concerns-300041108.html.

17. Confidence in Institutions: Trends in Americans' Attitudes toward Government, Media, and Business, Associated Press-NORC Center for Public Affairs Research, March 12, 2015, http://www.apnorc. org/projects/Pages/confidence-in-institutions-trends-in-americans-attitudes-toward-government-media-and-business.aspx.

18. Ye Hee Lee, "Has there been one school shooting per week since Sandy Hook?"

19. These are cases reported in Bloomberg's February 2014 report that received massive national news coverage. See *Analysis of School Shootings*, Moms Demand Action and Mayors Against Illegal Guns, http://crimeresearch.org/wp-content/uploads/2016/03/ Bloomberg-School-Shootings-Report.pdf.

20. It is possible that this couple was going to shoot more people, but that isn't clear. What is clear is that only a cat was killed. See Fox and Friends, "School Shooting Foiled When Bus Driver Uses Car to Run Down Armed Man," Fox News Insider, June 8, 2015, http:// insider.foxnews.com/2015/06/08/north-carolina-bus-driver-thwarts-potential-shooting-south-macon-elementary-school.

21. Andrew Goldstein, "Man accidentally shoots himself in leg outside Beaver County college," *Pittsburgh Post-Gazette*, April 2, 2015, http://www.post-gazette.com/local/west/2015/04/02/Man-accidentally-shoots-himself-near-Beaver-County-Airport/ stories/201504020165.

22. "Teen injured after shooting in parking lot of East English Village Preparatory Academy in Detroit," WXYZ TV, April 11, 2014, http://www.wxyz.com/news/region/detroit/person-shot-in-parking-lot-of-east-english-village-preparatory-academy-in-detroit.

23. Russell Westerholm, "Eastern Florida State College Shooter Allowed Back on Campus; Cops Determine Shot Fired Was in Self Defense," University Herald, February 4, 2014, http://www. universityherald.com/articles/7297/20140204/eastern-florida-state-college-shooter-allowed-back-on-campus-cops-determine-shot-fired-was-in-self-defense.htm.

24. Scott Feldman, "Mines professor apparently commits suicide on campus," *Rapid City Journal*, November 22, 2013, http:// rapidcityjournal.com/news/

mines-professor-apparently-commits-suicide-on-campus/article_
b75ce434-91b1-58df-b204-5bbe02cbd384.html.

25.   Katherine Klingseis, "Update: Police identify man found dead on
      Algona school property," *Des Moines Register*, November 1, 2013,
      http://blogs.desmoinesregister.com/dmr/index.php/2013/11/01/
      algona-schools-close-friday-after-police-find-body-on-school-
      property.

26.   Edward Murphy, "19-year-old kills himself at Gray-New Gloucester
      High School—The Portland Press Herald / Maine Sunday
      Telegram," *Portland Press Herald*, September 28, 2013, http://
      www.pressherald.com/2013/09/28/19-year-old-kills-himself-at-
      gray-new-gloucester-high-school/.

27.   Laura Anthony and Lilian Kim, "Friends, Family Gather at School
      to Mourn Teen," ABC Channel 7 News, February 14, 2013, http://
      abc7news.com/archive/8992648/.

28.   A total of sixty-five people were murdered in forty-five of the
      shootings. Out of those forty-five cases, one person was killed in
      thirty-eight shootings, three shootings had two killed, two cases
      had three killed, and in the two remaining cases six and nine people
      were killed. The two biggest shootings were the Umpqua
      Community College shooting in Oregon where nine people were
      killed in October 2015 and the Santa Monica College shooting in
      California where six were killed in June 2013. Both cases received
      massive news coverage.

29.   Out of all 170 shootings, at least thirty-four and possibly forty-
      seven are gang-related. That means that 28 percent of the cases are
      likely gang related.

30.   The data on school shootings are obtained from the following
      sources: *School Associated Violent Deaths*, The National School
      Safety Center, March 3, 2010, https://docs.google.com/viewer?a=v-
      &pid=sites&srcid=c2Nob29sc2FmZXR5LnVzfG5zc2N8Z3g6NW
      FlZDdjZjBjMGY1Yjc3Mw; Chris Kirk, "Since 1980, 297 People
      Have Been Killed in School Shootings," Slate, December 19, 2012,
      http://www.slate.com/articles/news_and_politics/map_of_the_
      week/2012/12/sandy_hook_a_chart_of_all_196_fatal_school_
      shootings_since_1980_map.html; *Analysis of School*

*Shootings,*Moms Demand Action and Mayors Against Illegal Guns, December 15, 2012–February 10, 2014, http://s3.amazonaws.com/ s3.mayorsagainstillegalguns.org/images/SchoolShootingsReport. pdf; and Ashely Fantz, Lindsey Knight, and Kevin Wang, "A closer look: How many Newtown-like school shootings since Sandy Hook?" CNN, June 19, 2014, http://www.cnn.com/2014/06/11/us/ school-shootings-cnn-number/. The National School Safety Center's data was used from 1991 to June 2010, Slate's data from August 2009 to June 2012, and Bloomberg's from August 2012 to June 2014.

31.   Centers for Disease Control and Prevention, "Injury Prevention Control," http://webappa.cdc.gov/sasweb/ncipc/dataRestriction_inj. html.

32.   National Center for Education Statistics, "Digest of Education Statistics," table 200, estimate for 2015, http://nces.ed.gov/ programs/digest/d11/tables/dt11_200.asp.

33.   A Study of Active Shooter Incidents in the United States Between 2000 and 2013, Federal Bureau of Investigation and Texas State University, September 16, 2013, http://crimeresearch.org/ wp-content/uploads/2014/10/U-_ActiveShooter13B_FBI.pdf.

34.   In 2014, the Obama administration changed the FBI's definition to include shootings with three or more fatalities (instead of the original standard of four or more). This change was presumably to increase the official number of mass public shootings. A higher number could then be used when trying to generate public concern. To keep our discussion consistent with past research, like Bloomberg's study, we will use that definition.

35.   Gene Maddaus, "Sheriff Lee Baca and the Gun-Gift Connection," *LA Weekly*, February 14, 2013, http://www.laweekly.com/news/ sheriff-lee-baca-and-the-gun-gift-connection-2612907.

36.   Michael Rushford, "Under realignment serious criminals are classified as 'low risk,'" Criminal Justice Legal Foundation, December 27, 2012, http://www.cjlf.org/releases/12-27.htm.

37.   Meg Kissinger, "Friend of Sikh Temple shooter feared what he might do," *Milwaukee Wisconsin Journal Sentinel*, August 9, 2012,

http://www.jsonline.com/news/milwaukee/friend-of-page-feared-what-he-might-do-426edmg-165668826.html.

38. Sean Robinson, "A long saga of crime," *The Olympian*, December 1, 2009, http://www.theolympian.com/2009/12/01/1054714/a-long-saga-of-crime.html.

39. Tom Breen, "Robert Stewart Sentenced To Life In Prison For Nursing Home Slayings," Associated Press, September 4, 2011, http://www.huffingtonpost.com/2011/09/04/robert-stewart-sentenced-nursing-home-slayings_n_948309.html.

40. Nick Allen, "Fort Hood gunman had told US military colleagues that infidels should have their throats cut," The Telegraph (UK), November 8, 2009, http://www.telegraph.co.uk/news/worldnews/northamerica/usa/6526030/Fort-Hood-gunman-had-told-US-military-colleagues-that-infidels-should-have-their-throats-cut.html.

41. Josh Green, "Spa victim foreshadowed violence in '06 restraining order," *Gwinnett Daily Post*, February 24, 2012, http://www.gwinnettdailypost.com/news/2012/feb/23/police-id-4-victims-shooter-in-spa-killing/.

42. Manny Fernandez and Nate Schweber, "Binghamton Killer Kept His Fury Private," *New York Times*, April 11, 2009, http://www.nytimes.com/2009/04/12/nyregion/12binghamton.html?pagewanted=all_r=1.

43. FBI and Texas State University, "A Study of Active Shooter Incidents in the United States Between 2000 and 2013," Federal Bureau of Investigation, September 16, 2013, http://crimeresearch.org/wp-content/uploads/2014/10/U-_ActiveShooter13B_FBI.pdf.

44. For examples of the extensive media coverage see Devlin Barrett, "Mass Shootings on the Rise, FBI says," *Wall Street Journal*, September 24, 2014, http://online.wsj.com/articles/mass-shootings-on-the-rise-fbi-says-1411574475. BBC, "FBI study: Deaths in mass shootings increasing," BBC, September 24, 2014, http://www.bbc.com/news/world-us-canada-29357199; Michael Schmidt, "F.B.I. Confirms a Sharp Rise in Mass Shootings Since 2000," *New York Times*, September 24, 2014, http://mobile.nytimes.com/2014/09/25/us/25shooters.html?emc=edit_th_20140925nl=todaysheadlinesn lid=67549140_r=1referrer=; and Evan Perez, "FBI: Mass shooting

incidents occurring more frequently," CNN, September 24, 2014, http://www.cnn.com/2014/09/24/justice/fbi-shooting-incidents-study/index.html?hpt=hp_t2.

One of the few publications that didn't make such a link in its headline was *USA Today*. See Donna Leger, "'Active shooter' incidents on the rise," *USA Today*, September 25, 2014, http://www.usatoday.com/story/news/nation/2014/09/24/active-shooter-incidents-rising-fbi-finds/16158921/.

45.   John R. Lott, Jr., "The FBI's Misinterpretation of the Change in Mass Public Shooting," Academy of Criminal Justice Sciences Today, March 2015, http://www.acjs.org/uploads/file/ACJS_Today_March_2015.pdf.

CHAPTER 7

1.   President Obama, "Transcript: President Obama's Remarks On Gun Violence," CBS Chicago Channel 2, January 5, 2016, http://chicago.cbslocal.com/2016/01/05/transcript-president-obamas-remarks-on-gun-violence/.

2.   Denis Slattery, "President Obama addresses tragic frequency of mass shootings in U.S. as gun massacre unfolds in California," *New York Daily News*, December 2, 2015, http://www.nydailynews.com/news/national/obama-addresses-tragic-frequency-mass-shootings-u-s-article-1.2453247.

3.   "President Obama Holds News Conference in Paris. Aired 8:30-9a ET," CNN, December 1, 2015, http://transcripts.cnn.com/TRANSCRIPTS/1512/01/nday.06.html.

4.   President Obama, "Remarks by the President to U.S. Conference of Mayors," The White House, June 19, 2015, https://www.whitehouse.gov/the-press-office/2015/06/19/remarks-president-us-conference-mayors.

5.   President Obama, "President Obama Answers a Question on Gun Violence During a Tumblr Q&A," The White House, June 11, 2014, https://www.youtube.com/watch?v=NDVFs2l6-fo.

6.   For other times that Obama has made similar claims, see President Obama, "Statement by the President on the Shootings at Umpqua Community College, Roseburg, Oregon," The White House,

October 1, 2015, https://www.whitehouse.gov/the-press-office/2015/10/01/statement-president-shootings-umpqua-community-college-roseburg-oregon; and President Obama, "Statement by the President on the Shooting in Charleston, South Carolina," The White House, June 18, 2015, https://www.whitehouse.gov/the-press-office/2015/06/18/statement-president-shooting-charleston-south-carolina.

7.   John Shiklam, "Nigeria: Kaduna–Suspected Fulani Herdsmen Kill 123 in Fresh Attacks," All Africa, June 25, 2014, http://allafrica.com/stories/201406260277.html; Luka Binniyat, "Nigeria: 123 Killed in Kaduna Attacks," All Africa, June 25, 2014, http://allafrica.com/stories/201406260256.html; Luka Binniyat, "Nigeria: Fulani – 'They Came From Different Directions, Killing Villagers'," All Africa, June 29, 2014, http://allafrica.com/stories/201406301825.html; and Staff, "Massacre: 258 Northern Christians killed in 7 days," News Express, June 30, 2014, http://www.newsexpressngr.com/news/detail.php?news=6433)

8.   Besides the Beslan School siege discussed in the text, the other four cases all involved the Chechen wars (1995 Samashki Massacre, 2000 Novye Aidi massacre, 1999 Staropromyslovski massacre, 1999 Grozny refugee convoy). Three of these cases allegedly involved Russian police doing the killings. See "Russia Condemned for Chechnya Killings," Human Rights Watch, October 12, 2006, https://www.hrw.org/news/2006/10/12/russia-condemned-chechnya-killings; "Civilian Killings in Staropromyslovski District of Grozny," Human Rights Watch, February 1, 2000, https://www.hrw.org/report/2000/02/01/civilian-killings-staropromyslovski-district-grozny; Major Gregory Celestan, "Wounded Bear: The Ongoing Russian Military Operation in Chechnyas," Global Security.org, August 1996, http://www.globalsecurity.org/military/library/report/1996/wounded.htm; Michael Wines, "New Reports Back Claims of Attack on Chechen Refugee Convoy," *New York Times*, December 5, 1999, http://www.nytimes.com/1999/12/05/world/new-reports-back-claims-of-attack-on-chechen-refugee-convoy.html.

9. David Satter, "The Truth about Beslan," The Weekly Standard, November 13, 2006, http://www.weeklystandard.com/article/14035.

10. "Dagestan shootings leave 11 dead," PressTV, November 11, 2010, http://previous.presstv.ir/detail.aspx?id=150595&sectio nid=351020602; "Islamists Stage Suicide Attack on Chechen Parliament," *The Moscow Times*, October 19, 2010, http://www.themoscowtimes.com/news/article/islamists-stage-suicide-attack-on-chechen-parliament/420597.html; "In a shootout with Chechen rebels killed five," NewsRU.com, December 5, 2010, http://newsru.com/russia/05feb2010/boi.html; and Gregory Zalasky, "Dagestan: Russia's Most Overlooked Hot Spot," *Foreign Policy*, February 9, 2010, http://foreignpolicy.com/2010/02/09/dagestan-russias-most-overlooked-hot-spot/.

11. "Nigeria confirms market massacre blamed on Boko Haram," BBC, May 8, 2014, http://www.bbc.com/news/world-africa-27323094.

12. Staff, "Over 200 killed in Boko Haram Led Attack in Nigerian Town," IANS, May 7, 2014, http://news.biharprabha.com/2014/05/over-200-killed-in-boko-haram-led-attack-in-nigerian-town/.

13. Zulfigar Ali and Shasbank Bengali, "Pakistan raises death total in Peshawar School attack to 148," *Los Angeles Times*, December 17, 2014, http://www.latimes.com/world/afghanistan-pakistan/la-fg-families-grieve-peshawar-pakistan-20141217-story.html.

14. Faith Karimi, "Kenya attack victims: Vigil mourns 147 slain by terrorists in Garissa," CNN, April 10, 2015, http://www.cnn.com/2015/04/07/africa/kenya-attack-victims-vigil/.

15. Jamie Schram, Isabel Vincent, and Bob Fredericks, "Paris under siege: At least 129 dead in terror attacks," *New York Post*, November 14, 2015, http://nypost.com/2015/11/14/paris-under-siege-more-than-150-dead-in-terror-attacks/.

16. Staff, "Boko Haram Islamists Massacre Christian Villagers in Borno State, Nigeria," *Morning Star News*, February 25, 2014, http://morningstarnews.org/2014/02/boko-haram-islamists-massacre-christian-villagers-in-borno-state-nigeria/.

17. "Nigeria's Boko Haram 'in village massacre'," BBC, February 16, 2014, http://www.bbc.com/news/world-africa-26220300.

18. Jayshree Bajoria, "Lashkar-e-Taiba (Army of the Pure) (aka Lashkar e-Tayyiba, Lashkar e-Toiba; Lashkar-i-Taiba)," Council on Foreign Relations, January 14, 2010, https://web.archive.org/web/20110108091314/http:/www.cfr.org/publication/17882/lashkaretaiba_army_of_the_pure_aka_lashkar_etayyiba_lashkar_etoiba_lashkaritaiba.html;

19. *Brief Chronology of War and Peace in the Philippines*, USC Conflict Data Base, http://www.usc.edu/dept/LAS/ir/cews/database/Moros/moros.pdf.

20. Peter Beaumont, "Norway attacks: at least 92 killed in Oslo and Utøya island," The Guardian, July 23, 2011, http://www.theguardian.com/world/2011/jul/23/norway-attacks.

21. Jason Straziuso, "NYPD report on Kenya attack isn't US gov't view," Yahoo News, December 13, 2013, http://news.yahoo.com/nypd-report-kenya-attack-isn-39-t-us-151711825.html.

22. AFP/Reuters, "Nigerian boarding school attack by Boko Haram gunmen leaves 59 pupils dead, officials say," ABC, February 25, 2014, http://www.abc.net.au/news/2014-02-26/scores-dead-in-boko-haram-nigeran-school-attack/5284250; and

23. Alastair McIndoe, "Behind the Philippines' Maguindanao Massacre," *Time*, November 27, 2009, http://content.time.com/time/world/article/0,8599,1943191,00.html.

24. "Troops seek killers of 53 in Philippines," *Ocala Star-Banner*, Wednesday, April 12, 1995, https://news.google.com/newspapers?id=TH9RAAAAIBAJ&sjid=xgcEAAAAIBAJ&pg=6372,6803892&dq=ipil&hl=en.

25. Adamu Adamu and Michelle Faul, "Boko Haram blamed after attack on Nigerian college leaves as many as 50 dead," *The Globe and Mail*, September 29, 2013, https://web.archive.org/web/20131002234600/http:/www.theglobeandmail.com/news/world/at-least-42-killed-18-injured-in-nigeria-college-attack-by-suspected-islamic-extremists/article14589188/.

26. "Pakistan gunmen kill 45 on Karachi Ismaili Shia bus," BBC, May 13, 2015, http://www.bbc.com/news/world-asia-32717321.

27. Damien McElroy, "Extremist attack in Nigeria kills 42 at boarding school," *The Telegraph*, July 6, 2013, http://www.telegraph.co.uk/news/worldnews/africaandindianocean/nigeria/10163942/Extremist-attack-in-Nigeria-kills-42-at-boarding-school.html.

28. Declan Walsh, "Pakistan militants launch deadly attack on Rawalpindi mosque," The Guardian, December 4, 2009, http://www.theguardian.com/world/2009/dec/04/militants-attack-rawalpindi-mosque-pakistan.

29. Heather Saul and Lizzie Dearden, "Isis claims responsibility for Tunisia museum attack and warns deadly shooting is 'just first drop of the rain'," Independent, March 19, 2015, http://www.independent.co.uk/news/world/europe/isis-claims-responsibility-for-tunisia-museum-attack-and-warns-deadly-shooting-is-just-the-first-10120321.html; and

30. John Shiklam, "Nigeria: Kaduna—Suspected Fulani Herdsmen Kill 123 in Fresh Attacks," All Africa, June 25, 2014, http://allafrica.com/stories/201406260277.html.

31. Ibid

32. Mukhtar Ahmad, "'Innocent civilians killed' in Kashmir cover-up," CNN, July 16, 2002, http://edition.cnn.com/2002/WORLD/asiapcf/south/07/16/kashmir.incident/index.html.

33. Shiklam, "Nigeria: Kaduna."

34. Matthew Grimson, "Port Arthur Massacre: The Shooting Spree That Changed Australia's Gun Laws," NBC News, October 2, 2015, http://www.nbcnews.com/news/world/port-arthur-massacre-shooting-spree-changed-australia-gun-laws-n396476.

35. Tehama Lopez, "Black September," International Encyclopedia of the Social Sciences, 2008, http://www.encyclopedia.com/doc/1G2-3045300204.html.

36. Emily Friedman, "Va. Tech Shooter Seung-Hui Cho's Mental Health Records Released," ABC, August 19, 2009, http://abcnews.go.com/US/seung-hui-chos-mental-health-records-released/story?id=8278195.

37. Gujarat Gandhinagar, "Terrorist Attack on Akshardham," BAPS Swaminarayan Sanstha, September 25, 2002, http://www.swaminarayan.org/news/2002/09/akshardham/report.htm.

38.   "1994: Jewish settler kills 30 at holy site," BBC, February 25, 1994, http://news.bbc.co.uk/onthisday/hi/dates/stories/february/25/newsid_4167000/4167929.stm.

39.   Mukhtar Ahmad, "29 killed in militant attack in Jammu," Rediff News, July 13, 2002, http://www.rediff.com/news/2002/jul/13jk2.htm.

40.   Marian Lebor, "Before Munich there was Lod: 40 years since the Lod Airport massacre," *The Times of Israel*, May 30, 2012, http://blogs.timesofisrael.com/before-munich-there-was-lod-40-years-since-the-lod-airport-massacre/; and

41.   Staff, "Quetta: 26 Shia pilgrims killed by gun men in Mastung," Pakistan News Service, September 21, 2011, http://paktribune.com/news/Quetta-26-Shia-pilgrims-killed-by-gun-men-in-Mastung-243789.html.

42.   "Report reveals new details about Newtown shooter's history," CBS News, November 22, 2014, http://www.cbsnews.com/news/adam-lanza-newtown-school-shooter-report-reveals-new-details-about-lanzas-history/.

43.   Thomas C. Hayes, "Gunman Kills 22 and Himself in Texas Cafeteria," *New York Times*, October 17, 1991, http://www.nytimes.com/1991/10/17/us/gunman-kills-22-and-himself-in-texas-cafeteria.html?pagewanted=all.

44.   Shiklam, "Nigeria: Kaduna."

45.   Amanda Covarrubias and Ernest Sander, "McDonald's Massacre: Time Can't Heal All Wounds Inflicted by 21 Slayings: Crime: San Ysidro lost its innocence in the violence 10 years ago. Survivors cope in different ways," *Los Angeles Times*, July 17, 1994, http://articles.latimes.com/1994-07-17/local/me-16553_1_san-ysidro.

46.   Staff, "Police detain two over Mali hotel attack: security sources," Yahoo News, November 26, 2015, http://news.yahoo.com/police-detain-two-over-mali-hotel-attack-security-170334399.html.

47.   Anissa Haddadi, "Gunmen Kill 19 in Church Attack in Central Nigeria," International Business Times, August 7, 2012, http://www.ibtimes.co.uk/gunman-kills-19-people-church-attack-central-371163.

48.   Edmund L. Andrews, "Shooting Rampage at German School," *New York Times*, April 27, 2002, http://www.nytimes. com/2002/04/27/world/shooting-rampage-at-german-school.html.

49.   Erlend Clouston and Sarah Boseley, "From the archive, 14 March 1996: Sixteen children killed in Dunblane massacre," The Guardian, March 14, 2013, http://www.theguardian.com/ theguardian/2013/mar/14/dunblane-massacre-scotland-killing.

50.   William Tuohy, "17 Killed in Airport Raids by Terrorists at Rome, Vienna: 116 Wounded in Attacks Apparently Aimed at El Al; Palestinians Blamed," *Los Angeles Times*, December 28, 1985, http://articles.latimes.com/1985-12-28/news/mn-29569_1_el-al.

51.   Lucas Tomlinson and The Associated Press, "Ivory Coast gunmen who killed 16 had sights set on Obama official, source says," Fox News, March 13, 2016, http://www.foxnews.com/ world/2016/03/13/gunmen-storm-ivory-coach-beach-resort. html?intcmp=hpbt1.

52.   Jan Mills, "Gunmen kill 16 at retirement home, handcuffing victims and shooting them in the head," Metro, March 5, 2016, http:// metro.co.uk/2016/03/05/gunmen-kill-16-at-retirement-home- handcuffing-victims-and-shooting-them-in-the-head-5734867/.

53.   Jeff Edwards, "Crimes That Shook Britain: The Hungerford Massacre," Mirror Online, May 8, 2012, http://www.mirror.co.uk/ news/uk-news/crimes-shook-britain-hungerford-massacre-823698.

54.   Shiklam, "Nigeria: Kaduna."

55.   Staff, "Ex-Soldier Kills 15 in Shooting Rampage," Los Angeles Times, May 24, 1997, http://articles.latimes.com/1997-05-24/news/ mn-62123_1_shooting-rampage.

56.   Carter Dougherty, "Teenage Gunman Kills 15 at School in Germany," *New York Times*, March 11, 2009, http://www.nytimes. com/2009/03/12/world/europe/12germany.html?mtrref=www. google.com&_r=0.

57.   On June 8, 2002, ten people were shot to death by the Guadalcanal Liberation Front (GLF), an Islamic organization. On April 2002, six Melanesian Brothers, who were Christian and working with the Catholic church, were murdered by the Islamic Guadalcanal Liberation Front. November 12, 2000: four people were shot and

killed by Bougainvilleans at the Gizo Hotel. See Sam Ata et al., *Solomon Islands Truth and Reconciliation Commission: Final Report*, Truth and Reconciliation Commission, February 2012, http://pacificpolicy.org/files/2013/04/Solomon-Islands-TRC-Final-Report-Vol1.pdf. For information on the Solomon Islands' gun control regulations, see David H. Capie, *Under the Gun: The Small Arms Challenge in the Pacific*, (Wellington: Victoria University Press, 2003), 34.

58. Joe Palazzolo and Alexis Flynn, "U.S. Leads World in Mass Shootings," *Wall Street Journal*, October 3, 2015, http://www.wsj.com/articles/u-s-leads-world-in-mass-shootings-1443905359.

59. Adam Lankford, "Public Mass Shooters and Firearms: A Cross-National Study of 171 Countries," *Violence and Victims* 31, no. 2 (2016): 1-13.

60. Palazzolo and Flynn, "US Leads World in Mass Shootings."

61. Melissa Healy, "Why the U.S. is No. 1—in mass shootings," *Los Angeles Times*, August 24, 2015, http://www.latimes.com/science/sciencenow/la-sci-sn-united-states-mass-shooting-20150824-story.html.

62. Tanya Basu, "Why the U.S. Has 31% of the World's Mass Shootings," *Time*, August 24, 2015, http://time.com/4007909/gun-violence-mass-shootings/.

63. Sarah Kaplan, "American exceptionalism and the 'exceptionally American' problem of mass shootings," *Washington Post*, August 27, 2015, https://www.washingtonpost.com/news/morning-mix/wp/2015/08/27/american-exceptionalism-and-the-exceptionally-american-problem-of-mass-shootings/.

64. Jen Christensen, "Why the U.S. has the most mass shootings," CNN, August 28, 2015, http://www.cnn.com/2015/08/27/health/u-s-most-mass-shootings/.

65. Susan Miller, "More guns are simply not the answer," *USA Today*, January 5, 2016, http://www.usatoday.com/story/opinion/voices/2016/01/05/voices-guns-ownership-mass-shootings/77756466/; Michael Melia, "Multiple shooters, including woman, set apart latest attack," Associated Press, December 3, 2015, http://bigstory.ap.org/article/7e3f85792aa6405886a0a12cabb

53eb3/multiple-shooters-including-woman-set-apart-latest-attack;
and Jane Clayson, "In San Bernardino, Yet Another Mass
Shooting," NPR's On Point with Tom Ashbrook, December 3,
2015, http://onpoint.wbur.org/2015/12/03/san-bernardino-mass-
shooting-latest.

66. The information on the worldwide coverage for Lankford's work is
available on his website. See http://adamlankford.com/pressroom.
htm.

67. John R. Lott, Jr. and Kevin A. Hassett, "Is newspaper coverage of
economics events politically biased?" *Public Choice* 160 (July 2014):
70, http://link.springer.com/article/10.1007/s11127-014-0171-5.

68. Viekki Dozier, "88 years ago: Bath School disaster kills 45," *Detroit
Free Press*, May 18, 2015, http://www.freep.com/story/news/local/
michigan/2015/05/18/bath-school-disaster-michigan/27521127/.

69. The data used in calculating the annual per capita death rate from
bombings in Russia is available in this table. The population used in
making the calculations is 146,270,033.

CHAPTER 8

1. President Obama, "Remarks by the President in Town Hall at
Benedict College, Columbia, SC," The White House, March 6,
2015, https://www.whitehouse.gov/the-press-office/2015/03/06/
remarks-president-town-hall-benedict-college-columbia-sc.

2. William Alex Pridemore, "Using Newly Available Homicide Data to
Debunk Two Myths About Violence in an International Context,"
Homicide Studies (August 2001): 267-275.

3. Charles M. Blow, "On Guns, America Stands Out," *New York
Times*, December 19, 2012, http://www.nytimes.com/2012/12/20/
opinion/blow-on-guns-america-stands-out.html?_r=1.

4. Elisabeth Rosenthal, "More Guns = More Killing," *New York
Times*, January 5, 2013, http://www.nytimes.com/2013/01/06/
sunday-review/more-guns-more-killing.html.

5. "A Loaded Question: Gun Ownership vs Gun Deaths Worldwide,"
Bloomberg Businessweek, March 12, 2013, http://businessweek.
tumblr.com/post/45192209697/a-loaded-question-gun-ownership-
vs-gun-deaths.

6.   For example, see http://www.smallarmssurvey.org/fileadmin/docs/
     F-Working-papers/SAS-WP15-Kenya-Policing-the-Periphery.pdf.
7.   United Nations Office on Drugs and Crime, "Global Study of
     Homicides: 2011," 2011, http://www.unodc.org/documents/data-
     and-analysis/statistics/Homicide/Globa_study_on_homicide_2011_
     web.pdf.
8.   David Bernstein and Noah Isackson, "The Truth About Chicago's
     Crime Rates," *Chicago*, April 7, 2014, http://www.chicagomag.
     com/Chicago-Magazine/May-2014/Chicago-crime-rates/.
9.   William Alex Pridemore, "Using Newly Available Homicide Data to
     Debunk Two Myths About Violence in an International Context,"
     Homicide Studies (August 2001): 267–275.
10. Roque Planas, "Venezuela Has World's Second-Highest Homicide
     Rate: NGO," Huffington Post, December 30, 2014, http://www.
     huffingtonpost.com/2014/12/30/venezuela-homocide-rate-
     2014_n_6395960.html.
11. With 65 percent of all people murdered being fifteen to twenty-nine
     years of age, 22 percent of violent deaths of just those young people
     were classified as "unknown intent." Charles Parkinson, "Argentina
     Youth Homicides Points to Rising Organized Crime," Insight
     Crime, October 15, 2013, http://www.insightcrime.org/news-briefs/
     leap-in-argentina-youth-homicides-points-to-rising-organized-
     crime.
12. Katy Barnato, "China's GDP may be much lower than you think,"
     CNBC, January 11, 2016, http://www.cnbc.com/2016/01/11/
     chinas-gdp-may-be-much-lower-than-you-think.html.
13. Janet Rosenbaum, "Gun Utopias? Firearm access and ownership in
     Israel and Switzerland," *Journal of Public Health Policy* 33
     (February 2012), http://www.ncbi.nlm.nih.gov/pmc/articles/
     PMC3267868/.
14. Associated Press, "Swiss Vote to Keep Mandatory Army Service,"
     New York Times, September 22, 2013, http://www.nytimes.
     com/2013/09/23/world/europe/swiss-vote-to-keep-mandatory-
     army-service.html?_r=0.
15. About two-thirds of Swiss males are found eligible to serve in the
     military. See "Zwei Drittel der Rekruten diensttauglich," Neue

Zürcher Zeitung, November 3, 2008, http://www.nzz.ch/zwei-drittel-der-rekruten-diensttauglich-1.687233.

16. In regressions, this one extreme data point for the U.S. has a disproportionate impact on the results. Regressions minimized the sum of the squared errors between the regression line and the observation. Pretending that the U.S. gun ownership is so high compared to other countries drives any regression results.

17. FBI, "2014 Crime in the United States," https://www.fbi.gov/about-us/cjis/ucr/crime-in-the-u.s/2014/crime-in-the-u.s.-2014/tables/expanded-homicide-data/expanded_homicide_data_table_8_murder_victims_by_weapon_2010-2014.xls; and Centers for Disease Control "Fatal Injury Reports 1999-2014, for National, Regional, and States (RESTRICTED)," http://webappa.cdc.gov/sasweb/ncipc/dataRestriction_inj.html.

18. Piers Morgan claims: "America has the worst incidents of gun murders of any of what they call the civilized world." "Mayor Bloomberg Speaks on Guns; The Right to Bear Arms; Acts of Heroism," *Piers Morgan Tonight*, July 23, 2012, http://transcripts.cnn.com/TRANSCRIPTS/1207/23/pmt.01.html.

19. Organization for Economic Co-operation and Development, "Better Life Index," http://www.oecdbetterlifeindex.org/topics/safety/.

20. Even if one excludes Russia, Brazil, and Mexico from the list of developed countries (though Mexico is a member of the OECD), what the U.S. can learn from the remaining countries is clear: more guns means less crime.

21. Kevin Smith et al., *Homicides, Firearm Offences and Intimate Violence 2010/11: Supplementary Volume 2 to Crime in England and Wales 2010/11*, Home Office, January 2012, https://www.gov.uk/government/uploads/system/uploads/attachment_data/file/116483/hosb0212.pdf. See Table 1.01 and the column marked "Offences currently recorded as homicide per million population."

22. Home Office, "Police workforce England and Wales statistics and Policing statistics," (https://www.gov.uk/government/statistics/police-service-strength-england-and-wales-31-march-2012 and https://www.gov.uk/government/collections/police-workforce-england-and-wales).

23. "An Garda Síochána Working Group on Review of Firearms Licensing," Irish Department of Justice and Equality, November 2014, http://www.justice.ie/en/JELR/2014.WG.Report.pdf/ Files/2014.WG.Report.pdf.

24. W. Calathes, "Gun Control in a Developing Nation: The Gun Court Act of Jamaica," *International Journal of Comparative and Applied Criminal Justice* 14, no. 1 (1992), https://www.ncjrs.gov/App/ publications/abstract.aspx?ID=160203. Enforcement continues through today. See " 'Get the Guns' campaign nets 68 guns, 800 ammo," *Jamaica Observer*, October 15, 2015, http://www. jamaicaobserver.com/news/-Get-the-Guns—campaign-nets-68- guns—800-ammo.

25. "Venezuela bans private gun ownership," BBC, June 1, 2012, http:// www.bbc.com/news/world-latin-america-18288430.

26. "Guns in the Solomon Islands," GunPolicy.org, http://www. gunpolicy.org/es/firearms/region/cp/solomon-islands. There are a large number of errors at the GunPolicy.org website. For example, the site claims that there were no gun murders after 1999, but as we will show in the text that was clearly not the case.

27. Jamaica's crime data were obtained from a variety of sources. Its murder data from 1960 to 1967 were obtained from Terry Lacey, *Violence and Politics in Jamaica*, 1960–70 (Manchester: Manchester University Press, 1977). Professor Gary Mauser obtained the data from 1970 to 2000 from a Professor A. Francis in Jamaica and the data from 2001 to 2006 from the Statistical Institute of Jamaica; see http://www.statinja.com/stats.html. Jamaica's population estimates were obtained from NationMaster. com; see http://www.nationmaster.com/graph/ peo_pop-people- population&date=1975.

28. "How Ireland was Always Violent," IrishSalem.com, http://www. irishsalem.com/irish-controversies/crime-in-ireland/wasireland- alwaysviolent-jun11.php.

29. Niame Hourigan, "Niamh Hourigan examines the true nature of gang crime in Ireland today and asks, has anything really changed post-austerity?" Garda Review, November 25, 2014, http://www. gardareview.ie/index.php/the-changing-face-of-irish-gangsters/.

30. Michael Lohmuller, "Jamaica Sees 20% Spike in Murders," InSight Crime, August 28, 2015, http://www.insightcrime.org/news-briefs/jamaica-sees-20-spike-in-murders-in-2015.

31. National Gang Intelligence Center, U.S. Department of Justice, "National Gang Threat Assessment 2009," January 2009, http://www.usdoj.gov/ndic/pubs32/32146/index.htm. See also Kevin Johnson, "FBI: Burgeoning Gangs Behind up to 80% of U.S. Crime," *USA Today*, January 29, 2009, A1, http://www.usatoday.com/news/nation/2009-01-29-ms13_ N.htm.

32. The homicide rates for the years after the gun ban were 5.7 per 100,000 in 2002, 4.4 in 2004, 5.5 in 2005, 4.8 in 2006, 5.2 in 2007, 3.7 in 2008, and 4.3 in 2012 compared to 1.9 in 1997.

33. Four Corners, "Guns and Money: Solomon Islands, a one-time South Pacific idyll, is on the brink of collapse," Australian Broadcasting Corporation, 2002, http://www.abc.net.au/4corners/stories/s559713.htm.

34. Phil Sylvester, "Solomon Islands safety in a nutshell," World Nomads, 2016, https://www.worldnomads.com/travel-safety/solomon-islands/solomon-islands.

CHAPTER 9

1. "Clinton: Australian-style gun control 'worth considering' for U.S.," Grabien, October 16, 2016, https://grabien.com/story.php?id=39363.

2. John Howard, "I Went After Guns. Obama can, Too," *New York Times*, January 16, 2013, http://www.nytimes.com/2013/01/17/opinion/australia-banned-assault-weapons-america-can-too.html?_r=0.

3. Nick Ralston, "Australia reloads as gun amnesties fail to cut arms," *Sydney Morning Herald*, January 14, 2013, http://www.smh.com.au/national/australia-reloads-as-gun-amnesties-fail-to-cut-arms-20130113-2cnnq.html.
   I have also been collecting data from individual states in Australia. For South Australia, a Freedom of Information Act application found that the number of registered guns grew from 313,593 in

2000 to 376,479 in 2010. Thus, while South Australia's population grew by 9 percent, the number of guns grew by 20 percent.

4. Figures A and B are from Andrew Leigh and Christine Neill, "Do Gun Buybacks Save Lives? Evidence from Panel Data," *American Law and Economics Review*, (2010), http://andrewleigh.org/pdf/ GunBuyback_Panel.pdf.

5. D. M. Cutler, E. L. Glaeser, and K. E. Norberg, "Explaining the Rise in Youth Suicide," in *Risky Behavior Among Youths: An Economic Analysis*, ed. J. Gruber (Chicago: University of Chicago Press, 2001), 219–69. See also Lott, Jr., *More Guns, Less Crime*.

6. Australian Institute of Criminology, "Victims of Violent Crime (rate per 100,000)," http://aic.gov.au/dataTools/facts/vicViolentRate. html.

7. John R. Lott, Jr. and William M. Landes, "Multiple Victim Public Shootings," Social Science Research Network, October 19, 2000, http://ssrn.com/abstract=272929. See also Lott, Jr., *More Guns, Less Crime*.

8. John R. Lott Jr., "Making up facts about guns," Fox News, June 16, 2014, http://www.foxnews.com/opinion/2014/06/16/making-up-facts-about-guns/; and Lott Jr., "Gun Control and Mass Murders," National Review, June 11, 2010, http://www.nationalreview.com/ articles/229929/gun-control-and-mass-murders/john-r-lott-jr.

9. Samara McPhedran and Jeanine Baker, "Mass Shootings in Australia and New Zealand: A Descriptive Study of Incidence," *Justice Policy Journal* 8, no. 1 (Spring 2011) http://ssrn.com/ abstract=2122854.

10. Charles F. Wellford, John V. Pepper, and Carol V. Petrie, eds., *Firearms and Violence: A Critical Review*, (Washington, D.C.: The National Academies Press, 2004).

CHAPTER 10

1. Editorial Board, "The Right to Sue the Gun Industry," *New York Times*, March 4, 2016, http://www.nytimes.com/2016/03/05/ opinion/the-right-to-sue-the-gun-industry.html?_r=1.

2. Editorial, "Gunmakers' War Profiteering on the Homefront," *New York Times*, December 11, 2015, http://www.nytimes.

com/2015/12/11/opinion/gunmakers-war-profiteering-on-the-homefront.html?_r=0.

3. Jack Healy, "Suspect Bought Large Stockpile of Rounds Online," *New York Times*, July 22, 2012, http://www.nytimes. com/2012/07/23/us/online-ammunition-sales-highlighted-by-aurora-shootings.html?_r=0.

4. As another example, take this claim about the Washington Navy Yard shooting in 2013. The lead sentence in a front page story asserted: "The gunman who killed 12 people at the Washington Navy Yard on Monday test fired an AR-15 assault rifle at a Virginia gun store last week but was stopped from buying one because state law there prohibits the sale of such weapons to out-of-state buyers, according to two senior law enforcement officials." It would have been interesting to know who these unnamed law enforcement officials were because if they did actually tell this to The New York Times, they were wrong. As with most states, Virginia law does not prohibit the sale of rifles (assault rifles or any other type of rifle) to U.S. citizens from out-of-state. What is needed is proof of residency and of U.S. citizenship. See Emily Miller, "New York Times gets it wrong, media obsessed with linking AR-15 with Navy Yard shooter," *Washington Times*, September 17, 2013, http://www. washingtontimes.com/news/2013/sep/17/miller-new-york-times-gets-it-wrong-about-navy-yar/?page=all.

5. Barack Obama, "State of the Union Address," CNN, December 16, 2012.

6. As of 2014, the states that banned deer hunting with .223 caliber bullets were: Colorado, Connecticut, Illinois, Iowa, Massachusetts, Virginia, Ohio, New Jersey, Washington, and West Virginia. Many other states, such as Alaska, ban that caliber of bullet for hunting larger animals such as caribou. The issue is even a little more complicated for other states. In many states, the standard is that the guns must release a certain level of force. For example, Maryland requires a minimum of 1200 foot-pounds of energy for a rifle bullet to be legal for hunting deer. Many .223 caliber bullets are below that. See Staff, "Which AR-15 can you hunt with," Stag Arms, April 25, 2014, http://info.stagarms.com/blog/bid/381895/Which-AR-15-Can-You-Hunt-With.

7. Some have cited Terry Petrosky's murder in the 1990s in Colorado as a case where someone was murdered by a .50 caliber rifle. But the testimony at Albert Petrosky's trial in 1996 indicates that was not the case. Indeed, the murder was committed using "a large-caliber handgun." A Jefferson County Sheriff, Sgt. Tim Mossbrucker, was shot with a rifle, but it was a .30-caliber SKS semiautomatic rifle. See Charlie Brennan, "Jury hears grim inventory of Petrosky's rampage," *Rocky Mountain News*, March 29, 1996, 23a.

8. See Barrett 2016 Retail Pricing, https://barrett.net/pdf/price-list.pdf; and Barrett 2016 M107A1 Product Brochure, https://barrett.net/pdf/products/M107A1/M107A1_Product_Brochure.pdf.

9. Other *New York Times* stories on the "bulletproof vest" include: David Goodman, Jennifer Preston, and Marc Santora, "Live Updates on Movie Theater Shooting in Colorado," *New York Times*, July 20, 2012, http://thelede.blogs.nytimes.com/2012/07/20/live-updates-on-movie-theater-shooting-in-colorado/.

10. For an example of the vest, see http://www.amazon.com/BLACKHAWK-Urban-Assault-Vest-Black/dp/B000VU34J8/ref=sr_1_1?s=sports-and-fitness&ie=UTF8&qid=1459240265&sr=1-1&keywords=urban+assault+vest.

11. Gary Kleck, "Large-Capacity Magazines and the Casualty Counts in Mass Shootings: The Plausibility of Linkages," (working paper, Florida State University, December 6, 2015).

12. Web staff, "Victim: Aurora theater shooting gun jam saved my life," Fox 31 Denver, July 23, 2012, http://kdvr.com/2012/07/23/suspects-gun-jammed-during-aurora-theater-shooting/; and John Emshwiller, Devlin Barrett, and Charles Forelle, "Suspect Fixated on Giffords," *Wall Street Journal*, January 10, 2011, http://www.wsj.com/news/articles/SB10001424052748703667904576071191163461466.

13. Comparing large capacity magazines (without multiple guns) and multiple guns (without large capacity magazines) finds that the different means (six and 8.5) are only statistically significantly different at the 37 percent level with an absolute t-statistic of 0.9456.
Comparing large capacity magazines (but not excluding cases that also had multiple guns) and multiple guns (but not excluding cases

that also had large capacity magazines) finds that the different means (11.5 and 10.1) are only statistically significantly different at the 68 percent level with an absolute t-statistic of 0.4143.

14. The authors wrote: "The evidence is not strong enough for us to conclude that there was any meaningful effect (i.e. that the effect was different from zero)." Koper and Roth suggested that after the ban had been in effect for more years it might be possible to find a benefit. Seven years later, in 2004, they published a follow-up study for the National Institute of Justice with fellow criminologist Dan Woods that concluded, "We cannot clearly credit the ban with any of the nation's recent drop in gun violence. And, indeed, there has been no discernible reduction in the lethality and injuriousness of gun violence." See Jeffrey A. Roth and Christopher S. Koper, "Impacts of the 1994 Assault Weapons Ban: 1994–96," National Institute of Justice, March 1999, https://www.ncjrs.gov/pdffiles1/173405.pdf. This was later published as Christopher S. Koper and Jeffrey A. Roth, "1994 Federal Assault Weapon Ban on Gun Violence Outcomes: An Assessment of Multiple Outcome Measures and Some Lessons for Policy Evaluation," *Journal of Quantitative Criminology*, 17, no. 1 (March 2001): 33–74. See also their later report; Christopher S. Koper, Daniel J. Woods, and Jeffrey A. Roth, *An Updated Assessment of the Federal Assault Weapons Ban: Impacts on Gun Markets and Gun Violence*, 1994-2003: Report to the National Institute of Justice, United States Department of Justice, June 2004, https://www.ncjrs.gov/pdffiles1/nij/grants/204431.pdf.

15. It isn't clear how many people actually obey this law. Los Angeles, San Francisco, and Sunnyvale, California have all banned magazines holding more than ten bullets, but in none of those cities were any magazines turned in during the amnesty periods. See Chip Johnson, "One gun control attempt that misfires," *San Francisco Chronicle*, January 28, 2016, http://www.sfchronicle.com/bayarea/johnson/article/One-gun-control-attempt-that-misfires-6791466.php; Emily Reyes, "L.A. to start enforcing new limit on ammunition magazine size next week," *Los Angeles Times*, November 12, 2015, http://www.latimes.com/local/lanow/

la-me-ln-ammunition-ban-20151112-story.html; and Alex Emslie, "What's the Impact of Local Gun Laws?" KQED, April 10, 2016, http://ww2.kqed.org/news/2016/04/10/whats-the-impact-of-local-gun-laws.

16. U.S. Army Chief of Staff Mark Milley, "Army Chief of Staff says unnecessary to let troops be armed on base, 8 min is a fast response time 'adequate'," YouTube video, posted by John Lott, April 8, 2016, https://www.youtube.com/watch?v=Om15eF2W32k.

17. I debated Adam Winkler on Larry Mantle's AirTalk, "Where should guns be allowed?" 89.3 FM KPCC Southern California Public Radio, April 28, 2014, http://www.scpr.org/programs/airtalk/2014/04/28/37169/where-should-guns-be-allowed/.

18. Rich Schapiro and Tim O'Connor, "Fort Hood shooter's spree lasted 8 minutes, filled with more than 35 shots: Army," *New York Daily News*, April 7, 2014, http://www.nydailynews.com/news/crime/fort-hood-shooter-spree-8-minutes-35-shots-long-article-1.1748803.

19. History Channel, "Army major kills 13 people in Fort Hood shooting spree," This Day in History, http://www.history.com/this-day-in-history/army-major-kills-13-people-in-fort-hood-shooting-spree.

20. Billy Kenber, "Nidal Hasan sentenced to death for Fort Hood shooting rampage," *Washington Post*, August 28, 2013, https://www.washingtonpost.com/world/national-security/nidal-hasan-sentenced-to-death-for-fort-hood-shooting-rampage/2013/08/28/aad28de2-0ffa-11e3-bdf6-e4fc677d94a1_story.html. CBS/AP, "Prosecution to Rest in Ft. Hood Massacre Trial," CBS News, October 21, 2010 (http://www.cbsnews.com/news/prosecution-to-rest-in-ft-hood-massacre-trial/).

21. At the San Bernardino terrorist attack in December 2016, the police arrived in four minutes, but it was not fast enough to save the fourteen people who were killed and the twenty-two injured. (Rong-Gong Lin II and Richard Winton, "San Bernardino suspects 'sprayed the room with bullets,' police chief says," *Los Angeles Times*, December 4, 2016, http://www.latimes.com/local/lanow/la-me-ln-san-bernardino-suspects-sprayed-the-room-with-bullets-

20151203-story.html. The two killers in that attack fired between sixty-five and seventy-five bullets in about three minutes—they had about 5.14 seconds to fire each bullet. At Sandy Hook, 154 bullets were shot in a little over five minutes—a rate of one bullet every two seconds. See Susan Raff, "154 shots in 5 minutes: Sandy Hook warrants released," CBS 46, April 25, 2013, http://www.cbs46.com/story/21814424/154-shots-in-5-minutes-sandy-hook-warrants-released. At least a half-dozen of Adam Lanza's rounds were fired in a couple of seconds "to open a hole big enough to step through in one of the school's glass doors." See Edmund Mahony and Dave Altimari, "A Methodical Massacre: Horror And Heroics," *Hartford Courant*, December 15, 2012 (http://www.courant.com/news/connecticut/newtown-sandy-hook-school-shooting/hc-timeline-newtown-shooting-1216-20121215-story.html. For a discussion of some other attacks see William Saletan, "The Volume Killers," Slate, December 18, 2012, http://www.slate.com/articles/health_and_science/human_nature/2012/12/sandy_hook_and_assault_weapons_is_newtown_a_warning_of_worse_school_shootings.html.

22. Shawn Ley, "FBI: Dearborn Heights ISIS supporter planned to attack Detroit church," WDIV-TV, February 5, 2016, http://www.clickondetroit.com/news/dearborn-heights-isis-supporter-planned-to-attack-detroit-church.

23. For a copy of the relevant page from Holmes' diary is available here, see http://crimeresearch.org/wp-content/uploads/2015/06/james-holmes-notebook-dragged.pdf.

24. John R. Lott Jr., "Did Colorado shooter single out Cinemark theater because it banned guns?" Fox News, September 10, 2012, http://www.foxnews.com/opinion/2012/09/10/did-colorado-shooter-single-out-cinemark-theater.html.

25. Some have misleadingly claimed that Holmes picked the movie theater because of its layout and exits, but that detailed discussion by Holmes was over which room in the Century Cinemark movie theater to do the attack, not over the choice of movie theaters. See the discussion on pages forty-nine to fifty-one in his diary at http://extras.denverpost.com/trial/docs/notebook.pdf.

The movie theaters were: Aurora Plaza 8 Cinemas, 777 Peoria St., Aurora, CO 80011; Harkins Northfield 18 (Billed as the home of Colorado's largest auditorium) 8300 E. Northfield Blvd., Denver, CO 80238; Aurora Movie Tavern, 18605 East Hampden Avenue, Aurora, CO 80013-3533; THE MOVIE TAVERN AT SEVEN HILLS 18305 E. Hampden Ave., Aurora, CO 80013; Landmark Theatre Greenwood Village 5415 Landmark Place, Greenwood Village, CO 80111; and UA Colorado Center Stadium 9 and IMAX, 2000 S. Colorado Blvd., Denver, CO 80222. For more details, see http://johnrlott.blogspot.com/2012/08/so-are-movie-theaters-in-aurora.html.

26. "Do mentally ill, multiple victim killers purposefully pick targets where victims are most vulnerable: The case of Elliot Rodger," Crime Prevention Research Center, May 26, 2014, http://crimeresearch.org/2014/05/do-mentally-ill-multiple-victim-killers-purposefully-pick-targets-where-victims-are-most-vulnerable-the-case-of-elliot-rodgers/.

27. "The Moncton, New Brunswick Shooter: Another killer who clearly understood the advantage to him of gun-free zones," Crime Prevention Research Center, June 6, 2014, http://crimeresearch.org/2014/06/the-moncton-n-b-shooter-another-killer-who-clearly-understood-the-advantage-to-him-of-gun-free-zones/.

28. Crime Prevention Research Center, "The Moncton, New Brunswick Shooter: Another killer who clearly understood the advantage to him of gun-free zones."

29. Bob Orr and Pat Milton, "Newtown shooter motivated by Norway massacre, sources say," CBS Evening News, February 19, 2013, http://www.cbsnews.com/news/newtown-shooter-motivated-by-norway-massacre-sources-say/.

30. Brian Hernandez, "25 revealing things we learned Monday in Aurora theater shooting trial," Denver ABC Channel 7, June 1, 2015, http://www.thedenverchannel.com/news/movie-theater-shooting/25-revealing-things-we-learned-monday-in-the-aurora-theater-shooting-trial06012015.

31. Jake Berry, "Examining the last 20 years of mass shootings through the lens of 'gun free' zones," The Nashua Telegraph, January 13,

2013 (http://www.nashuatelegraph.com/news/990499-469/
examining-the-last-20-years-of-mass.html).

32. "Police say 'drifter' killed 2, injured 9 in Lafayette, La. movie
theater shooting," Fox News, July 24, 2015, http://www.foxnews.
com/us/2015/07/24/gunman-reportedly-opens-fire-at-la-movie-
theater.html. For information on the policies of the other movie
theaters in the area, see "Lafayette, Louisiana Movie Theater
Shooting was yet another gun-free zone, other movie theaters in
area didn't have that policy," Crime Prevention Research Center,
July 23, 2015, http://crimeresearch.org/2015/07/lafayette-louisiana-
movie-theater-shooting-was-yet-another-gun-free-zone/.

33. Evidence of the Trolley Square Mall being a gun-free zone is
provided for me at the time in a picture obtained by Clark
Aposhian. See http://johnrlott.tripod.com/uploaded_images/
HPIM0240-724381.jpg; and "Media Coverage of Mall Shooting
Fails to Reveal Mall's Gun-Free-Zone Status," Fox News, December
6, 2007, http://www.foxnews.com/story/2007/12/06/media-
coverage-mall-shooting-fails-to-reveal-mall-gun-free-zone-status.
html. While I had called up the other malls in the area at the time,
few places in Nebraska had posted signs banning permitting
concealed handguns. See http://4.bp.blogspot.com/_2SW2_lbrxgY/
R1gZwy1WaWI/AAAAAAAAAE8/a6HSha-Arys/s1600-h/
Picture+5.png; but the Westroads Mall was an exception.

34. Major Garrett, "Face the Nation Transcripts May 25, 2014:
Blumenthal, Thune, Kinzinger," Face the Nation, CBS News, May
25, 2014, http://www.cbsnews.com/news/face-the-nation-
transcripts-may-25-2014-blumenthal-thune-kinzinger/.

35. The *New York Times* analysis concluded: "At least half of the killers
showed signs of serious mental health problems." See Ford
Fessenden, "They Threaten, Seethe and Unhinge, Then Kill in
Quantity," *New York Times*, April 9, 2000, http://www.nytimes.
com/2000/04/09/us/they-threaten-seethe-and-unhinge-then-kill-in-
quantity.html?pagewanted=all. However, the *New York Times*
sample is quite problematic. Fessenden admitted that they had
concentrated mainly on cases for the years after 1994. For the early
years, they had only retrieved the "easily obtainable" cases. He said

that there was nothing magical about the number one hundred, but it had simply seemed like a convenient number at which to stop searching. See John R. Lott Jr., *The Bias Against Guns: Why Almost Everything You've Heard About Gun Control Is Wrong* (Washington, D.C.: Regnery Publishing, 2003).

36. "Face the Nation Transcripts May 25, 2014: Blumenthal, Thune, Kinzinger," CBS News, May 25, 2014, http://www.cbsnews.com/news/face-the-nation-transcripts-may-25-2014-blumenthal-thune-kinzinger/.

37. Elliot Rodger, "My Twisted World: The Story of Elliot Rodger," http://abclocal.go.com/three/kabc/kabc/My-Twisted-World.pdf.

38. Ibid.

39. Philip Rucker and Robert Costa "In Elliot Rodger, authorities in Calif. saw warning signs but didn't see a tipping point," *Washington Post*, May 25, 2014, http://www.washingtonpost.com/national/sheriff-calif-shooter-rodger-flew-under-the-radar-when-deputies-visited-him-in-april/2014/05/25/88123026-e3b4-11e3-8dcc-d6b7fede081a_story.html.

40. Javier Panzar, "Elliot Rodger's dad to Barbara Walters: 'My son was a mass murderer'," *Los Angeles Times*, June 26, 2014, http://www.latimes.com/local/lanow/la-me-ln-peter-rodger-barbara-walters-isla-vista-interview-20140626-htmlstory.html.

41. Crime Prevention Research Center, "Why we shouldn't depend on mental health professionals to detect mass killers: Elliot Rodger's slipping 'under the radar' is hardly rare," May 26, 2014, http://crimepreventionresearchcenter.org/2014/05/why-we-shouldnt-depend-on-mental-health-professionals-to-detect-mass-killers-elliot-rodgers-slipping-under-the-radar-is-hardly-rare/.

42. Craig Whitlock and Carol D. Leonnig, "Fort Hood shooter had psychiatric issues but showed no 'sign of likely violence,' officials say," *Washington Post*, April 3 2014, http://www.washingtonpost.com/world/national-security/fort-hood-shooter-showed-no-sign-of-likely-violence-official-says/2014/04/03/d6d39986-bb30-11e3-9a05-c739f29ccb08_story.html?tid=pm_world_pop.

43. Virginia Tech Review Panel Presented to Governor Kaine Commonwealth of Virginia, "Mass Shooting at Virginia Tech,"

April 16, 2007, http://www.washingtonpost.com/wp-srv/metro/documents/vatechreport.pdf, 23, 47.

44. Ibid.

45. Ned Potter and David Schoetz, "Va. Tech Killer Ruled Mentally Ill by Court; Let Go After Hospital Visit," ABC News, April 18, 2007, http://abcnews.go.com/US/print?id=3052278.

46. Tom McGhee, "Theater shooting victim's wife sues Holmes' psychiatrist," *The Denver Post*, January 15, 2013, http://www.denverpost.com/ci_22378331/theater-shooting-victims-wife-sues-holmes-psychiatrist.

47. American Psychiatric Association, "APA President Calls for Gun Control Measures in Wake of Oregon Tragedy," Psychiatric News Alert, October 3, 2015, http://alert.psychnews.org/2015/10/apa-president-calls-for-gun-control.html?utm_source=feedburner&utm_medium=feed&utm_campaign=Feed%3A+PsychiatricNewsAlert+%28Psychiatric+News+Alert%29.

48. Kelly Riddell, "Hillary's gun-control stance a drastic departure from her 2008 bid," *Washington Times*, October 5, 2015, http://www.washingtontimes.com/news/2015/oct/5/clinton-gun-control-view-drastic-departure-2008/.

49. John R. Lott, Jr., "Reaction to D.C. Gun Ban Decision," Fox News, July 1, 2016, http://www.foxnews.com/story/2008/07/01/john-lott-reaction-to-dc-gun-ban-decision.html; and John R. Lott, Jr., "Obama and Guns: Two Different Views," Fox News, April 7, 2008, http://www.foxnews.com/story/2008/04/07/obama-and-guns-two-different-views.html.

CHAPTER 11

1. Michael Graham, "Doc, what's up with snooping?" *Boston Herald*, October 4, 2007, http://www.bostonherald.com/news_opinion/opinion/op_ed/2007/10/doc_what's_snooping.

2. Kevin Gipson, *Submersions related to non-pool and non-spa products, 2012 Report*, Consumer Productive Safety Commission, September 2012, http://www.cpsc.gov/PageFiles/129419/nonpoolsub2012.pdf.

3. For the Centers for Disease Control and Prevention data, see http://
    webappa.cdc.gov/sasweb/ncipc/dataRestriction_inj.html.

4. Associated Press, "Toddler shot in hospital waiting room when
    mom's gun in purse fires," Fox News, April 14, 2016, http://www.
    foxnews.com/us/2016/04/14/toddler-shot-in-hospital-waiting-room-
    when-moms-gun-in-purse-fires.html.

5. Associated Press, "Girl, 2, grazed by bullet after mother drops purse
    and gun inside goes off in Miss," *New York Daily News*, April 14,
    2016, http://www.nydailynews.com/news/national/girl-2-grazed-
    bullet-mother-drops-purse-gun-article-1.2601520; and Associated
    Press, "Toddler shot in hospital waiting room when mom's gun in
    purse fires," Fox News, April 14, 2016, http://www.foxnews.com/
    us/2016/04/14/toddler-shot-in-hospital-waiting-room-when-moms-
    gun-in-purse-fires.html.

6. For a video from ABC News on January 31, 2014, see http://
    abcnews.go.com/video/embed?id=22258370; John R. Lott, Jr.,
    "ABC News reports on guns mislead Americans," Fox News,
    February 7, 2014, http://www.foxnews.com/opinion/2014/02/07/
    abc-news-reports-on-guns-mislead-americans.html.

7. Lott Jr., *The Bias Against Guns*.

8. Centers for Disease Control and Prevention, "Injury Prevention &
    Control," January 2015, http://webappa.cdc.gov/sasweb/ncipc/
    dataRestriction_inj.html.

9. Gary Kleck and Marc Gertz, "Armed Resistance to Crime: The
    Prevalence and Nature of Self-Defense with a Gun," Journal of
    Criminal Law and Criminology 86 (Fall 1995); see also Kleck,
    "Critique of Cook/Ludwig Paper," (undated manuscript, Dept. of
    Criminology, Florida State University); John R. Lott Jr., The Bias
    Against Guns (Washington, D.C.: Regnery, 2003); and Lott Jr.,
    More Guns, Less Crime, 3rd ed. (Chicago: University of Chicago
    Press, 2010).

10. Lott Jr., *The Bias Against Gu145*

11. Associated Press, "More people in Tennessee died from guns than
    car accidents," *San Francisco Chronicle*, January 24, 2016, http://
    www.sfgate.com/news/article/More-people-in-Tennessee-died-from-
    guns-than-car-6780726.php; "Bangers v bullets," *The Economist*,

January 10, 2015, http://www.economist.com/news/united-states/21638140-gun-now-more-likely-kill-you-car-bangers-v-bullets; Jason Millman, "Many more people are dying from gun suicides than gun-related homicides," *Washington Post*, January 14, 2015, https://www.washingtonpost.com/news/wonk/wp/2015/01/14/many-more-people-are-dying-from-gun-suicides-than-homicides/; Jim Gorzelany, "Safer Cars Could Make Guns The Leading Cause Of Death Among Young Americans," Forbes, January 20, 2015, http://www.forbes.com/sites/jimgorzelany/2015/01/20/safer-cars-could-make-guns-the-leading-cause-of-death-among-young-americans/#6f13df5f3ce3); Adrienne LaFrance, "America's Top Killing Machine," *The Atlantic*, January 12, 2015, http://www.theatlantic.com/technology/archive/2015/01/americas-top-killing-machine/384440/; Ken Jennings, "Play the Slate News Quiz," Slate, January 2015, http://www.slate.com/articles/news_and_politics/the_slate_quiz/2015/01/the_slate_quiz_with_quizmaster_ken_jennings_play_the_news_quiz_for_jan_16.html); and German Lopez, "Report: Guns will probably kill more young Americans than car accidents in 2015," Vox, January 12, 2015, http://www.vox.com/2015/1/12/7531603/guns-cars-deaths.

12.   "Guns To Surpass Car Accidents As Leading Cause Of Deaths Among Young People," Think Progress, February 22, 2014, http://thinkprogress.org/justice/2014/02/22/3320751/gun-deaths-surpass-car-accidents-leading-cause-young-people/.

13.   "Bangers v bullets,"http://www.economist.com/news/united-states/21638140-gun-now-more-likely-kill-you-car-bangers-v-bullets.

14.   There were 742 more motor vehicle deaths in 2014 than for firearms.

15.   With only about one to two hundred suicides committed with motor vehicles, the variability of motor vehicle suicides is fairly large—rising by 33 percent between 2000 to 2006, falling to just 1 percent over the number in 2000 by 2009, and then finally rising to 72 percent in 2014.

16. Emily DePrang, "Why Asking Texas Drivers about Mental Illness is Dumb," *Texas Observer*, January 17, 2014, http://www. texasobserver.org/dps-asks-drivers-theyre-mentally-ill/.

17. Wellford, Pepper, and Petrie, eds., *Firearms and Violence: A Critical Review*, 192.

18. John R. Lott, Jr. and John E. Whitley, "Safe Storage Gun Laws: Accidental Deaths, Suicides, and Crime," *Journal of Law and Economics* 44, no. 2 (2001); and Lott, Jr., *More Guns, Less Crime*.

19. Josh Sugarmann, "Gun Deaths Exceed Motor Vehicle Deaths in Ten States," Huffington Post, May 22, 2012, http://www. huffingtonpost.com/josh-sugarmann/gun-deaths-exceed-motor-v_b_1536793.html.

20. Sam Peltzman notes: "Progress in auto safety would likely have continued whether or not NHTSA had been created, and it would not surprise me if the vehicle mile death rate falls at 3-4% per year for the rest of your lifetime, whether that agency issues another MVSS or not." Sam Peltzman, "Regulation and the Natural Progress of Opulence," AEI-Brookings Joint Center for Regulatory Studies, September 2004, https://www.aei.org/publication/regulation-and-the-natural-progress-of-opulence/.

CHAPTER 12

1. Andrea Noble, "No changes—yet—to D.C. gun sales law after federal ruling in Texas," *Washington Times*, February 12, 2015, http://www.washingtontimes.com/news/2015/feb/12/dc-gun-sales-law-remain-the-same-after-federal-rul/?page=all. In New York City, the lowest cost for transferring a gun is $125 at John Jovino Gun Shop on 183 Grand Street. In New York State, eighty dollars is common, but costs have been up to one hundred dollars; see http://nyfirearms.com/forums/off-topic/27264-ffl- transfer-fees.html and http://www.usacarry.com/forums/new-york-discussion-and-firearm-news/28142-ffl- transfer-cost-ny.html.

2. Even proponents of Initiative 594 in Washington State that enacted background checks estimated that these checks would add up to sixty dollars to the price of each gun. See http://crimeresearch.org/

wp- content/uploads/2014/11/6.14.14-FINAL-Law-Enforcement-FAQ.pdf.

3. For example, on April 8, 2013, President Obama said: "Background checks have kept more than 2 million dangerous people from getting their hands on a gun." See President Obama, "Remarks by the President on Reducing Gun Violence—Hartford, CT," White House, April 8, 2013, https://www.whitehouse.gov/photos-and-video/video/2013/04/08/president-obama-speaks-reducing-gun-violence#transcript.

4. Sara Kehaulani Goo, "Sen. Kennedy Flagged by No-Fly List," *Washington Post*, August 20, 2004, A1, http://www.washingtonpost.com/wp-dyn/articles/A17073-2004Aug19.html; Staff Reports, "The truth on background checks," *New York Post*, February 14, 2013, http://nypost.com/2013/02/14/the-truth-on-background-checks/; "Ted Kennedy Got Off The No-Fly List, But What About Joe Normal?," Aero News Network, August 23, 2004,m http://www.aero-news.net/index.cfm?do=main.textpost&id=38d1ce4a-5a84-4d67-908d-621b2264cb8; and Eric Bradner, "Trump would consider gun ban for no-fly list members that rest of GOP balks at," CNN, December 6, 2015, http://www.cnn.com/2015/12/06/politics/2016-election-guns-no-fly-list/.

5. There are five stages of review for background check denials. The first stage of review is done at the BATF's national offices. In 2010, there were 72,659 denials and 94 percent of those were dropped at the first stage of review. There is no discretion at this stage. Those doing the review are merely looking to see whether the paperwork was accurate and whether the cases actually involved violations of the law. See Ronald Frandsen, "Enforcement of the Brady Act, 2010: Federal and State Investigations and Prosecutions of Firearm Applicants Denied by a NICS Check in 2010," National Criminal Justice Reference Service, August, 2012, https://www.ncjrs.gov/pdffiles1/bjs/grants/239272.pdf.

Of the cases referred in the next review step to the BATF field offices there were still a number of false positives. A 2004 sample found out that about 21 percent of these cases were found to be false positives (the percentage is slightly higher if a weighted sample is used). See "Review of the Bureau of Alcohol, Tobacco, Firearms, and Explosives' Enforcement of Brady Act Violations Identified Through the National Instant Criminal Background Check System," USDOJ/OIG, July 2004, https://oig.justice.gov/reports/ATF/e0406/results.htm#prohibit.

6. Frandsen, "Enforcement of the Brady Act, 2010."

7. Palash Ghosh, "Why Are So Many Vietnamese People Named Nguyen?" *International Business Times*, February 18, 2014, http://www.ibtimes.com/why-are-so-many-vietnamese-people-named-nguyen-1556359.

8. Steven Greenhut, "California Gun Law Paves the Way for Confiscation," Reason, January 3, 2014, https://reason.com/archives/2014/01/03/california-gun-law-paves-the-way-for-con; Robert Farago, "And So It Begins: New York Sending Out Gun Confiscation Notices," Guns.com, November 27, 2013, http://www.thetruthaboutguns.com/2013/11/robert-farago/begins-new-york-sending-gun-confiscation-notices/; and Staff, "Sheriff's team working to seize guns from thousands in Illinois," Fox News, July 28, 2013, http://www.foxnews.com/us/2013/07/28/sheriffs-team-working-to-seize-guns-from-thousands-in-illinois.html.

9. Staff, "From Veep to Lobbyist: Biden Pressures CO Democratic Lawmakers to Pass Gun Control," Colorado Peak Politics, February 15, 2013, http://coloradopeakpolitics.com/2013/02/15/from-veep-to-lobbyist-biden-pressures-co-democratic-lawmakers-to-pass-gun-control/.

10. Four hours of training is required in Maryland to own a handgun. The least expensive class is $125, though many others are $150 or more. The fee for the three-year permit is fifty dollars, and the renewal cost is twenty dollars. The cost of fingerprinting is thirty dollars. For information on the Handgun Qualification License in Maryland, see http://mdsp.maryland.gov/Organization/Pages/CriminalInvestigationBureau/LicensingDivision/Firearms/HandgunQualificationLicense.aspx.

11. For example, on December 6, 2015, Hillary Clinton claimed: Roof "should have never been given a gun, but the universal background check was not fast enough." See "'This Week' Transcript: Hillary

Clinton and Jeb Bush," ABC, December 6, 2015, http://abcnews.
go.com/Politics/week-transcript-hillary-clinton-jeb-bush/
story?id=35596885.

12. Presidential Candidate Hillary Clinton in Portsmouth, New
Hampshire, C-SPAN, December 29, 2015, http://www.c-span.org/
video/?402565-1/hillary-clinton-town-hall-meeting-portsmouth-
new-hampshire.

13. The FBI's statement on the Dylann Roof's case is as follows:
"Dylann Roof was arrested in Lexington County, South Carolina
and according to an incident report dated March 1, 2015 Roof
admitted possessing Suboxone, a Schedule III narcotic, without a
prescription which would have prohibited the transfer of the firearm
based on the protocol the NICS Section uses for a final
determination in establishing inference of current use for 18 USC
§922 (g)(3) based upon the definition as provided below, 27 C.F.R.
§478.11.
The Bureau of Alcohol, Tobacco, Firearms and Explosives (ATF)
Regulation Title 27, Code of Federal Regulations (C.F.R.), Section
478.11, defines an unlawful user of or addicted to any controlled
substance as "A person who uses a controlled substance and has lost
the power of self-control with reference to the use of a controlled
substance; and any person who is a current user of a controlled
substance in a manner other than prescribed by a licensed physician.
Such use is not limited to the use of drugs on a particular day, or
within a matter of days or weeks before, but rather that the
unlawful use has occurred recently enough to indicate that the
individual is actively engaged in such conduct. A person may be an
unlawful current user of a controlled substance even though the
substance is not being used at the precise time the person seeks to
acquire a firearm or receives or possesses a firearm. An inference of
current use may be drawn from evidence of a recent use or
possession of a controlled substance or a pattern of use or
possession that reasonably covers the present time, e.g., a conviction
for use or possession of a controlled substance within the past year;
multiple arrests for such offenses within the past five years with the
most recent arrest occurred within the past year; or persons found

through a drug test to use a controlled substance unlawfully, provided that the test was administered within the past year."

14. "Friend of SC Church Shooter: 'He's Racist,' Mom 'Didn't Trust Him' With Gun," Fox News Insider, June 18, 2015, http://insider.foxnews.com/2015/06/19/dylann-roofs-longtime-friend-i-think-he-racist.

15. Clinton in Portsmouth, New Hampshire.

16. *Mass Shootings at Virginia Tech: Report of the Review Panel Presented to Governor Kaine Commonwealth of Virginia*, Virginia Tech Review Panel, April 16, 2007, 47, http://www.washingtonpost.com/wp-srv/metro/documents/vatechreport.pdf.

CHAPTER 13

1. John R. Lott, Jr., *More Guns, Less Crime*, 3rd ed. (University of Chicago Press, 2010).

2. There were thirty-eight Democrats in the State House at that vote, and the Democrats were almost equally divided on the issue. For the legislative history for "HB 249 CS—Protection of Persons and Property" see http://www.myfloridahouse.gov/Sections/Bills/billsdetail.aspx?BillId=15498.

3. At the time that the law was passed in Illinois, it was illegal to carry handguns in public (either openly or concealed). However, with the change in the state concealed handgun law in 2014, those provisions now apply to a much broader area. See "Stand Whose Ground: President Obama vs. Senator Obama," *Wall Street Journal*, July 23, 2013, http://online.wsj.com/article/SB10001424127887324783204578622102597966828.html.

4. John Fund, "Obama Voted to Strengthen Illinois's Stand Your Ground Law in 2004," National Review Online, July 22, 2013, http://www.nationalreview.com/corner/354059/obama-voted-strengthen-illinoiss-stand-your-ground-law-2004-john-fund.

5. Alyssa Giannirakis, "Tavis Smiley: You Can 'Stand Your Ground Unless You Are A Black Man'," ABC News, July 14, 2013, http://abcnews.go.com/blogs/politics/2013/07/tavis-smiley-you-can-stand-your-ground-unless-you-are-a-black-man/. There is a long list of others who have made similar statements. For example, see E.J.

Dionne, "Repeal 'stand your ground' laws," *Washington Post*, February 19, 2014, http://www.washingtonpost.com/opinions/ ej-dionne-repeal-stand-your-ground-laws/2014/02/19/38fd3d64- 999f-11e3-80ac-63a8ba7f7942_story.html.
Attorney General Eric Holder claimed that repealing "Stand Your Ground" laws would help blacks. See Patrick Howley, "Blacks benefit from Florida 'Stand Your Ground' law at disproportionate rate," The Daily Caller, July 16, 2103, http://dailycaller. com/2013/07/16/blacks-benefit-from-florida-stand-your-ground- law-at-disproportionate-rate/.
President Obama has made many comments on the subject. In one comment, President Obama noted: "If I had a son, he'd look like Trayvon." See Jeff Mason and Daniel Trotta, "Obama gets personal over killing of black Florida teenager," Reuters, March 23, 2012, http://www.reuters.com/article/2012/03/23/us-florida-shooting- obama-idUSBRE82M0QF20120323.

6. The information from the *Tampa Bay Times* was last viewed on October 13, 2014. See http://www.tampabay.com/stand-your- ground-law/fatal-cases. The census data for Florida for 2013 was available from http://quickfacts.census.gov/qfd/states/12000.html.

7. Elizabeth Flock, "Trayvon Martin's Father Urges Congress to Amend 'Stand Your Ground'," US News & World Report, July 24, 2013, http://www.usnews.com/news/articles/2013/07/24/trayvon- martins-father-urges-congress-to-amend-stand-your-ground.

8. Hussein and Webber, "Florida's 'Stand Your Ground' Statute," visited April 15, 2016, http://www.husseinandwebber.com/case- work/criminal-defense-articles/floridas-stand-ground-statute/. The 2011 Florida Statutes, Title XLVI, CRIMES, Chapter 776 Justifiable Use of Force, 776.012: Use of force in defense of person http://www.husseinandwebber.com/florida-stand-your-ground- statute.html. The provisions are the same for other states, such as Pennsylvania. See http://www.legis.state.pa.us/WU01/LI/LI/CT/ HTM/18/00.005.005.000..HTM.

9. "Jury Sent Home, to Return and Continue Deliberations," Associated Press Newswire, September 28, 1999; "Man Killed After Argument," Associated Press Newswire, February 26, 1999;

and"Wallace Found Guilty of Negligent Homicide," Associated Press Newswire, September 29, 1999.

10. Allison Klein, "Judge acquits two men who shot intruder," *Baltimore Sun*, January 24, 2003.

11. Phillip D. Mielke, "Pastor acquitted in fatal shooting of intruders at his church," Associated Press (AK), October 27, 2003.

12. Nancy L. Othon, "Free but in fear of reprisal man acquitted of murder, but living under threat," *South Florida Sun Sentinel*, July 1, 2007.

13. "Wilson man released from Georgia prison after six years," WRAL, February 13, 2013, http://www.wral.com/wilson-native-who-maintained-innocence-to-go-free-tuesday/12096265/.

14. Lucia McBath, " 'Stand your ground' killed my son," *USA Today*, February 20, 2014, http://www.usatoday.com/story/opinion/2014/02/20/stand-your-ground-michael-dunn-jordan-davis-column/5655819/; and Chuck Ross, "Trayvon Martin's mother testifies in Senate 'stand your ground' hearing," Daily Caller, October 29, 2013, http://dailycaller.com/2013/10/29/trayvon-martins-mother-testifies-in-senate-stand-your-ground-hearing/.

15. Dunn faced two trials. During his first trial he was convicted of four charges, but the jury was deadlocked on the first-degree murder charge. During his second trial, he was convicted of first-degree murder. See Dan Abrams, "No, Florida's Stand Your Ground Law Did Not Determine Either Zimmerman or Dunn Cases," ABC News, February 17, 2014, http://abcnews.go.com/US/floridas-stand-ground-law-determine-zimmerman-dunn-cases/story?id=22543929; and Michelle Quesada, "Jordan Davis' parents greet, hug demonstrators after guilty verdict," First Coast News, October 1, 2014, http://www.firstcoastnews.com/story/news/local/2014/10/01/jordan-davis-parents-after-verdict-demonstrators/16568039/.

16. MCT Regional News, "Angela Corey: Florida prosecutor reflects on high-profile cases," *Orlando Sentinel*, October 13, 2014, http://www.orlandosentinel.com/news/trayvon-martin-george-zimmerman/os-angela-corey-george-zimmerman-20141013-story.html#page=1.

17. Gillian Mohney, "Florida Extends 'Stand Your Ground' to Include Warning Shots," ABC News, June 21, 2014, http://abcnews.go.com/US/florida-extends-stand-ground-include-warning-shots/story?id=24244906.

18. These are cases from the beginning of 2006 to July 24, 2013. See "Florida's Stand Your Ground Law," Tampa Bay Times, August 10, 2013, http://www.tampabay.com/stand-your-ground-law/fatal-cases. A breakdown of fatal cases, where they classify the accused as black and the victim as white, finds four cases where the charges were dropped or the black defendant was found "not guilty."

19. Randy Wimbley, "Detroit man says 'stand your ground' kept him out of prison," Fox 2 News, August 2, 2013, http://www.myfoxdetroit.com/story/23035397/detroit-man-says-stand-your-ground-kept-him-out-of-prison.

20. Leslie Coursey, "Man says 'stand your ground' law saved his life," WTEV Channel 47 in Jacksonville, July 26, 2013, http://www.actionnewsjax.com/content/topstories/story/Man-says-stand-your-ground-law-saved-his-life/SQNPxo275UqMpfF-7g8iOQ.cspx.

21. I dropped the Zimmerman case from their sample because it is clear that Zimmerman did invoke the Stand Your Ground defense. In three cases, the race of the victim was unknown. In another case, the race of the defendant was unknown. A fifth case involved an American Indian who was the defendant.

22. Using earlier data, the Tampa Bay Times had reported the percent of those who killed a black person and faced no penalty as 71 percent.

23. John Roman, *Race, Justifiable Homicide, and Stand Your Ground Laws*, The Urban Institute, July 2013, http://www.urban.org/UploadedPDF/412873-stand-your-ground.pdf. Roman concluded that when white defenders kill black attackers, "the justifiable homicide rate is 34%," compared to a 3 percent rate when the defender is black and the attacker is white. Roman concludes that this proves racism, but there is one big problem with this discussion: it assumes that the underlying true rate of justifiable homicides for the two groups of cases is the same. If the underlying rates are different, there could be no discrimination or even the opposite discrimination of what is claimed.

This paper also doesn't understand how the FBI's justifiable homicide data is measured. While often about thirty-five states report this data, a large percentage of the jurisdictions in even those states don't report the data. What states and what jurisdictions within those states report this data changes dramatically over time. The implication is any changes over time might simply arise from changes in the states or portions of states that are reporting this data. The biggest problem involves how this data is collected. Police initially report the cases as criminal homicides. If it is later determined to be justifiable, they don't frequently go back and recode the data. The problem is greatest for those deaths where the greatest amount of time elapses between the death and when it is determined justifiable. There is also some evidence that recoding is less likely to occur in the larger urban areas where you are likely to have a greater percentage of crime involving blacks. If so, the larger changes in shootings by whites found in Roman's study would simply result for jurisdictional differences. See John Barnes, "Justified to kill: Why there are more self-defense killings in Michigan than anyone knows," MLive, June 12, 2012, http://www.mlive.com/news/index.ssf/2012/06/justified_to_kill_why_there_ar.html.

24.   Lott Jr., *More Guns, Less Crime*, 3rd ed.

25.   Roman, *Race, Justifiable Homicide, and Stand Your Ground Laws: Analysis of FBI Supplementary Homicide Report Data*.

26.   Ibid.,11.

27.   Roman notes: "Several facts about the Martin homicide are known. Zimmerman and Martin were strangers, they were the only two people involved in the incident, neither was law enforcement, a handgun was used in the homicide, Zimmerman was white, Martin was black, and Zimmerman was older than Martin." But this is only a small portion of the information available in the Tampa Bay Times data set that is listed out in the appendix. Ibid.,9.

28.   Note that Roman's analysis is hardly typical. The preferred way academics analyze such data is a panel analysis where the change in a state's justified homicide rate would be looked at before and after a state adopts a Stand Your Ground law. Looking at changes in each

state before and after a law changes is crucial for trying to take into account differences across states. But his analysis, with no explanation, departs from the traditional analysis: arbitrarily lumping states into ten different groups makes it impossible to see if there is a change in a state's justifiable homicide rate after that particular state changes its law.

29. Roman provides information on whether these estimates are statistically significantly different from zero, but not on whether they are statistically different from each other.

30. The estimates in Roman's Table 4 could have dealt with this question by interacting the coefficients for black on black, white on black, and black on white with the Stand Your Ground dummy variable to see how those race coefficient variables change with whether the Stand Your Ground law is in effect.

31. Only about thirty-five states report data on justifiable homicides, and a large percentage of the jurisdictions even within those states don't report such data. Police initially report the cases as criminal homicides. However, if a homicide is later determined to be "justifiable," they frequently never go back and recode the data. The problem is greatest for deaths where the greatest amount of time has elapsed between the death and when it is determined to be justifiable. Some evidence suggests that recoding is less likely to occur in the larger urban areas, where a greater percentage of crimes involves blacks. If so, the larger changes in shootings by whites found in Roman's study could simply result from jurisdictional differences. See "More Killings Called Self-defense," *Wall Street Journal*, April 2, 2012, http://online.wsj.com/news/interactive/STA ND0330?ref =SB10001424052702303404704577311873214574462; and Barnes, "Justified to kill."

32. Mark Hoekstra and Cheng Cheng, *Does Strengthening Self-Defense Law Deter Crime or Escalate Violence? Evidence from the Castle Doctrine* (working paper, Texas A&M University, December 17, 2012), 4, http://ssrn.com/abstract=2079878.

33. See Lott, Jr., *More Guns, Less Crime*, 3rd ed., 332 for a list. For example, even during the period from 2000 to 2004, state law

changes were ignored. Utah's 2003 change is not included. And major changes in Illinois' law in 2004 are also not included.

34. Ibid., 330–333.

35. *State of Washington v. Studd*, 137 Wn.2d, 533 (April 1, 1999).

CHAPTER 14

1. For example, after the Newtown massacre Obama noted: "A majority of Americans support laws requiring background checks before all gun purchases so that criminals can't take advantage of legal loopholes to buy a gun from somebody who won't take the responsibility of doing a background check at all." President Obama, "President Obama's remarks on gun control, fiscal cliff, December 19, 2012 (Transcript)," *Washington Post*, December 19, 2012 , https://www.washingtonpost.com/politics/president-obamas-remarks-on-gun-control-policy-dec-19-2012-transcript/2012/12/19/08f5f7fe-49fb-11e2-b6f0-e851e741d196_story.html.

2. President Obama, "On the Shooting in San Bernardino," The White House, December 5, 2015, https://www.whitehouse.gov/blog/2015/12/02/president-obama-shooting-san-bernardino. This type of claim was made frequently by the president. See President Obama, "Obama talks about Umpqua shooting for second time (full transcript)," *The Oregonian*, October 2, 2015, http://www.oregonlive.com/pacific-northwest-news/index.ssf/2015/10/obama_talks_umpqua_shooting_fo.html.

3. This is from a talk that Hillary Clinton gave in Manchester, New Hampshire. See "Clinton Calls for Gun Control in Wake of Planned Parenthood Shooting," ABC Radio, November 30, 2015, http://wbt.com/clinton-calls-for-gun-control-in-wake-of-planned-parenthood-shooting/.
   After the Oregon shooting Clinton claimed that "Republicans refuse to do anything to protect our communties" and pushed background checks by saying "too many people who should never have gotten guns in the first place." See presidential candidate Hillary Clinton in Davie, Florida, C-SPAN, October 2, 2015, http://www.c-span.org/video/?328503-1/hillary-clinton-grassroots-campaign-event-davie-

florida; Matt Wilstein, "Hillary Speaks on WDBJ Shooting: I Will Take on Gun Violence," August 26, 2015, http://www.mediaite. com/tv/hillary-speaks-on-wdbj-shooting-i-will-take-on-gun-violence/; and https://twitter.com/HillaryClinton/ status/672149874046083072.

4. Some academics claim that mass public shootings would be avoided as a result of background checks, but they don't address that the background check laws on private transfers wouldn't have stopped any of the mass public shootings that they point to. For example, John Donohue at Stanford notes: "From the Gabby Giffords shooting in Arizona to the Batman movie theater shooting in Colorado, disaster strikes when guns end up in the hands of deeply troubled individuals. Bringing federal law in line with common sense rules on gun possession would clearly help in reducing mass shootings." See Clifton Parker, "Improved gun buyer background checks would impede some mass shootings, Stanford expert says," Stanford Report, December 31, 2015, http://news.stanford.edu/ news/2015/december/guns-donohue-law-121915.html.

5. The Colorado shooting is usually not listed as a mass public shooting because three people were killed there.

6. Even proponents of Initiative 594 in Washington State that enacted background checks estimated that these checks would add up to sixty dollars on to the price of each gun. See http://crimeresearch. org/wp-content/uploads/2014/11/6.14.14-FINAL-Law-Enforcement-FAQ.pdf. The cost of transferring a gun in 2011 for Washington, D.C. was $125, but the cost has reportedly gone up since then. See Emily Miller, "Transferring a gun into D.C.," *Washington Times*, January 24, 2012, http://www. washingtontimes.com/blog/guns/2012/jan/24/miller-transferring-gun-dc/. See also Andrea Noble, "No changes—yet—to D.C. gun sales law after federal ruling in Texas," *Washington Times*, February 12, 2015, http://www.washingtontimes.com/news/2015/ feb/12/dc-gun-sales-law-remain-the-same-after-federal-rul/?page=all). In New York City, the lowest cost for transferring a gun is $125 at John Jovino Gun Shop on 183 Grand Street. In New York State, $80 is common, but costs have been up to $100 (http://

nyfirearms.com/forums/off-topic/27264-ffl-transfer-fees.html and http://www.usacarry.com/forums/new-york-discussion-and-firearm-news/28142-ffl-transfer-cost-ny.html.

7. For example, the National Resource Council in its survey noted: "the Brady Act had no direct effect on homicide rates." See Wellford, Pepper, and Petrie, eds., *Firearm and Violence: A Critical Review*. For another more recent survey that looks at both state and federal background checks, see Lott, Jr., *More Guns, Less Crime*, 3rd ed.. For other recent discussions not covered in those surveys, see Carlisle Moody and T.B. Marvell, "On the Choice of Variables in the Crime Equation," *Oxford Bulletin of Economics and Statistics* (2010): 696–715; and Cramer, "Background Checks and Murder Rates," (working paper, College of Western Idaho,April 11, 2013), http://ssrn.com/abstract=2249317. The lack of evidence that background checks have little impact on crime rates may not be too surprising given that even before dealers in most states were not required to conduct background checks, only one-fifth of prisoners reportedly obtained their guns directly from a licensed gun dealer. See James D. Wright and Peter H. Rossi, *Armed and Considered Dangerous: A Survey of Felons and Their Firearms* (New York: Aldine de Gruyter, 1986). For a history of these laws see David Kopel, "Background Checks for Firearms Sales and Loans: Law, History, and Policy," *Harvard Journal on Legislation* 53 (2015), http://ssrn.com/abstract=2665432.

8. Caroline Wolf Harlow, Firearm Use by Offenders, U.S. Department of Justice, November 2001, http://bjs.gov/content/pub/pdf/fuo.pdf.

9. AWR Hawkins, "Puerto Rican Court: 2nd Amendment means to license required for Open Carry," Breitbart, June 22, 2015, http://www.breitbart.com/national-security/2015/06/22/puerto-rican-court-2nd-amendment-means-no-gun-registry-required-for-open-carry/.

10. The FBI report notes: "Specifically, shootings that resulted from gang or drug violence—pervasive, long-tracked, criminal acts that could also affect the public—were not included in this study. In addition, other gun-related shootings were not included when those incidents appeared generally not to have put others in peril (e.g., the

accidental discharge of a firearm in a school building or a person who chose to publicly commit suicide in a parking lot)." The first paper to use this definition was by Lott and Landes; see John R. Lott, Jr. and William M. Landes, "Multiple Victim Public Shootings, Bombings, and Right-to-Carry Concealed Handgun Laws: Contrasting Private and Public Law Enforcement," Social Science Research Network, April 21, 1999, http://ssrn.com/abstract=161637. See also John R. Lott Jr. and William Landes, "Multiple Victim Public Shootings," Social Science Research Network, October 19, 2000, http://ssrn.com/abstract=272929. Lott Jr., More Guns, Less Crime has additional discussions. Some, such as the *New York Times*, refer to the attacks being studied here as so-called "rampage" killings. See Ford Fessenden, "They Threaten, Seethe and Unhinge, Then Kill in Quantity," *New York Times*, April 9, 2000, http://www.nytimes.com/2000/04/09/us/they-threaten-seethe-and-unhinge-then-kill-in- quantity. html?pagewanted=all. Politifact and CNN also define these mass shootings in the same way; see http://www.politifact.com/truth-o-meter/statements/2014/jun/13/everytown-gun-safety/have-there-been-74-school- shootings-sandy-hook-clo/; and http://www.cnn.com/2014/06/11/us/school-shootings-cnn- number/.

11. Larry Buchanan, Larry et al., "How they got their guns," *New York Times*, updated December 3, 2015, http://www.nytimes.com/interactive/2015/10/03/us/how-mass-shooters-got-their-guns.html?hp&action=click&pgtype=Homepage&module=second-column-region&region=top-news&WT.nav=top-news.

12. Statisticians call this "state fixed effects."

13. The quote is from Fox KTVU Channel 2 in San Francisco on Thursday, December 3, 2015, from 12:15 to 12:23 PM EDT. See http://crimeresearch.org/2015/12/cprc-on-san-franciscos-fox-affiliate-ktvu-to-debate-about-gun-laws-after-the-san-bernardino-shooting/.

14. Alexis bought the gun in Virginia because that is where he lived and San Marco bought her gun while she lived for a couple of years in New Mexico. She literally drove from her home in New Mexico to where she did the attack in California at her old place of

employment. While Alexis and San Marco had histories of mental illness, neither had ever been "adjudicated as a mental defective" or "committed to a mental institution" and would not have been prohibited from being able to buy a shotgun under either D.C. or federal law. Thus Alexis and San Marco could have purchased their guns, respectively, in D.C. and California, though some gun control advocates have claimed that San Marco should have been stopped. Referring to San Marco: "How she managed to purchase it is 'the million-dollar question yet,' he said." Regarding Jennifer San Marco's history see her entry in Murderpedia, http://murderpedia.org/female.S/s/san-marco-jennifer.htm. For Aaron Alexis' case, see Glenn Kessler, "Marco Rubio's claim that no recent mass shootings would have been prevented by gun laws," *Washington Post*, December 10, 2015, https://www.washingtonpost.com/news/fact-checker/wp/2015/12/10/marco-rubios-claim-that-no-recent-mass-shootings-would-have-been-prevented-by-gun-laws/. Even gun control advocate Josh Horwitz has this post "How Aaron Alexis Passed a Background Check and Bought a Gun," Huffington Post, November 19, 2013, http://www.huffingtonpost.com/josh-horwitz/how-aaron-alexis-passed-a_b_3955687.html.

15. The lack of statistically significant results in columns (3) and (4) appears to be driven by not including 2015 in the sample, not by the inclusion of additional control variables. When 2015 data is omitted, columns (1) and (2) yield much the same results as columns (3) and (4) for background checks.

16. Mark Zaretsky, "Police Not Challenging Report Adam Lanza Planned Newtown Massacre on Spreadsheet," *County Times*, March 18, 2013, http://www.countytimes.com/articles/2013/03/18/news/doc5147b6f199d4e250356419.txt.

17. Editorial Board, "Keep Guns Away from Abusers," *New York Times*, January 16, 2016, http://www.nytimes.com/2016/01/17/opinion/sunday/keep-guns-away-from-abusers.html?_r=0.

18. Everytown for Gun Safety, "Gun Background Checks Reduce Crime and Save Lives," examined on May 8, 2016, http://everytown.org/documents/2014/10/background-checks-reduce-crimes-and-save-lives.pdf.

19. Lott Jr., *More Guns, Less Crime*, 3rd ed., 327-331.

CONCLUSION

1. President Obama, "Remarks by the President in Town Hall at Benedict College, Columbia, SC," The White House, March 6, 2015, https://www.whitehouse.gov/the-press-office/2015/03/06/remarks-president-town-hall-benedict-college-columbia-sc.

2. Obama, "Remarks by the President in Town Hall at Benedict College."

3. President Obama, "President Obama Answers a Question on Gun Violence During a Tumblr Q&A," The White House, June 11, 2014, https://www.youtube.com/watch?v=NDVFs2l6-fo.

4. See "Bloomberg ad on gun free zones in Nevada," Youtube video, posted by Jon Lott, March 3, 2015, https://www.youtube.com/watch?v=AxzY4mqABhE.

5. John J. Donohue, "Gun lunacy rides high in America," CNN, September 13, 2013, http://johnrlott.blogspot.com/2013/09/comments-on-piece-on-gun-control-at-cnn.html.

6. These comments by John Donohue were directed at myself and an academic coauthor of mine, David Mustard. See John Donohue, "The Final Bullet in the Body of the More Guns, Less Crime Hypothesis," *Criminology and Public Policy* 2, no. 3 (2003): 397–410; and John J. Donohue, "Can You Believe Econometric Evaluations of Law, Policy, and Medicine?" address given at the University of Virginia Law School, October 24, 2008.

7. James L. Meriner, "The Shootout," *Chicago magazine*, June 7, 2007, http://www.chicagomag.com/Chicago-Magazine/August-2006/The-Shootout/.

8. Cherrie Anne Villahermosa, "Gun-law measure now with governor," *Marianas Variety*, April 7, 2016, http://www.mvariety.com/cnmi/cnmi-news/local/85161-gun-law-measure-now-with-governor.

INDEX